CANADA

Harvard University, Cambridge

Boston Grammar School Boston

Bowdoin College Brunswick

MAINE

Dartmouth College, Hanover

Middlebury College, Middlebury

VT.

N.H.

MASS.

Amherst College, Amherst

Williams College, Williamstown
Mount Holyoke, South Hadley

CONN.

Roxbury School, Roxbury

Yale University, New Haven

NESOTA

Northland College, Ashland

MICHIGAN

N.J.

Princeton University Princeton

Ripon College, Ripon

WISCONSIN

Olivet College, Olivet

Hillsdale College Hillsdale

on College, thfield

Beloit College, Beloit

Western Reserve University, Cleveland

Rockford Colleges, Rockford

Wheaton College, Wheaton

Oberlin College, Oberlin

nell College, Grinnell

IOWA

ILLINOIS

Defiance College, Defiance

OHIO

Howard University, Washington, D.C.

VIRGINIA

Knox College, Galesburg

University of Illinois, Urbana

Marietta College, Marietta

Illinois College, Jacksonville

KENTUCKY

Hampton Institute, Hampton

MISSOURI

Monticello College, Alton

Drury College, Springfield

Berea College, Berea

TENNESSEE

Fisk University, Nashville

Talladega College, Talladega

Tougaloo College, Tougaloo

ALABAMA

LOUISIANA

MISSISSIPPI

AS

Juston-Tillotson College, Austin

Dillard University, New Orleans

ATLANTIC OCEAN

N

GULF of MEXICO

The winner of two Guggenheim fellowships, **Marion Starkey** is one of America's most distinguished popular history writers. A New Englander by birth, she discovered, while doing research for this book, that she herself is a direct descendant of the early Pilgrims of the "Congregational Way." Newspaper and free-lance journalistic work have led to travel to most parts of the world, but Miss Starkey now makes Saugus, Massachusetts, her permanent residence.

THE CONGREGATIONAL WAY

MARION L. STARKEY

The Congregational Way

THE ROLE OF THE PILGRIMS
AND THEIR HEIRS
IN SHAPING AMERICA

90

DOUBLEDAY & COMPANY, INC., GARDEN CITY, NEW YORK, 1966

LIBRARY OF CONGRESS CATALOG CARD NUMBER 66–12199

COPYRIGHT © 1966 BY MARION L. STARKEY

ALL RIGHTS RESERVED

PRINTED IN THE UNITED STATES OF AMERICA

FIRST EDITION

For those good Vermonter Congregationalists
Francis and Lillian Irons

RELIGIONS IN AMERICA

A Statement by the Editor

We know about the Pilgrims and the Puritans. Or do we? But who were the Congregationalists? And what? And what are they now? What had churches under that name to do with the shaping of American society? With education? The movement West? The democratic idea?

It is fitting that the first book in an extended series, each volume being given over to the story of a single denomination or persuasion, should begin with the Congregationalists. They were first in order, and at times you would think that they were first in color. They offered both an enactment and a preview of the drama and tumult in the American religious story. There is hardly an exciting or picturesque element missing. Even evangelism is present in the preaching of Jonathan Edwards and others who stirred The Great Awakening, foreshadowing the convulsive periods of emotion that were to follow.

There is vastly more. The connection with, and complete departure from, European backgrounds mark the beginning of American religion as a distinct phenomenon, baffling to Europeans—and to many Americans, too. It is made up of "multitudes brought hither out of many kindreds and tongues." And the variety of religious experience on these shores is demonstrated at the very outset.

The groups forming the first American churches represented two distinct traditions. The Pilgrims of Plymouth were wanderers who had withdrawn from the Church of England and brought with them leanings that led to tolerance and good will. The severe Puritans of Massachusetts Bay were reformers and brought with them a harsh and exacting theology that led to intolerance and persecution. Differing in policy and polity, coming from separate heritages and classes and occupying separate territories, the two groups in time nonetheless became the Congregationalists.

The story of religions in America is not one story, but scores of stories, each expressing diversity of mood and belief and yet all pointing

toward a unity of aspiration. It is history made by people of conviction and the strength to translate conviction into deeds. It resounds
with outcries of protest and pleas for reform. It is touched at times
with hysteria. It is also marked by moving evidence of patience and
insight and penetrating searches after inner truth. In a word, it is a
story of emotions back of events, of forces that are a part of the
mainstream of American life and yet dwell apart and are slow to
affect conduct. It affords some sense of a fourth dimension in history.
On more practical grounds, it rounds out and completes history.

A series dealing with the emotional aspects of our culture comes at a
good time. The stirring in popular interest is apparent these days in the
frequent use of the term ecumenical, deriving from the Greek word
for house and suggesting that all phases of faith may one day be
brought together under one roof. The ecumenical movement prompts
persons within denominations to want to know more about the lineage
of their own faith and makes them more alert than formerly to the
beliefs of others. Among the unchurched the widespread talk of unity
provokes curiosity about the peculiarities and differences within the
religious spectrum.

We lack a common body of usable information about religion in this
country. Persons versed in ordinary dates and occurrences find themselves hard put to answer simple questions about Americans grouped
in churches, chapels, cathedrals, tabernacles, temples, and synagogues.
A scrupulous neglect of information about religion is built into the very
system of education. Dr. Harry Emerson Fosdick once pointed out that
schoolteachers under the present arrangements are allowed to teach
whatever they wish about the Emperor Nero but nothing about the
Apostle Paul.

The effects of religious illiteracy are many and none of them is
good. One effect is illustrated by a sequence of dialogue that appeared
in the comic column, Peanuts. One piece of small fry asked his sister,
"Do you ever pray, Lucy?" To which Lucy replied, "That's a kind of
personal question, isn't it? Are you trying to start an argument?" Religious controversy, at high levels or in the backyard, thrives on ignorance and misinformation. There may be argument, but there is not
likely to be discussion unless there is shared knowledge.

To provide a rich fund of common knowledge is the central purpose of the Religions in America Series. Fortunately, a wealth of detail is available and needs only to be mortised into the mores. Church historians have kept voluminous records. Churchmen have never been inarticulate and have held few views back. Stories abound. Personalities flourish under stress nourished by religious conviction. Sequestered in files are narratives that often attain epic proportions, peopled with gifted, eloquent, unquenchable and, not infrequently, theatrical characters. There are triumphs that come from strength not natural to the human frame, accounts of strong men on horseback, and records of gentle impulses and meditations.

Questions touching distinctions among and within denominations cannot be dealt with by quick reference. They demand full accounts of people acting out their beliefs and managing their affairs in the light of these beliefs. American religion is best seen as people rather than doctrines.

To this end, the Religions in America Series will employ writers trained in history and research and skilled in expression to seek out and present the story of religions in America through the lives and deeds of the men and women daily involved. The aim of the Series is to make the story of each group so vivid that it will be unforgettable and will become familiar.

Charles W. Ferguson

CONTENTS

THE CONGREGATIONAL WAY

I

GENESIS

On Thanksgiving Eve the Pilgrims still come to Plymouth. Some bear names that its founding father William Bradford would recognize; many do not. Some come from the settlements on Massachusetts Bay, some from points in New England, the West and Midwest, of which the early Pilgrims never heard. Like the first Pilgrims they bring their children with them, confident now that there is no want of "inns to refresh their weather-beaten bodies."

They sup at a counter in Jim's Lunch, and finding it companionable, think well of having Thanksgiving dinner there, if they find other restaurants reserved for family reunions. They wander uptown into a gift shop to buy neat replicas of Plymouth Rock. "Made in Japan" it says on the underside; good that the fame of the Pilgrim fathers has spread so far.

In motels and guest houses they make plans for Thanksgiving Day. There will be open house at many points, where cranberry juice and doughnuts are served to all comers. There will be a visit to the faithful reproduction of the *Mayflower,* moored as the first *Mayflower* was unable to do, at the town wharf hard by Plymouth Rock. They must get to "Plimouth Plantation," two miles out of town, to visit the replica of the fort where the Pilgrims worshiped so long, and explore the reproductions of their homes. They must visit Pilgrim Hall, where the genuine artifacts are, and point out to a small boy the wicker cradle of his great-great-grandfather, Peregrine White.

"Now can we take it home?" the child asks. "We'll tell them it's great-granddaddy's cradle and they'll let us. I want it."

It's an emergency. Peregrine's small descendant is not wholly appeased that Pilgrim Hall will let him take home as a Thanksgiving Day gift, a steeple-crowned Pilgrim hat.

All these things and many others can be seen on any visit to Plymouth. The special objective of the Thanksgiving pilgrimage is the memorial service in the Church of the Pilgrims. At midmorning the bells begin to sound, and the newer Pilgrims go up Town Square to take their places in the church pews. It is not the original structure; indeed, it is at least the fifth. It is built of stone with a porch modeled after that of the English church in which the infant William Bradford was baptized. The rich colors of the stained glass windows, representing the signing of the Mayflower Compact and the preaching of John Robinson, would be a surprise to Pilgrims who in America worshiped first in the rude common house and then in the fort. The singing of the interchurch choir would please them; they had not heard such full-throated song since they left Holland. And the prayers and sermons by ministers of varied denominations (for this service is under the auspices of the Greater Plymouth Council of Churches) would not displease them.

Some of the late-come Pilgrims, fluttering their bills into the collection plates, are bewildered. By examination of the hymnals, by literature picked up in the foyer ("Good Men in Hell"), they have learned that the Church of the Pilgrims is Unitarian. Why Unitarian? Were not the first Pilgrims Congregational, founders of the Congregational Churches of America?

That is a long story, which it is one purpose of this book to recount. There is next door a Congregational Church, the Church of the Pilgrimage, housed in a white painted frame structure in the New England and Congregational tradition. But the memorial service is always held in the First Parish Unitarian.

To the first Pilgrims the term Congregational would have been as unfamiliar as Unitarian. There never was and is not now a Congregational Church in the formal corporate sense that there is a Methodist or Episcopal Church. There were Congregational Churches, but even this phrase would ring strangely in the ears of the first settlers of Plymouth and Massachusetts Bay.

When they used the term church at all, they applied it to the communion of "visible saints," those men and women who had covenanted themselves to live according to the Word of God, in contrast to the "strangers" who had not done so. (Strangers were not necessarily sinners, and the sanctity of the saints lay in their intention rather than their accomplishment.) The saints were a congregation, not a church, and the structure that housed them was called a meetinghouse, a term accurately descriptive of its multiple functions. On the Sabbath it sheltered the congregation, on weekdays town meeting and court sessions. The phrase that covers this practice is not the Congregational Church but the Congregational Way, and this practice did originate among the Pilgrims.

Even so they did not invent the term or call themselves Congregationalists. A congregation they were; their saints had so covenanted themselves before they left Holland, and in America they continued to elect and ordain their officers. The name adopted by most twentieth-century Congregational Churches, Church of Christ, would have suited them well; it described their intention, which was to follow, so far as human frailty would permit, their leader Christ.

The Way of the Pilgrims

It was the Puritan minister, John Cotton, who coined the phrase Congregational Way. It obtained general currency after 1648 when the Pilgrims and Puritans united in formulating the Way in what they called the Cambridge Platform. What was most strange was that the humble Pilgrims, who in England had been despised as Separatists by the Puritans, and in America were far inferior in number and power to the aggressive settlers of Massachusetts Bay, somehow imposed their Way upon the latter.

"Impose" it, literally, however, they did not and could not. A little community which had for years no minister empowered to administer the sacraments was in no position to impose its will upon a people who had come to America with a near plethora of ministers, among them the most gifted and highly cultivated clergymen of England. Sometimes the Plymouth Pilgrims were moved to feeble protest against the aggressions of the Bay Puritans, but mostly they deferred. They had to. Yet their Way became the Congregational Way of Puritan Massachusetts. How did it happen?

The simplest answer is that the Pilgrims got to America first, had demonstrated the viability of New England well before 1628 when the Puritans sent the advance party of their "great migration" to settle Naumkeag, the later Salem. Befriended in their need by the neighborliness of Plymouth, those Salem settlers who gathered themselves into a

congregation, adopted the Pilgrim practice; and when the Puritans followed en masse in 1630 they found a congregational church polity
already in operation. That it had originated among a Separatist group
gave them some misgivings. That they adopted it had less to do with
political or theological preconceptions than with the fact that nothing
else suited the pioneering communities so well.

One aspect of the Way became distinctively Puritan: the local autonomy of the separate congregations, each maintaining fellowship with its
neighbors, but governing itself according to its own lights. The Pilgrims, long concentrated in Plymouth, had no occasion to invent this
practice; the Puritan settlers, scattering at once, evolved the local
autonomy which one might say anticipated the doctrine of states' rights.

It is also true that the town meeting, that most characteristic of
New England secular institutions, arose first among the Puritans, at
least in a clearly recognizable form. It was so natural an extension of
congregational practice, so suitable to the time and place, that the
Pilgrims presently followed it. Thus the Way took on a dual aspect,
secular as well as spiritual.

The Way was to prevail throughout New England. When the colonies
became a nation, when pioneers moved into the West, they took it with
them. There it would never dominate as it had in New England, but in
Illinois, Iowa, and finally the Pacific Coast, what now called themselves Congregationalists, would command an influence disproportionate
to their numbers. Even the turmoil of the Unitarian Separation would
not extinguish the Way, for most Unitarians continued to follow it. The
ancient Calvinism of the first settlers would be modified; a new order
of ministers would renounce the doctrines of natural depravity and
predestination; they would address themselves not only to spiritual but
to social problems, to relations between capital and labor, to the rights
of minorities. At long last later-come Pilgrims, who could not say with
Bradford "our fathers were Englishmen," would unite with the followers of the Way and form with them the United Church of Christ.

These newcomers, many of them of German ancestry, also looked
back to the New England past, and when they did so, they identified
themselves not with the powerful Puritans, but the humble Pilgrims.
Why did they not look to Boston, the "city set on a hill" rather than to
little Plymouth for their spiritual beginnings?

Perhaps only because the story of Plymouth is simpler. It is easier to follow the human experience of the Pilgrims who were few than that of the Puritans who were many. But there is also a latter-day aversion to the extremes to which the Puritans went when for half a century they governed themselves under a theocratic oligarchy, somewhat after the order of Calvin's Geneva. The Pilgrims were no theocrats; not only did they lack the power to establish so rigid a regime, but they were deterred by the preaching of their beloved pastor John Robinson, by his references to "further light" yet to be expected from God's holy word. Men who waited on the revelation of more light could not be rigidly self-righteous.

Yet the Puritan heritage deserves honor. Among them no less than among the Pilgrims there was honest seeking after righteousness, neighborly kindness, and finally, after the terrible chastening of the Salem witchcraft, a healing humility. They revered education; their ministers had a truer appreciation of science than their medical men; without their thrusting vigor, the little Pilgrim settlement might not have endured. To them no less than to the Pilgrims we owe the founding of democratic institutions and the staying power of the Congregational Way.

A Personal Note

Much of my childhood was spent with Congregational grandparents. Their Sabbath was holy, but not in the austere Puritan sense of cold meals prepared the day before. My grandmother got the roast into the oven before she rustled into her Sabbath silks. My uncle, who sang in the choir, left first; when the bells began to sound my grandfather fetched his hat and his Bible and led us up the hill to take our places in the Gray pew in the Hyde Park First Congregational Church.

I think that my grandfather, a man of great simplicity and goodness, who in church leaned forward, cupping his good ear, not to miss a word of the sermon, best represented the ancient Scrooby congregation. My grandmother belonged with the Puritans; like them she was capable of kindness, but like them also she could be fiercely righteous and conscious of class; it was an affliction to her that the Gray pew had to be shared with communicants who did not meet her standards.

If the sermons ever touched on hell, that was a point I missed. I did, however, hear of the devil; I was fascinated by a character known to me as the Christian Devil.

My knowledge of him came through my aunt, who hurried through Sunday night supper to keep her rendezvous with him. I begged to go with her. But no, said my aunt firmly; it wasn't for little girls; it was like prayer meeting and I wouldn't like it a bit.

I knew better. Without asking questions I had worked out the mythology of the Christian Devil. I knew that Lucifer was an angel who had fallen; obviously there was another devil who had risen, had become a Christian. Relentlessly I importuned my aunt until she gave in.

She was quite right; it was like prayer meeting and of no interest to little girls. The Christian Devil was nowhere in sight. There was only a velvet banner bearing the legend Christian Endeavor. Bleakly it was borne in upon me that my bright mythology was based on a simple confusion of terms.

The Lack of Pageantry

This episode would seem of small significance in a history of the Congregational Way, yet it has relevance. The devout Pilgrims and Puritans of the first days, the gathered "saints" of the congregation, needed no colorful ritual, no adornments in the plain meetinghouses where they worshiped. The beauty of holiness was all their ornament. But with them sat others unfitted by youth or temperament to respond to so austere a beauty, and their attention sometimes wandered in strange directions.

Young Cotton Mather, consecrated to saintliness in infancy, but endowed nonetheless with a wayward fancy, was visited by angels in his dreams, and they appeared to him not in ministerial black, but gorgeously bejeweled and caparisoned, as if they wore the richly embroidered vestments of a priesthood which the Puritans had long ago renounced.

If the children of Mather's time were not bemused by a fantasy of a "Christian devil," they found abundant scope for fancy in devils of another sort, nasty little beings who pinched and tormented, and who seduced good church members into service most foul. The Puritans had hitherto eschewed superstition, but in an evil day the hallucinations of these children impressed Cotton Mather and most of the community, impelling the Bay Colony into a disastrous witch hunt.

They came out of this tragedy sobered and humbled, but not disposed to give rein to fancy or return to the pageantry of their forebears. Yet some of them were capable of being unexpectedly moved by exposure to it. Thus in 1774 on a visit to Philadelphia, John Adams of Boston visited what he called a Romish chapel to hear "a discourse on the duty of parents to their children." The discourse pleased, but what struck him, and what he recorded in his journal, was the magical beauty of the service: "The Scenery and the Musick is so callculated to take in Mankind that I wonder the Reformation ever succeeded. The Paintings, the Bells, the Candles, the Gold and Silver. Our Saviour on the Cross over the Altar, all his wounds a-bleeding. The chanting is exquisitely soft and sweet."

It was the reverse of his own experience in New England. Even organs still had no place in the meetinghouses of John Adams' time, and though the "new style" of singing by note was coming in, the sensitive Adams ear was affronted by the "quavering discords" of worshipers who sang the psalms each at his own tempo and to his own tune.

In the old "ship meetinghouse" in Adams' Hingham there were no paintings, no candles, no gold, nor were there in any of his time. The Pilgrims and Puritans, like the Moslems and Jews of old, renounced pictorial art in their worship. But children growing up deprived of it, often hungered for they hardly knew what.

This was notably true of John Adams' great-grandson Henry, who studying the Norman and Gothic cathedrals of medieval France came to a pause before Chartres, most beautiful of them all. There he found something that had been wanting in the religious instruction of his Boston childhood, which had seemed to him dry and unconvincing. Here he found the very opposite of his childhood experience, exquisite beauty on every hand, from the two disparate yet harmonious towers without to the soaring of the Gothic vaults within, the grave and lovely figures of the divine mother and son in the north porch, and the many-faceted radiance of the light that blazed through the jeweled stained glass of the windows.

He responded not only to the aesthetic beauty of Chartres, but even more to the moral beauty of its conception, to its existence as a monument to the radiant *ambience* of faith of the twelfth century. He pored over the records of its construction, when rich and poor, noble and peasant, all chosen after as rigid a test of their dedication as the "elect" of his Puritan ancestors, harnessed themselves to wagons to draw the great stones from the quarry. He studied the details of the north porch, which best represented the century of faith, and found a consecration inspired not by the terrors of damnation or the misery of the human condition, but the joy of salvation.

Christ was represented, not as in a thousand Puritan sermons as the dreadful judge of mankind in the Day of Doom; He sat enthroned by His mother, as compassionate as she, the Saviour, not the destroyer. Nor were His earthly sufferings depicted; a series of sculptures presenting scenes in the human life of mother and son had one remarkable omission: the crucifixion.

The sight wrung from Henry Adams, aging then, and dourly intellectual, a cry of rare poignance which he inserted among much scholarly detail in his *Mont-Saint-Michel and Chartres:* "People who suffer beyond the formulas of expression—who are crushed into silence and beyond pain—want no display of emotion—no bleeding hearts— no weeping at the foot of the Cross—no hysterics, no phrases. They want to see God and know that He is watching over His own."

His Catholic friends, reading this cry of the heart and expressions of his chivalric devotion to the Virgin, supposed that he was about to become one of them. But they were wrong; Adams could appreciate their faith; he could not embrace it. Too many centuries had passed since his ancestors had foresworn that which his great-grandfather had remarked was so well calculated to "take in mankind."

The Reformation in Europe

But why did a people capable of responding to such beauty and wonder foreswear it? Why did the Puritans abandon the English equivalents of Chartres to worship in what they called, and not impiously, "the Lord's barns"? Why did they abandon the jollity of religious festivals, suppressing even Christmas, the glorious windows, the protection of the saints, from Mary who would intercede even for the damned to the lesser figures who consented to perform homely offices for the faithful, like St. Christopher guiding the wayfarer, or St. Anthony recovering the lost article? As John Adams had asked himself, how had the Reformation ever succeeded?

It had begun while Chartres Cathedral was still abuilding. The construction, interrupted once by fire, had taken centuries. Those parts that most enchanted Henry belonged to the twelfth century; it was the early sixteenth before the second spire was raised to stand by the classic simplicity of the first. In the meantime acknowledgments of misery and damnation had invaded the cathedral. Two windows represented the crucifixion, another the Day of Judgment. Even so the former were inconspicuous, the latter so suffused with jeweled light that the joy of the saved eclipsed the sorrows of the damned. Chartres remained a hymn to salvation.

Many things had happened, however, since the first great stones were laid. The Crusades had come and gone; the Black Death had ravaged Europe and begun the social and economic upheavals which during the Renaissance were to destroy feudalism. A new spirit of inquiry was abroad, leading to the discovery of America, of the phases of Venus, and a general intellectual ferment which was to challenge the basis of the old faith. Even in France there were some, notably the Waldensians of Lyons, who were demanding a newer and simpler order of worship.

In one of the Germanies a young monk named Luther was about to launch the Protestant Reformation by attacking the hierarchy of the Church, its corruptions of power and wealth, its self-appointed right to remit sins through the sale of indulgences. Eventually the Church would be impelled to self-criticism and the reforms of the Counter-Reformation, but its natural first posture was self-defense. The Inquisition was instituted to hunt down heretics, especially those who worshiped the devil and practiced witchcraft. Since Luther also believed in the devil, his Protestant followers hunted witches as zealously as the Catholics. Curiously the whole course of the Renaissance, with its emphasis on intellect, was attended by a massive witch hunt. Nor was that the worst: Europe was torn by religious wars. To quote Dickens out of context, "It was the best of times and the worst of times."

The Puritans and the Separatists in England

While these things developed on the Continent, England was entering the Protestant Reformation at its own pace, in its own way. It too would have a witch hunt; it too would have a revolution. If the scale of both was smaller than those of Europe, particularly the culmination of the Reformation in the Thirty Years' War which devastated the Germanies, details were hard enough on the people intimately concerned.

Before Europe had a Luther, England had Wycliffe, protected like Luther by its princes, and engaging like him in what was to be the mainstay of Protestantism, the translation of the Bible into the vernacular. Wycliffe also had his followers, known as the Lollards, the sort of derisive term that usually gets attached to dissenting sects, meaning in this case "loafers." They were, however, less a sect, a "gathered church," than a miscellaneous movement; after Wycliffe's death they had no protection from royal authority. By the time Henry VIII for his own private reasons broke with Rome, they survived only as an obscure yeasty element in the population.

It was not Tudor Henry's purpose to institute a Protestant Reformation in England. He prized the title of Defender of the Faith given him by Pope Leo X, and retained it even when he divorced the English Church from the Pope's authority, and took the occasion to seize the wealth of the monasteries. Life was not easy for the devout under Henry; those who like Sir Thomas More adhered to their Roman allegiance, lost their heads; so did some who renounced Roman dogma.

Only during the short reign of his young son Edward was it safe to be openly Protestant, and Edward was followed by Mary, who being the loyal daughter of Henry's Queen Catherine of Aragon, naturally returned to her mother's faith. She became Bloody Mary; it is the persecutions of her reign that form the substance of Foxe's *Book of Martyrs*. In spite of burnings at Smithfield and beheadings at Whitehall, or perhaps because of them, Protestantism took a firmer foothold in Britain under Mary than it had under Edward. When Anne Boleyn's daughter Elizabeth succeeded Mary to the throne and the title of Defender of the Faith, she was faced with dissenters who followed two well-defined paths, the Puritans and the Separatists.

The first, being the less radical of the two, in Elizabeth's time suffered derision rather than persecution. Shakespeare satirized them in the person of Malvolio. It is to be noted that though Malvolio's jealous fellow servants mocked him ("Dost thou think because thou art virtuous there shall be no cakes and ale?"), he commanded the respect of his mistress.

The Elizabethan Puritans and their early successors did not eschew cakes and ale, especially the latter; beyond an occasional ascetic, no Englishman of the time voluntarily drank water. Their leaders were highly educated—Cambridge University had become the forcing ground of Puritanism—and many were in the humanistic tradition of the Renaissance. Certainly that was true of Milton; though in later life he veered from Presbyterian Puritanism to the more radical order, he was no man to forbid organ music or urge Cromwell's soldiers to break stained-glass windows. This was true of Milton's young friend Andrew Marvell, and of the American Puritans, it was eminently true of the younger and enormously popular John Winthrop, and indeed, until circumstances forced austerity upon him, of the elder Winthrop who founded Massachusetts Bay.

These had no desire to break with the Anglican Church; they only asked that it be "purified." Part of what they objected to was the Romish ritual, for which the persecutions of Mary had given them a violent distaste: vestments, candles, incense, readings and chantings of Holy Scripture without priestly explication. They also wanted it cleared of the same sort of corruption that had drawn Luther's fire against the Roman Church, especially as exemplified in the character of many rectors. They did not want men who, to quote Milton, accepted a pulpit merely as a "living," whose "hungry sheep looked up and were not fed." They did not want "blind shepherds . . . who for their bellies' sake creep and climb and intrude into the fold." They wanted dedicated men, and they wanted them to consecrate their followers not by bell, book, and candle, but by preaching them sermons in plain, understandable English.

Their initial demands were simple, and the reforms they asked reasonable. An early compromise on the part of authority might conceivably have averted the whole train of events that led to the hegira to Massachusetts and the outbreak of civil war. Elizabeth was a sovereign who knew how to compromise, but in this respect she was wanting in perception. Though she also prized her inherited title of Defender of the Faith, she had little appreciation of true religious fervor; besides, her attention was taken up by international crises including the attempted invasion from Spain. She suffered the Puritans, and gave some a grudging respect; but she did not exert herself to grant their demands.

There was another, austerer element in Puritanism. During Mary's reign some had taken flight to the Continent; when they returned many had adopted the stern doctrines of Calvin, which also infiltrated from John Knox's Scotland. Eventually some of their remote descendants would renounce such dogma as predestination and natural depravity as "immoral theology." At this time it was an eminently moral theology. It marked the same advance from the Church's recent arrogation of power to remit sins though the sale of indulgences as the Mosaic precept of an eye for an eye was an advance from the primitive concept of unlimited vengeance. It was a doctrine which brooked no favoritism, and reduced the King to the level of the plowman.

These were the Puritans. The Separatists were another order entirely. They deemed the establishments, Anglican or Roman, too corrupt to be purified. Like Henry VIII they wanted divorce; they wanted to set up their own congregations, subject to no bishop, no royal Defender of the Faith, subject only to Christ. They were the radicals. Elizabeth would not put up with them; the Puritans had no high opinion of them.

The difference between Puritan and Separatist was not only ideological, but to some extent class-structured. As a whole the Puritans were more prosperous, more highly educated, better pedigreed. Some leaders came from the nobility, many from the gentry and upper middle class. Though some Separatist leaders had their training at Cambridge and were moderately prosperous, more were of a humbler sort who without the translation of the Bible and the timely invention of Gutenberg would not have been in a position to derive subversive doctrine from their Testaments. They were the meek, who, it is said, will inherit the earth. In a sense they were to do so, for it was among this group that the movement which the Puritans were to adopt as "the Congregational Way" first originated.

The Gospel for Every Man

Without the zeal of the leaders of reform to translate the Bible into the vernacular, Protestantism might never have taken root. Protest began among scholars able to read their Testaments in Latin, Greek, Hebrew, but to accomplish their purpose they needed a following, and for that they had to make the Bible available to both prince and peasant in their native tongue.

The enterprise began as early as the twelfth century when Peter Waldo, a devout merchant of Lyons, employed a scholar to translate and clerks to make copies for distribution. Wycliffe worked out an English translation, and by the time Luther and Calvin applied themselves to German and French versions, Gutenberg had invented movable type, and printing presses were springing up in Europe. In the Middle Ages, the Bible had been a precious document that only the rich could afford; now it was accessible to men of more modest means and in their own language. Thanks to the printing press, literacy was no longer an exclusive prerogative. Education of the masses did not begin so early, but the books and pamphlets coming off the presses gave ordinary people an incentive to learn their letters. In any event they could listen in their churches to readings from the sacred books in a language they could understand.

The effect was to bring simple people into the glory of the Renaissance. They shared the same exhilarating shock of discovery that the scholars had known when after the fall of Constantinople they came upon the manuscripts of forgotten Greek philosophers. The Apostles were newly revealed not as aloof dignitaries in vestments of richly embroidered silver and gold, chanting litanies in strange tongues, but people as simple as themselves, whose hands were also grimed and calloused, and who followed a man no more princely than a carpenter. Their way of life was simple and its virtues comprehensible. To follow in the way of such goodness and mercy one would be willing to suffer much.

It was the Church's contention that opening the Bible to the interpretation of common men who lacked priestly discipline and learning to guide them was perilous. And so it was, as the Protestants discovered soon enough. A document which covers human history from the Stone Age to the mysteries of the Apocalypse can give rise to as many interpretations as there are men to interpret it. Protestant emphasis on individual study of the Word of God meant that there might never be a Protestant Church in the sense that there was a Catholic Church. Individual readers, their studies supplemented by their private visions, would come to conclusions that would dismay Luther as much as the Pope. Multiplication of interpreters who cared intensely about things of the spirit would be an important factor (though there were many others) in bringing about the bitter religious wars that shattered what one might call the "Pax Romana" of the medieval Church.

The Congregational Way

What was in substance the Congregational Way evolved spontaneously in many times and places. Among people studying the Gospels and the Book of Acts arose a craving to re-establish the primitive Christian Church as they understood it, in its purity and simplicity.

Some of the monkish orders of the Middle Ages were founded on these same principles. Though by no means denying the authority of the Pope, they did make themselves virtually independent of the hierarchy by their withdrawal from the world and adoption of rules supervised by their own elected officers. The Waldensians, nearly exterminated by the Inquisition, were apparently so motivated. In England a clear expression of the fundamentals of Congregationalism was made about 1580 by Robert Browne. According to his philosophy a church existed wherever two or three were gathered together to attempt to live by the law of Christ. He therefore considered that such a church was organized when its members bound themselves by a convenant and elected their elders. No temporal power had authority over such a church, whose only allegiance was to Christ, its true head. Separate churches owed each other fellowship in aid and counsel, but could not command each other.

Usually a new minority faith resigns itself to the name given by its enemies, Methodist, Quaker, and the like. The Separatists became known as Brownists, but they did not accept the designation, especially the group which became the Plymouth Pilgrims. The connotations were radical and of ill repute. Browne himself was better at stating a principle than at carrying it out. His congregations in England's Norwich and Holland's Middelburg fell into uncontrolled bickering when he imposed on them the discipline of "church watch," whereby each member was to assess his neighbor's degree of virtue. The practice, which was to be resumed in New England, could be profitably exercised only with a measure of charity and good sense found here in neither pastor nor congregation.

Browne retired in defeat and went back to the Church of England. Somehow he died in prison. So many dissenters in these times did so that it was hardly a mark against him, but the fact remained that "Brownist" became an insulting epithet that Separatists avoided.

But an obscure group meeting as privately as they could arrange in a manor house in an obscure country village called themselves only Christians, the true Christians. Much later, when circumstances drove them elsewhere, they would be happy with the title of Pilgrims.

II

EXODUS

On the highway known as the Great North Road, which ran between London and Berwick, there was an obscure hamlet called Scrooby. The highway was barely superior to those presently to be beaten out through the virgin forests of America; though it ran through level, open country, strangers needed a guide to prevent their straying aimlessly among the fields. But it was sometimes dignified by a royal progress from London to Berwick, and being also a post road, little Scrooby was a postal station. From 1590 to 1607 the postmaster was William Brewster.

He was a man of education, some means, and good connections. A kinsman who was a trusted servant of Queen Elizabeth had once taken him on a mission to the Netherlands. In 1590 Brewster got the lucrative postmastership and with it the use of the Scrooby Manor House, once the property of the Archbishop of York. By the time of Elizabeth's death he was putting it to a use which neither Her Majesty nor her successor, the son of Scottish Mary, would have approved.

Not only was Brewster cultured; he was devout, and driven by a social conscience. The country people in and about Scrooby were Milton's hungry sheep who "looked up and were not fed." What shepherds the Anglican bishops appointed for them took small interest in flocks so obscure and gave them scant attention. And yet this was a region where religious fervor was as indigenous as corn or hops might be in another, and where more dissenting creeds than one were to be born. There was here a natural hungering after righteousness, a craving for the Word, and this Brewster made it his business to supply.

Himself a layman, though he was to become an elder once a congregation was gathered, he made a search for pastors. Those people who could get to Gainsborough could hear the Separatist John Smyth, but getting there was not easy. To Scrooby, Brewster brought another Separatist, Richard Clyfton, and then John Robinson. He opened the Manor House to pastor and flock, and when the preaching was done, he fed the little multitudes at his own expense.

Illicit Meetings at Scrooby

In the Manor House a congregation was gathered on the ancient New Testament principle. Men and women covenanted with each other and with God to live rightly and preserve fellowship with each other. Among them was a youth named William Bradford, who braved the mockery of his Anglican kinsmen to join. Unlike his mentor Brewster, who had put in a few terms at Cambridge, Bradford had no university education. He was well educated nonetheless, especially in the Bible, as intelligent as he was devout, and possessed of natural qualities of leadership. One day he would write the history of the great adventure that began humbly in Scrooby.

The meetings in the Manor House were illicit. Elizabeth, who put up more or less with the Puritans, forbade on the pain of death any sect so radical as to deny her title of Defender of the Faith. After the hanging of Barrow and Greenwood in 1586, Parliament passed an Act to Retain the Queen's Subjects in Obedience, under which any person over sixteen who refused to attend Anglican service was liable to three months' imprisonment; if that did not cause him to mend his ways, he must either go into exile or suffer the fate of Barrow.

Members of a London group fled to Holland, and by 1587, after uneasy beginnings, achieved in Amsterdam the congregation known as the Ancient Brethren. So remote and inconsiderable a spot as Scrooby was less likely to draw attention. Still the unlawful assemblies at a postal station on a route that occasionally saw a royal progress could not hope to be ignored indefinitely. In 1607 Brewster resigned his postmastership. He and John Robinson were actively canvassing the means of transporting their flock to safety in Holland.

It took doing. Brewster had moderate means, and in spite of the fact that it was long since the bishops had granted him a living, Robinson was not a poor man. But much more was required than the cost of transportation. These saints were farmers; the only trade they knew was husbandry which they could not hope to practice in the land they were going to. They must learn new trades, and while learning them, they and their families must eat and have shelter.

Why did they accept a transplanting so difficult? What did Eliza-

beth's act require of them after all? Merely that once a month they find
their way to divine service and sit through it, thinking what thoughts
they would. If Paris had once been described as worth a Mass, surely
England was worth the Book of Common Prayer. There must have
been some who reasoned thus and sorrowfully withdrew from the company of emigrés. What impelled the latter? Faith of course; they had
covenanted with God and with each other and would not depart from
that covenant. They had their own renaissance in the vision of the
good life as revealed in the Acts of the Apostles. Fear too. What
vengeance might not God visit upon those who having learned the
truth would not abide in it? And anger, an emotion that during the
stormy course of the Protestant Reformation often turned to bloody
hatred of those who did not share the same vision. The wisdom and
charity of John Robinson preserved them from the sterile extremes of
religious hatred, but that there was passionate anger is demonstrated
by the opening passages of the history that Bradford wrote decades
later. They were freeborn Englishmen and would not suffer that bishops
and monarchs enslave their consciences.

Flight across the Channel

And so they embarked on the first stage of their difficult pilgrimage,
and it took courage and ingenuity. Though Elizabeth's act prescribed
exile for their kind, other subsequent acts made exile difficult to achieve.
When a ship was hired to ferry them across the Channel, its English
captain betrayed them to the magistrates, so that they lost their money
and got nowhere. Some were briefly imprisoned.

This was in the fall of 1607. In the spring another attempt was
made, this time with a Dutch captain. Again mishap befell them,
though not this time through perfidy. The longboat containing women
and children got grounded, and the captain, unable to stay, took off
with only the men. His ship was caught in storms that drove it nearly
to Norway; the passage took two weeks, the men meantime wracked
with anxiety for their families. The magistrates, however, did not commit them to prison.

This was their last attempt to emigrate in a body. Thereafter small
parties took passage separately as opportunity arose, "some at one time

and some at another," reported Bradford, "and met together again according to their desires with no small rejoicing." Robinson, who considered it his duty to enhearten the rear guard, was one of the last to arrive.

The joyous reunion took place in Amsterdam, a natural refuge in that so large a city afforded opportunity for the industrious, and also because the Ancient Brethren were there. Within a year the newcomers were on the move again, this time to Leyden, and their motives included a desire to get away from the Brethren. They did not say so; Bradford would write his history with only a passing reference to them, though he found his sixteen-year-old bride Dorothy May among them. The fact was that the Brethren were too contentious to make good company.

They were perhaps more "Brownist" than the Scrooby people. Like Browne's congregation they had set up a "church watch" and with similar results. Women must have pursued it with particular diligence, for who but they would have made so much of the *haute couture* affected by the wife of the pastor, Francis Johnson: her gold ring, her showy hat, her "excessive deal of lace," and above all her stays fitted with scandalously expensive whale bones. Women had been forbidden by Paul himself to preach before men, and perhaps it was just as well, but they could watch and report what they saw, with unpleasant results in Amsterdam. Mrs. Johnson did not take kindly to reproof; her husband said that her money was her own and she was free to spend it as she pleased. Other Brethren, including the pastor's brother, would not let the subject drop, and there were other bones of contention besides those in Mrs. Johnson's stays. Though the Scrooby congregation worshiped separately they could not keep themselves entirely apart from such garboils. In 1609 they petitioned the Court of the City of Leyden for permission to settle, giving their numbers as "one hundred persons or thereabouts," and certifying their ability to support themselves "without being a burden in the least to anyone."

Leyden made gracious reply that it would "refuse no honest persons . . . provided that such persons behave themselves and submit to the laws and ordinances; and therefore the coming of the Memorialists will be agreeable and welcome." And for a dozen years Leyden was home.

The Years in Holland

The years in Holland occupied a somewhat similar place in the Pilgrim experience that the years spent wandering in the wilderness did for the children of Israel. Orderly, well-kept Leyden, with its paved streets and its canals, was no wilderness, especially in comparison with what lay ahead of them when they left it. But it was here that their character was formed under the leadership of their own Moses, John Robinson, who like his Biblical predecessor was to be denied entrance to the Promised Land.

The effect of oppression in England had been to make Puritans more Puritanical and Separatists more Separatist. The earliest Puritans had by no means been inimical to all phases of life enjoyed in "merrie England." The elder John Winthrop craved tobacco and on his voyage across the Atlantic set the young people to playing such games as they had enjoyed on the village green. At no time were educated Puritans blind to the intellectual glories of the Renaissance, including scientific experiment. It was in large part the increasing stress of life under the bishops that forced them into austerity and theological rigidity.

Leyden, with its excellent university hard by the house where Robinson lived and preached, offered a different climate altogether. Holland was the one country in Europe which offered what many considered the supreme heresy, freedom of worship for all creeds. It had gone through its own religious strife under the Duke of Alva. Now that he was expelled, it wanted no more; the policy was live and let live, and under this genial permissiveness, even John Robinson's strict Calvinism underwent a mellowing.

He by no means accepted any creed repugnant to his faith. At Leyden University, in which he took membership to continue his theological studies, he engaged in debate with Episcopius, follower of Jacobus Arminius. He attacked the heresy of grace through works as opposed to the Calvinist doctrine of election, and did so with fury, not only in formal debate but in the pamphlets he now found opportunity to write and publish. All this, however, came under the head of honest dispute, not persecution, and he showed a large spirit in giving his congregation permission to communicate with the Reformed Churches

of the French and Dutch. Earlier, when he had to fight for his way
of life in England, it is possible that had there been such congregations,
he would have held his people firmly apart.

His writings, and though one doesn't have them, quite certainly his
sermons, revealed his discovery that though the Bible was the whole
fountainhead of wisdom, sufficient wisdom had been given no man to
make a final interpretation. "The custom of the Church is but the
custom of men; the sentence of the fathers but the opinion of men . . .
so was their testimony but human. . . . We are therefore to beware
that we neither wrong ourselves by credulity nor others by unjust suspicion."

He made such an admission of Calvin and his followers: "For
though they were precious shining lights in their time, yet God had not
revealed His whole will to them. And were they now living . . . they
would be as ready and willing to embrace further light, as that they had
received. . . . It is not possible the Christian world should come so
lately out of such thick Antichristian darkness and that full perception
of knowledge should break forth at once."

An even more famous phrase that "the Lord had more truth and
light yet to break forth out of His holy Word," would be invoked two
centuries later by those members of the Pilgrim Church, founded by
Robinson's followers, who embraced what the orthodox called the Unitarian heresy. Would Robinson have joined them? No telling. But in
such statements he was a true founder of a denomination that was
slow to adopt the name Congregationalist because its communicants
cared little about denominationalism. Far more than the Massachusetts
theocrats, he who never saw Massachusetts pointed out the road its
churches would eventually follow. And his flock, trained under his
ministry in Leyden, would never make the more egregious blunders of
the powerful Puritan theocrats. They would hang neither witch nor
Quaker; hangings there would be in Plymouth, but only for rational
cause. Calvinists they were and remained, but because their pastor had
filled them with the knowledge of God's love rather than His wrath,
they were less obsessed than most with doom and hellfire. Their way
was to be hard for all that. Overbearing Massachusetts would swallow
up their poor little Plymouth; but they were the meek who inherit the
earth; they were the leaven that makes the loaf to rise.

Yearning for a Better Land

The problem of earning a living was solved in Leyden. Though few had known anything but husbandry in England, at their distance from the Industrial Revolution, farming meant not only planting and harvesting, but functioning as general handymen, and during the slack season of winter practicing other crafts like cobbling and giving the women a hand at the loom. The Dutch then had a near monopoly of textile manufacture; the English often sent their cloth to Holland for finishing. The business prospered and there were openings for men willing to work as carders and weavers. Most of Robinson's congregation entered such employ.

They were, however, eligible for only the less skilled work. To be received into the guilds where they could learn the whole mystery of the craft required Dutch citizenship, and this they would not seek. Thus they could not rise above the subsistence level of the lowlier artisans.

Edward Winslow and William Brewster entered a higher craft— they became printers. Brewster seized the opportunity to publish pamphlets defending Separatism, and smuggled them into England, to the embarrassment of the Dutch authorities. He was welcome to his convictions, but the dissemination of these tracts in England brought protest from King James, with whom the Dutch had to remain on good terms. Even in Holland Brewster had to walk warily and sometimes go into hiding.

Much of the congregation lived as a compact enclave in little houses built in the *hof* in the rear of the big house Robinson had bought for himself. The purchase of so large a parsonage, paid for in installments over a number of years, implied no vanity on the part of the parson. It served not only as his residence with his Bridget and their six children, but as meetinghouse for his flock.

And thus for a dozen years the Pilgrims lived in close communion, the men going out from their compound to ply their trades, and on the Sabbath leading their families to the great house to hear the Word of God. Brewster served the pastor as assistant and by vote of the congregation achieved the dignity of elder. Contentions arose sometimes; now and then a communicant proved "incurable and incorrigible" and was expelled. But under a pastor "very helpful to their outward estate and so [in] every way [like] a common father unto them," this happened rarely. "Such was ye humble zeal and fervent love of these people (whilst they thus lived together) towards God and His ways, and ye single heartedness and sincere affection one towards another, that they came as near ye primitive pattern of ye first churches as any church of these later times."

And they left these homely communal comforts to face perils that made nearly everything they had experienced before insignificant.

Good as Leyden was, it wasn't good enough. Honest poverty was their lot as long as they stayed there, and like most people, however godly, they wanted to better themselves. Adaptable as they were in learning trades, they had a hankering for the good life on the land. The seasons turned, spring came again, and the only planting they could have was in the pots and boxes of herbs in their yards. It wasn't enough. In England few of them had owned the land they tilled, but there were reliable reports that in the New World beyond the sea (if they could summon the courage to cross it) good virgin soil could be had for the asking.

They were Englishmen and stubbornly so remained, but there was danger that their children would grow up Dutch. It was impossible in houses so small to find enough chores to keep small children from running into the streets and along the canals. They came back speaking in tongues, and not in the spirit of Pentecost, but in what Bradford called the "uncouth" language of the Dutch. Their own parents couldn't understand them, especially the women, who, unlike the men at their trades, had small occasion to practice the strange speech. Children could plot mischief in the presence of the mother and she be none the wiser.

Older children were in worse plight. There was no way of giving them an education; grinding labor pursued from dawn to dusk gave even literate fathers small leisure to instruct them, and necessity required that the more likely sons join early in the toil. Some youths became restive and broke out to what looked like freedom by joining the Dutch Army or running away to sea.

The very tolerance of the Dutch was a problem. Freedom to worship as one pleased could mean freedom not to worship at all. The Sabbath was by no means kept holy. Members of Robinson's congregation apparently made an attempt to call the attention of the Leyden authorities to the need of reform in this respect, but without result. The Dutch held to the view that the Sabbath had been made for man and not man for the Sabbath, a questionable, almost apocryphal text, which ministers, Puritan and Separatist, seem to have avoided, or if they preached on it at all, they drew quite other conclusions than the Dutch.

If the young were to be kept uncontaminated from the world, if the little enclave on Bell Lane was to remain English and not undergo assimilation, a better refuge than Leyden had to be found. There was another and urgent consideration. The ten-year truce between Spain and the Netherlands would end in 1620. Already the Dutch were preparing for defense in the event that the war was resumed. Unwilling to be caught in the middle, the English looked about them for a new sanctuary.

Homesick as they were for England, they could not return. Their only hope lay in the New World. For a time they gave serious thought to Guiana. Like most Englishmen they assumed at first that life in the tropics required no more effort than reaching up to pluck fruit from the trees. Then, however, they heard that the equatorial climate was unwholesome to "English bodies." Regretfully they dismissed Guiana.

What of the territory claimed by the Dutch along the Hudson? They had trading posts there and there was talk of serious colonizing. A first sounding of the will of the Estates General brought no result, for the latter were of two minds about the wisdom of planting a colony. They had before them the experience of the London Company of Virginia which had so far achieved a series of disasters and near bankruptcy for the stockholders. Yet the Dutch had not abandoned the idea, and when negotiations were resumed there was a possibility that the Leyden group might have been granted not only land, but free transportation and generous supplies in cattle and provision. This time it was the congregation which broke off negotiations. They wanted to found not a Dutch but an English colony, and what appeared to be good news had come from London.

The Offer from London

They had not neglected consideration of the most obvious prospect, the settlement the English had already in Virginia. Two circumstances had deterred them. Virginia had an establishment, Anglican, and recently a royal governor who made failure to attend divine service a capital offense. Unless they were guaranteed their right to worship in their own way they might better return to England, and the guarantee was not forthcoming. They also needed transportation. Few of them had even a pittance to invest in the undertaking, and Dutch merchants who had considered investing in their proposed colony in Guiana lost interest when they turned elsewhere. Nor could the nearly bankrupt London Company pay their way.

Then Thomas Weston of London came to Leyden in person to make an offer. The stockholders of Weston and Company would transport and supply the settlers provided they engage themselves to work seven years for the profit of the company. They would have a patent to a northern part of Virginia, well away from Jamestown, where they would be safe from molestation. This offer, coming just when the end of Holland's truce with Spain was imminent, looked good.

To John Robinson it did not. He was as zealous as any to found an English colony and had accurate foresight of the course it would follow. From his contacts in England he knew that the position of the Puritans under King James was becoming as uncomfortable as that of the Separatists. Once the latter established a foothold in the New World, they were certain to be reinforced by a wave of emigration direct from England.

But Weston's terms distressed him. "The greatest part of the colony is like to be employed constantly not upon dressing their particular land and building houses, but upon fishing, trading. . . . The same consideration of common employment by the most is a good reason not to have two days in a week denied the planters for private use. . . . Consider also how much unfit that you and your likes must serve a new prenticeship of seven years and not a day's freedom from tasks."

His point was well taken. It would be impossible to fulfil the contract as stipulated in America; when at long last Plymouth managed to buy its way out of its obligations, it would be at usurious cost.

At the moment nothing better offered. The contract was signed, the departure arranged. It was impossible to ship the entire congregation at once; it now numbered about three hundred, thanks to increments from England and Amsterdam. A division was made; the strongest and most stouthearted were to go first under the direction of Elder Brewster; John Robinson would remain in Leyden to shepherd the part of his flock whom age or infirmity made unfit for the more rugged degree of pioneering. When the way was prepared in North Virginia, these people would follow in relays as ships were available, Robinson tarrying to the last to bring up the rear guard.

And thus it was done. Other members of the congregation did follow, but never the rear guard and hence never John Robinson. A remnant would remain, presently to be merged undistinguishably with the Dutch.

The Great Pilgrimage

Late in July 1620 the travelers left Leyden to embark on the *Speedwell* at Delfthaven. Friends who could manage the trip came with them, not only from Leyden but Amsterdam, and Robinson was one of them.

For these Pilgrims, bringing themselves so far had been a high act of courage. No one was so stout of heart as to be immune to fear, of the voyage itself, of the "miseries of the land" when it ended. They had heard of the general sickness and the starving time in Jamestown; they knew that "they should be liable to famine and nakedness and the want in a manner of all things. The change of air, diet and drinking of water would infect their bodies with sore sickness." Worst of all would be the American "salvages." For all that Pocahontas had visited England and they knew the writings of John Smith, to hear Bradford tell it, they had heard only of atrocities. Yet here they were, committed to the sea, committed to the unknown land and its salvages, committed also to their faith that "all great and honorable occasions are accompanied with great difficulty, and must be both enterprised and overcome with answerable courage."

They spent a last night in Delfthaven with their friends. In the morning, the "wind being fair," there was no putting off their embarkation on the little *Speedwell*. Parting wrenched them unbearably; even "the Dutch strangers that stood on the keys as spectators could not refrain from tears." Robinson fell on his knees and "with watery cheeks commended them with most fervent prayer to the Lord and His blessing." They made their last embraces, and as the ship hoisted sail and moved past the key, they made their last salute in a volley of small shot and ordnance. Their great pilgrimage had begun.

III

THE PROMISED LAND

The *Speedwell,* a pinnace of forty tons, made short work of the trip across the Channel to Southampton. Many passengers there transferred to the *Mayflower,* whose poop deck rose tall out of the water and whose 180 tons dwarfed the *Speedwell.* The two ships began their voyage on August 5, as the date was computed under the "Old Style" Julian calendar, which the English used until 1752. By the "New Style" Gregorian calendar, August had already run half its course. It was a late start for crossing the Atlantic, and what was worse, the ships had to turn back, and then turn back again.

The trouble was with the *Speedwell,* which had sprung a leak. The first return was a minor delay, but the second was a heartbreaker, for they had got into the Atlantic a hundred leagues beyond Land's End, and even the women were finding their sea legs when word came that the pinnace might founder. At Plymouth no serious fault was found in her except that she was overmasted and possibly overladen. The Pilgrims suspected treachery on the part of the crew; this ship had been appointed to remain a year at their service in the New World, and lacking enthusiasm for the assignment, the men were alleged to have made the most of the *Speedwell's* defects.

Wherever the fault lay, it was plain that trying to get the pinnace across the Atlantic was like entrusting themselves to the Flying Dutchman. It must be left behind and its cargo and passengers sorted out for transfer to the *Mayflower.* So at the start of their journey the Pilgrims were faced with a serious handicap.

Without the *Speedwell* for use in fishing for the profit of Weston and Company, it would be hard to live up to their contract. So much time had been lost setting out and returning that now in late September they were committed to a crossing in the season avoided by the weatherwise fishermen who best knew the American coast. Worst of all, though the *Mayflower* was a goodly ship, much larger than most of the craft that carried emigrants to Virginia, its capacity was not inexhaustible; the company had to be divided.

The Saints and the Sinners

Those who had borne the voyage ill or had excessively large families were asked to wait for a later sailing. Some, their nerve shaken by the false starts, were glad to do so. One such was Robert Cushman, who had been active in negotiating the contract with Weston, but was unpopular because of new stipulations that confronted the travelers when they came in from Leyden. He and his wife remained behind with the others, and it so happened that when the *Mayflower* set out alone, of the forty-one grown men on the passenger list, only seventeen were "saints," that is, communicants of John Robinson's church. The rest were "strangers," some servants of the saints, others in Weston's employ.

The disparity was not as great as it looked. Most strangers were single men, most saints heads of families, whose wives were also saints and whose baptized children were saints presumptive. On that basis approximately half the passengers were of the congregation. As for the strangers, while there were troublesome characters among them, some were steady fellows who would eventually seek the communion of the saints. One who did not was the godly, the indispensable Miles Standish. That he never joined the congregation did not prove that he was without faith; it is possible that he was a Catholic.

Left to herself, the *Mayflower* made on the whole a prosperous voyage, though there were times when no one thought so. She was what was called a "sweet ship," having lately been employed carrying wines in the Mediterranean. She was free of the bilge whose stench made many ships insupportable. Even crowded 'tween decks for most of the voyage, with one exception the passengers remained healthy; William Butten, Samuel Fuller's servant, died as they neared the coast. The only other death was that of a seaman, "a proud and profane young man," who mocked and cursed the seasick passengers, and it was God's judgment upon him. That most passengers suffered nothing worse than queasiness in an age when Atlantic transports often became pest ships was remarkable. In midocean Mrs. Stephen Hopkins was safely delivered of a man-child and called his name Oceanus.

Storms met them, buffeted them severely, and brought near-disaster. Young John Howland, caught on deck in a sudden swell which washed him overboard, almost drowned. But he had his share of the tenacity that had brought the company thus far; he held on to the halyards until the seamen could haul him to the surface and fetch him aboard with a boathook. Though much the worse for wear, he survived to ripe old age.

Another mishap, the cracking of a main beam, very nearly sent the *Mayflower* back to England. Though the ship was then past the halfway mark, the crew muttered that continuing the voyage was suicidal, and the passengers anxiously conferred with Captain Christopher Jones. The latter held that though the ship was leaking in "her upper works," she was "strong and firm under water." When he learned that the Pilgrims had brought with them a screw to help them in building, he used it to raise the beam in place, and had the carpenter brace it with a post set firmly into the lower deck.

Change of Destination

In November they rejoiced in their first landfall, Cape Cod. But it was not their journey's end; their destination lay to the south, to northern Virginia, "some place about Hudson's River," as Bradford put it. Were they so ungrateful to the Dutch who had used them kindly as to lay claim to what the Dutch also claimed? But a casual trading post or two was an unstable basis for a territorial claim, and when recently a Virginia governor had found Dutch traders on Manhattan Island, he had warned them off what he called English territory. "About Hudson's River" may almost as well have meant about the Delaware, where so far no one had made any claim at all, except as it was loosely included in the Virginia patent.

No one will ever know their destination because they never got to it. Sailing south got them into "dangerous shoals and roaring breakers." Rather than risk being driven ashore, the ship turned back and anchored in the shelter of Cape Cod Harbor.

God's providence was manifest. Somewhere hereabouts lay the land which He had promised them. The longboats were lowered and the people piled into them. On the yellow sands they gathered for a service of thanksgiving and praise. Then they set to work, the women to washing the bales of linen they had brought ashore, the men and children to digging the mussels. There must have been something wrong with the latter, or else after more than two months of monotonous ship diet, they were consumed too greedily. Back on shipboard that night there was as much retching and groaning as there had been on the high seas.

The change of destination presented new problems. The crew still included some profane fellows who wanted to dump passengers and stores on Cape Cod and go home. Since this was obviously too narrow and sandy a strip for planting, scouts had to be dispatched to find a better place.

Another problem demanded even more prompt action. Cape Cod was a landmark that no one could mistake; even those who had no access to the charts in the wheelhouse knew very well that it was no part of northern Virginia, the grant specified in the company patent. Their indentures, drawn up in reference to the patent, were accordingly void; servants pronounced themselves free of their contracts and so entitled to strike out on their own.

They had legal justification. This area was loosely included within a territory for which Sir Ferdinando Gorges was about to receive a patent; that the Pilgrims had hardly better than squatters' rights to it was to remain a perennial vexation. Five members of the congregation conferred in Elder Brewster's cabin. These leaders were John Carver, whom they elected governor, Bradford, William White, Edward Winslow, and Brewster. "We . . . do by these presents solemnly and mutually . . . covenant and combine ourselves together into a civil body politic for our better ordering and preservation . . . and by virtue hereafter to enact, constitute, and frame such just and equal laws, ordinances, acts, constitutions and offices from time to time as shall be thought most meet and convenient for the general good of the colony, unto which we promise all due subjection and obedience."

To this, the famous Mayflower Compact, the majority of the adult males among the passengers, saints and strangers, were induced to affix their signatures or marks. The grumblers thereby bound themselves to a new contract. Few needed much persuading; they had only to look at the wild land with winter already settling over it to lose their appetite for independent adventure. But the compact also gave them a remarkable opportunity. What Virginia had only lately achieved after a dozen years would be theirs from the start. May one identify the conference in the *Mayflower* cabin as the first New England town meeting, which was to become an inseparable concomitant of the Congregational Way? Not in any literal sense. Only one officer was elected, a governor; this official, later aided by assistants, would give the Pilgrims their first civil government. The evolution of this arrangement into the characteristic New England town meeting is difficult to determine. Bradford's history gives no details; George F. Willison, whose *Saints and Strangers* gives so carefully researched an account of the Pilgrim adventure, alludes to it only in much later days.

Nevertheless, the Mayflower Compact was the first step in the evolution of the civil aspects of the Congregational Way. Those who drew it up had nothing like Jeffersonian democracy in mind. Their reason for getting "strangers" to sign it as well as the "saints" of their congregation was only to bring them under control, by binding them, as it were, to a new indenture. But so signing was an act of consent whose significance could not be denied. The government of the congregation would remain in the hands of the saints; but in the long run strangers would not be excluded from the secular government of the colony.

The *Mayflower* put down its anchors near Clarke Island on December 16. The spot had been chosen five days earlier after several expeditions in search of an area which would combine the advantages of fertile land, fresh water, and a fair harbor. Once the captain, and always members of the crew, accompanied them, and a nameless seaman was the hero in the discovery of Plymouth. During a stormy twilight their pilot mistook his landmark, and they were nearly driven ashore into the breakers when their steersman "bade those which rowed, if they were men, about with them, or else they were all cast away." Under his vigorous direction they got to the shelter of a small island, and when morning came they found themselves near a promising site. They did not immediately explore it, for this was the Sabbath and the saints were in charge, but on Monday "they marched into the land and found diverse cornfields and little running brooks and a place (as they supposed) fit for their situation; at least it was the best they could find, and the season and their present necessity made them glad to accept it."

The harbor was not so good as that at Cape Cod; the *Mayflower* had to anchor a mile offshore, which made unloading tedious. But they got men and tools into the longboat and set to work constructing the common house designed to house their stores and serve as a dormitory for the workmen. Building began on Christmas Day, but Christmas, despised as a Papist feast, was only another working day. Later Bradford as governor would speak sharply to those strangers who planned to spend the day bowling. If their consciences forbade their working on Christmas, he would excuse them, he said; but in that case, they must spend the day indoors at their devotions and not abroad in levity.

"The General Sickness"

The common house was completed and the unloading had begun when a disaster befell them that was to delay construction of most of their homes until spring and keep the *Mayflower* riding at anchor until April. They who had made the voyage so well now fell mortally ill of what they called "the general sickness." There was scurvy, there were rheumatoid complaints, especially among the hardiest of the men who had been scouting, sleeping out in snow and rain, wading in all weathers. There were seldom half a dozen able-bodied men about at a time, and they were needed to wait on the sick. Given the impossibility of building shelter, Governor Carver risked (and incurred) the wrath of Weston by ordering the *Mayflower* to remain as shelter for the women and children.

At first the crew was churlish. When asked for beer to refresh the men lying desperately ill in the common house, the bosun's answer was rude: "If he were their own father he should have none." The crew might have defied the governor, dumped women and children ashore and sailed home but for the fact that the illness spread among them and became so general that there was no question of sailing. After this, and beholding the kindness of the saints, who nursed profane seamen as tenderly as they nursed their own, the captain "was something strucken and sent to the sick ashore and told the governor he should send for beer that had need of it though he drunk water homeward bound."

Elder Brewster, the saint, then in his fifties, and Miles Standish, the stranger, escaped the illness and were tireless in their service to the stricken. They "did all the homely offices for them which dainty and queasy stomachs cannot endure to be named; and all this willingly and cheerfully without any grudging in the least, showing their true love unto their friends and brethren." The tribute came from Bradford, who though only in his thirties barely made it through the winter. He had been doubly stricken, for returning with a severe chill from the discovery of Plymouth, he had learned that in his absence his young wife Dorothy had somehow fallen overboard and drowned.

When spring came half the company was dead. The children had made out better than their elders; even little Peregrine White, born to William and Susanna while the *Mayflower* waited at Cape Cod, had survived, but he was now fatherless. Many other children were motherless; of eighteen women, only five had lived to see the spring. Not all Miles Standish's skill in nursing could save his wife Rose.

Nor did spring end the mortality. On the first hot day in April, Governor Carver, working with the rest to set corn, suffered a fatal sunstroke, and his wife Mary lived not long after. Bradford, now shakily convalescent, was made governor in his stead. To him was it given to reply to the fierce anger of Thomas Weston when the *Mayflower* returned at last without any of the lading in fish and furs expected to found the fortune of Weston and Company.

The Call to Worship

There is a curious oversight in Bradford's history of these first years. One looks in vain for details of the founding of the church. Aside from his references to God's providence one would hardly know that the impetus to found this colony had come from men determined to worship as they would.

As governor his office was that of Martha rather than Mary, and he was cumbered with many cares. He was beset with the difficulty of managing both strangers and saints. "It is our calamity that we are (beyond expectation) yoked with some ill-conditioned people, who will never do good, but corrupt and abuse others." He had to direct allotments when, after an unsatisfactory year of communal planting prescribed by Weston rather than by any notions of primitive Christian communism, families were assigned each their own lot or meerstead, and under the free enterprise system even women and children worked the fields with a will. He had to see that supplies were rationed in lean seasons (these were usually May and June, and without the availability of shellfish, people would have gone hungrier than they did) lest the improvident consume them in one gulp. He had to find lading for new supply ships (and a fine cargo of beaver skins on the *Fortune* went only to French pirates). He had above all to maintain correct relations with the Indians.

The Indians, whose atrocities had been so much feared, were a great surprise. There had been one volley of arrows aimed at the scouts, but harmlessly deflected by their armor; during the desperate first winter there had been a sense of being stalked by mute observers, and sometimes tools were stolen.

But when there was real harm done, the shoe was on the other foot. The Pilgrims had looted the seed corn they found in mysterious mounds on the Cape (later they paid for it). The Indian Squanto, who taught them to plant Indian corn and served them as interpreter, owed his command of English to the perfidy of an English adventurer who had kidnaped him and two dozen others to sell in the European slave market.

The worst English atrocity was unintentional. Strange ailments imported by the fishermen who frequented the coast long before the Pilgrims came had become plagues among the Indians and nearly exterminated them. Squanto had returned to his native village near Plymouth to find only skeletons. It was for this reason that the scouts had found abandoned cornfields along the shore, and why the Indians had become too few to give the white men serious trouble. Not only Plymouth but the whole of Massachusetts Bay had been decimated by the Indian sickness. This fact was to be one of its major attractions to others planning settlement.

But what of the Pilgrim church? Surely having gone to such lengths to found it, they did not neglect it. Elder Brewster's ministry to the sick aboard the *Mayflower* and in the common house included prayer; his office resembled that of those members of the Dutch Reformed Church designated as "comforters of the sick." After the *Mayflower* sailed he had no place to preach and pray other than the common house. One may picture his congregation sitting on barrels or kegs, uneasily, since some of them contained gunpowder, to hear him read the good Word and enlarge upon it. One has to picture for oneself; Bradford gives no details.

The only authentic picture was drawn years later, in 1627, when the little colony had achieved a fairly stable footing, and it was drawn by a visitor from New Netherland, Isaac de Rasières. The Dutch had by then planted a real colony on the Hudson and had sent de Rasières to explore possibilities of trade with its little neighbor, once of Leyden. By good fortune his visit included a Sabbath.

He heard the drums beat the call to worship, and then saw the congregation assemble to march to church. It was a military procession; Miles Standish marshaled it, the governor with the minister at his side led it, and the men carried their arms. The church was still more martial; a twelve-hundred-pound cannon was mounted on its roof. "A mighty fortress is our God," the congregation might have sung, for this was in fact a fort, built on a hill so that the rooftop cannon could rake the countryside. It was also, as was to be true of the first churches in New England, the town hall.

Bradford does describe the construction of the fort, with an offhand reference to its other functions. It was begun late in the summer of 1622 after a visit from a fishing sloop whose captain brought terrifying news from Virginia. There, just when the colony seemed about to flourish, the Indians had risen on Good Friday and massacred 347 whites. The atrocity stories they had heard in Leyden were true after all, and what was most frightening, the Indians had plotted concerted action, attacking at the same moment throughout Virginia, at a time when peace seemed universal and no white man hesitated to welcome an Indian to his home.

There was peace in Plymouth, but often an uneasy peace. They had concluded a treaty with the local chief, Massasoit, but the latter had lately become angry at their interpreter. Squanto, to whom they owed so much, was not entirely the noble red man; his European education had perhaps taught him other things than linguistics, for lately he had been caught in double dealing, playing the white man against the Indians to the wrath of both. Nor was that all; the Narragansetts to the south had recently made the rude gesture of sending a rattlesnake skin stuffed with arrows.

One must not trust alone on treaties. In spite of the exigencies of harvest, men were spared to begin work on the fort, and when that was finished, they built a stockade around the village. Apparently the work took the better part of a year. When the fort was ready, the congregation had a place for worship.

But they had no pastor, only John Robinson in Holland. When the supply ship *Fortune* arrived in November 1621, they had great hopes, but though it brought a few saints from the Leyden congregation (and still more strangers) it did not bring their pastor. Robert Cushman had come on a flying visit; during the two weeks that the *Fortune* lay offshore he found time to preach them a proper sermon. Then the *Fortune* sailed, laden with the beaver skins which the pirates got, and they were left again with the ministry of Elder Brewster.

The colony had no better man; the faithful must have taken comfort in his readings from Scripture and his homely commentary, but what form the latter took no one knows, for if anyone took notes, they were not preserved. He had one defect; not being ordained he could not administer the sacraments. Longingly, good people remembered the grace they had received from the Lord's Supper, served weekly in Leyden; they could not have it here. Women, troubled for the health of their newborn babes, must have worried that they could not be baptized. Did they hold in these harsh circumstances to the Calvinist doctrine, derived like that of predestination itself from the Roman Church, that the baby dying unbaptized went to hell? What did Brewster tell them? No one knows, but remembering what Robinson had said about "further light," his common sense may well have found a means of allaying their anxieties. Plymouth would never be so severely doctrinal as the much greater colony founded after.

The Absent Pastor

Why didn't the orphaned congregation solve their difficulties by ordaining Brewster as pastor? It was the essence of Separatist polity that a congregation choose and ordain its officers. Why did they not elevate Brewster to such rank that he could administer the sacraments? But they would not take so momentous a step without the approval of Robinson, and when they suggested it, he demurred. Perhaps because the precedents of Congregationalism were not yet firmly established, he "judged it not lawful . . . nor convenient if it were lawful." He may have considered Brewster's education inadequate, for though he had studied at Cambridge, he had taken no degree.

One difficulty lay in the decision taken before the departure from Leyden, a resolve as touching as it was unwise. Though the congregation was to be physically divided, it was to remain in spirit one, and Robinson its pastor. The congregation would be united in America as soon as it was possible to transport pastor and the remnant of his flock. And the pastor never came.

When Weston had come to Leyden to invite the congregation to America, he had little interest in advancing the cause of Separatism. He headed a stock company prepared to finance a settlement, and needed settlers. He had heard that the Leyden group was prepared to go; that and not its religious eccentricities was what interested him. He knew also that in spite of their poverty they had a high reputation among the Dutch as a sober, hard-working people who could be trusted to live up to their obligations. He judged them good prospects for pioneering, and he was not mistaken.

During the brief stay in Southampton, while the *Mayflower* and its ill-fated sister ship prepared for the voyage, he may have become disillusioned. These sober, industrious people were also capable of stiff-necked obstinacy. There is an echo of that experience in the letter he wrote when the *Mayflower* returned without cargo. They could, he implied, have assembled one had they given to practical matters "a quarter of the time you spend in discussing, arguing and consulting." Much argument had taken place in Southampton when the travelers found that Cushman had committed them to new obligations to Weston of which they had not been told. They had refused to sign the revised contract.

Weston and Company soon lost interest in transporting the remainder of the Leyden group, though some arrived in relays on the *Fortune,* the *Anne,* and a second *Mayflower*. They were especially disinclined to transport John Robinson, who had been a shrewd critic of their offer from the first. Some members of the company were friendly to him and willing to grant Plymouth its dearest wish, but they were in a minority. The majority were Puritans who had as low an opinion of the

Separatists as the latter had of the Dutch Arminians. They persisted in calling them "Brownists," a term which Robinson had expressly warned his departing brethren to avoid.

Yet they had pity on a people living in a far land without the sacraments, and sent them a minister, John Lyford, who could preach a good sermon. Give them the benefit of the doubt that they did not know that he was also a lecher. The Pilgrims found him out and sent him away. They had ill luck with any pastor but Brewster; another sent them also had to be shipped back; he was deranged.

In 1626, a year after it occurred, they heard ill news indeed. Robinson was dead. Yet his spirit sustained them still; in the substantial colony that the Puritans were about to plant, the Pilgrim example would play an important part.

IV

THE GREAT MIGRATION

Toward the end of its first decade, Plymouth heard that there was sickness among new neighbors across Massachusetts Bay at Naumkeag. These being good neighbors, Dr. Samuel Fuller was sent to do what he could.

Lonely as was this coast, there had been other neighbors. Weston and Company had made a second planting at Wessagusset. It sent men only, probably all "strangers," and their behavior was an affliction to Plymouth. One man was said to keep an Indian mistress; others in want, to hire themselves to Indian masters. They stole from both the Indians and Plymouth, and had incurred the contempt of the former. It was a relief when such as survived hired themselves out to passing fishing craft in the hope of getting home.

When Weston undertook to visit his colony, he found it was no longer there. He had other bad luck, losing his shallop in Ipswich Bay and being stripped by the Indians. He made his way to Plymouth in sorry plight; there the people fed him, clothed him, and reluctantly gave him some of their small store of beaver skins when his transport was available. Weston was not grateful.

Other godless settlements had followed. When Lyford was expelled from Plymouth, he and another ne'er-do-well, John Oldham, pitched first at nearby Nantasket and then at Cape Ann, where they took over a fishing station which the Pilgrims had left for the winter. (A decade later the slaying and scalping of Oldham on an expedition to Long Island gave New England a real atrocity story and an excuse to commit one worse.)

Strays from fishing parties from England sometimes wandered into Plymouth, and recently there had been a very troublesome settlement at Mount Wollaston, the later Quincy, ruled by "Morton of Merrymount." Thomas Morton was a pagan who wrote scurrilous verses and marshaled his men in a heathenish ritual around a maypole. Since this took place on foreign soil, as it were, Plymouth might have put up with the may-pole. What they could not countenance was that Morton was luring their servants to his settlement and selling arms to the Indians. The only martial superiority the Pilgrim would have over the latter if any rattlesnake stuffed with arrows led to war, lay in their blunderbusses, whose noise scared the red men as much as their accuracy. Standish was dispatched with an armed guard to Mount Wollaston, and after an easy conquest (Morton's company was allegedly too drunk to resist), seized Morton and shipped him back to England.

Better live forever lonely than put up with such neighbors, but the settlement at Naumkeag was of another sort. Its beginnings had been annoying in that it had been some of its settlers who had invited Lyford and Oldham to Cape Ann. The venture had prospered no better than it deserved, and the company had withdrawn to Naumkeag, where it was joined in 1628 and 1629 by a much larger group under responsible leadership. It was the forerunner of the great Puritan migration to America; of that venture, whose inception is cloudy even to historians, Plymouth as yet knew nothing, but it knew that Naumkeag, or Salem as it was to be called, was suffering the familiar afflictions of first set-tlers. Charitably, Governor Bradford sent Dr. Samuel Fuller to do what he could for the ailing, especially Governor John Endicott, who had scurvy.

As a medical man, Dr. Fuller's rating was probably not high. Enemies to Plymouth claimed that his skill derived from his having been "bred a butcher." In Holland he had earned his keep as sergemaker; what medical lore he had picked up on the side had little availed the Pilgrims during the "general sickness," perhaps because he was as ill as any. But he represented what medical science there was on the coast, and he knew scurvy. He also knew the way to Salem. The Pilgrim fathers, who had known only husbandry in England and the textile business in Holland, by now knew something of seamanship. When the cod came into Massachusetts Bay, relays took turns in manning the shallop to go after it. Their fishing venture on Cape Ann had acquainted them with Naumkeag, and admiring its superior anchorage and the breadth of good land that bound it, they sometimes wished that winter had not forced them into the precipitate choice of narrow Plymouth.

God prospered Fuller at Salem. His treatments were successful; anyway the governor got over his scurvy. What was even more gratifying to the deacon, he had godly converse with the pious governor and the two ministers, Francis Higginson and John Skelton. He converted all three to the polity of the Plymouth church.

That is one story. There is another that all three were inclined to Congregational practice before they left England. There were Congregationalists among the English Puritans; these did not advocate separation, but they held to the Separatist belief that the true church of Christ consisted not of the parish at large, but of the elect who covenanted with God, and that under Christ they should be governed not by bishops or magistrates but by their own elect. The concept had been gaining ground in England, and some who advocated it had also gone to Holland. Robinson had met them and had been sufficiently impressed to permit his own congregation to worship with them.

According to this interpretation, Fuller did not "convert" his new friends, who did not in any case accept the necessity of separation, but confirmed and suggested practical application of ideas they already held.

The Salem congregation was appointed to be gathered on August 6, 1629, and Plymouth was invited to the ceremony. Crosswinds delayed Bradford and Brewster from reaching Salem until the afternoon, when they offered the right hand of fellowship to a congregation already covenanted and its pastors chosen. The elect, thirty men, had solemnly subscribed to their covenant, and had elected Skelton as their minister, and Higginson as their teacher. Everything had been done according to the old custom of Scrooby, Leyden, and Plymouth, except that there were as yet no deacons. Other settlers were expected from England, and the congregation chose to wait to see who came.

So it happened that a year later, when the Puritans poured into the Bay in such numbers that it looked as if all England were emigrating, they found a precedent already established, the Congregational Way. Some were better pleased than others. Puritan was a term describing not a denomination but an intention. It included ministers and communicants who held to the Scotch form of Presbyterianism, which did not so strictly limit church membership to the elect and preferred church government through an administrative body of presbyters to autonomous rule by each congregation. Many of them, however, even their ministers, would have been hard put to it to distinguish whether they were Presbyterian or Congregational. In the New World, Plymouth's practice was to prove so suitable to conditions that congregations adopted it without quibbling over terms, except that they would not call themselves Separatists; to the extent that they became so in time, it was accomplished *de facto* rather than *de jure*.

John Robinson had accurately foreseen that the unseparated Puritans would one day look to America for the same reasons that had impelled the Scrooby-Leyden congregation to do so. The Puritans had good hope when Scottish James succeeded Tudor Elizabeth, and had lost no time in presenting them their "millinary petition," so called because it was signed with a thousand names. James had been reared under the aegis of Calvinism. That, however, was exactly the trouble. James had had all he intended to take of Calvinist austerity. He gave the petition scant attention, and presently outraged the Puritans by publishing his *Book of Sports*. His intentions were good; he had composed it to end controversies about Sabbath-keeping by specifying what pleasures might be lawfully enjoyed after attendance at divine service: vaulting, archery, and in their season, maypole and morris dancing. After this the Puritans expected no more of King James, and when he died in the same year as Robinson, they looked hopefully to his son Charles.

King Charles and His Archbishop

Charles was a righteous man who was to prove his willingness to die for what he deemed holy. The difficulty was that his concept of righteousness and theirs were very different.

The first English King born within the Anglican Church and bred to its faith, he revered it, and in its defense placed his trust in Archbishop William Laud. To many of Charles' courtiers Laud was an odd companion for a king so aristocratic in his tastes. He was the son of a tradesman who had not taught him courtly manners. There was ill-suppressed laughter at the dedication of St. Catherine Cree when after the mighty invocation, "Be ye lifted up, ye everlasting doors, and the King of Glory shall come in," what came in was the fat little archbishop, "a little, low, redfaced man." But Laud shared Charles' concept of righteousness, and he too would die for it. He zealously undertook to reform the Church, but not according to Puritan prescription.

What were these misguided people after? They clamored for preaching instead of ritual. Let them go to London's St. Paul's as Charles often did, and listen to John Donne. What Puritan parson could command such magnificent eloquence? They said that what was true of London was not so in the country. Let them go into Wiltshire and listen to George Herbert, nobly born, who had abandoned a worldly career to preach sermons and write hymns in a spirit whose childlike sweetness would have won the simple people of Scrooby.

Both Laud and the Puritans were right. There were such men as these in the Church; there were also debauched characters who took "livings," as many as they could get, for what they would pay, and often never went near them. Sometimes they delegated their office to curates so ill paid that they had to take handyman jobs to earn their keep, and so unlettered that they could hardly spell out the Book of Common Prayer, let alone expound it.

Laud applied himself sincerely to reforming the Church according to his lights. He built it more stately mansions, set Inigo Jones to designing new churches or remodeling old ones in the Renaissance manner known as "Laudian Gothic." He imported gilded organs from Germany, set new standards of choir singing, encouraged musicians to compose works worthy of being sung before the King.

Even more strenuously he applied himself to ridding the Church of its enemies who would incontinently destroy the beauty of holiness, who would have none of candles, images, gilded organs. These enemies were the Puritans. Laud made it his business to harry them out of England, and when they took refuge in Holland, harry them there as well.

It happened that Charles had a Catholic Queen, Henrietta Marie of France. When the Puritans saw his courtiers thronging to worship in her chapel, they saw Bloody Mary come again and the Anglican Church united with Rome. And indeed union with Rome was not beyond the scope of Laud's ambition; he craved it, but only provided Rome would accept Anglican reforms and modifications. In this he was curiously akin to the Puritans, who asked not to leave the Anglican Church but only that it adopt their ways.

If Bloody Mary had come again, the Puritans could expect a return of the terrors described in Foxe's *Book of Martyrs*. In this their fears were unjustified. Sometimes under Laud's direction the High Commissioner sentenced a detractor of the bishops to the Tower, first putting him through the indignity, even if he were noble, of slitting his nostrils and cropping his ears; but fires were not relit to burn heretics and schismatics at Smithfield, and the chief martyrdom imposed on the Puritans was that their preachers were subjected to a kind of inquisition, and if they did not pass it, they were "silenced," that is, denied a license to preach.

Deprived of their livings, forbidden to preach, Puritans invented the "lecture"; it was delivered Sunday afternoon or on a market day, and since the Puritans commanded the best eloquence in England this side of John Donne, the lectures became immensely popular. But Laud's informers were as watchful as the Puritans were ingenious; lecturing was also forbidden by Charles' decree. Some noblemen gave Puritan ministers a limited hearing in their private chapels until Laud required that even here they be examined for licensing.

It was still possible to fight back. Having failed with royalty, the dissenters turned to Parliament, and with greater success. Though Parliament was not yet overwhelmingly Puritan in its sympathy, many members of the legal profession had small patience with His Majesty's interpretation of the divine right of kings to construe any opposition as treason and blasphemy. They especially objected to the conduct of the Star Chamber and the High Commission, and they attempted to force the royal hand by insisting on the parliamentary prerogative of controlling the money bags. Taxation originated in Parliament, and it would not tax except as the King made compromises.

His Majesty brooked no such insolence from what he called a "nest of vipers." In 1629 he cut the Gordian knot; he sent some parliamentary leaders to the Tower, dissolved Parliament, and did not call it again for eleven years. For all anyone then knew he would never call it again.

And now the Puritans had no hope at all in England. If they were not faced with martyrdom, they were faced with the impossibility of constructive action. Ministers deprived of livings, magistrates out of office, could no doubt find other means of livelihood, and if they worked quietly at it, would not be molested. But it was not to this that God had called them, that they blind the light within and live voiceless. God asked of them to be a loud voice crying. If England would not hear them, a newer England awaited them overseas, less wilderness than this had become.

It happened that six days before Charles dissolved Parliament he had granted a charter entitling a group of Puritan adventurers to plant a colony in Massachusetts Bay.

Beginnings of the Bay Colony

Interest in the New World was no novelty to the Puritans. They were largely of the substantial middle class, which included businessmen with a natural interest in opportunities for sound investment. They had been represented in the now dissolved London Company of Virginia, had largely backed the Pilgrims through Weston and Company, had taken over the unsuccessful fishing station at Cape Ann, and recently settled Naumkeag. They had also looked to the West Indies, and had formed the Providence Company which planted a settlement on the island now known as Santa Catalina, where the strictest notions of Puritan propriety were enforced.

Such ventures had not yet made the fortunes of the stockholders, but the latter had been learning. By now they no longer expected the quick return the Spaniards had from the gold and silver looted from Central America; in the parts available to them there was no such commodity to loot. Virginia had finally found profit in its tobacco (and was grateful to Charles for permitting them to raise it), but to bring Virginia to the point where it could raise a salable crop had meant year after year of investment without return. A colony took root with difficulty and in the meantime required long and expensive support.

They had glowing reports of life in New England, for even the Pilgrims, hard pressed though they were to scrabble out a living, put their best foot forward when writing for publication; they wrote of the abundance of wild turkeys and geese, of the succulence of berries and grapes. Francis Higginson of Salem had written of the beauty of the yellow "gillyflowers" that floated out to meet his ship as it neared shore. More to the point, he had written of the scarcity of Indians, of the mysterious sickness which had virtually cleared the Bay area of red men who might contest the arrival of the white. They knew also that the little Plymouth group had not pre-empted the choicest lands; those about Massachusetts Bay were far richer in fields of good black loam and stands of virgin forest.

Preparations had already begun with the sending of Governor Endicott with a company to Salem. Now when the dissolution of Parliament faced them with a total impasse in England, they planned a far greater venture. They had a patent to lands extending indefinitely west from a line drawn between the Charles and Merrimac Rivers; they prepared for a systematic, large-scale planting. In obscure conferences held variously in London and Lincolnshire, where the Earl of Lincoln (and to some extent even the bishop) was their friend, they made elaborate arrangements. Profit was not their prime motive, though they would not disdain such profits as became available. The men who invested in their company or joined the migration, like Isaac Johnson, whose wife was the Lady Arbella, daughter of the Earl of Lincoln, must hazard all to found a commonwealth dedicated to the glory of God.

The plans were perfected, a little fleet of ships engaged, supplies bought by the ton, migrants assembled, servants contracted for, and in April 1630, one of the most gifted of Puritan ministers came to Southampton to bid them Godspeed. His name was John Cotton, and he was still permitted to preach in his church in England's Boston. He was not silent now: he gave not a lecture but a sermon, "God's Promises to His Plantation." His text was II Samuel 7:10: "Moreover I will appoint a place for my people Israel. And I will plant them, that they may dwell in a place of their own and move no more."

If he spoke like Robinson on a similar occasion "with watery cheeks," no one made note of the fact. His sermon was not one of his more poetic flights of eloquence in which a woman member of his congregation recognized "the voice of the beloved." He had no need to stir hearts that were already stirred almost beyond bearing; he spoke practically in justification of the venture. He was addressing both a congregation and a stockholders' meeting, and did not neglect to cite as one reason for removal "merchandize and gaine-sake."

Their work was "to plant a colony, that is, a company that agree together to remove out of their own country to settle a city or commonwealth elsewhere." They were going "for the liberty of ordinances" to purify their worship of "mixtures and man-made corruptions." They would establish new ordinances in their commonwealth; "You shall never find that God ever rooted out a people that had the ordinances planted among them, and themselves planted into the ordinances; never did God suffer such plants to be pulled up." Difficulties ahead? God "hath given us hearts to overlook them all, as if we were carried up on eagles' wings."

Not all of his listeners proceeded with the voyage; heart was not given everyone to be "carried up on eagles' wings." Since the previous October when the company held its first general court under its charter, the membership had been volatile, some deciding not to risk it, not now, and being replaced by others. Even after embarking on the flagship *Arbella,* John Humfrey, who had been elected to serve Governor John Winthrop as deputy, suddenly decided against the trip (he came two years later) and Joseph Dudley was elected in his stead.

"It is not a wonder that they discovered so great a want of resolution," later wrote Thomas Hutchinson, a descendant of Cotton's most ardent admirer. "It is strange that so many persevered. . . . What must we think . . . of persons of rank and good circumstances in life bidding a final adieu to all the conveniences and delights of England . . . and exposing themselves, their wives and children to inevitable hardships . . . to land upon a most inhospitable shore, destitute of any kind of building to secure them from the inclemency of the weather."

Actually New England was not inhospitable in June when the *Arbella* and the forward ships of the fleet got there. The children piled happily ashore at Cape Ann to pick strawberries. Governor Endicott entertained the gentry, including Lady Arbella, in his quite presentable house in Salem. Where the Pilgrims had reached a weatherbeaten coast without shelter of any kind and the snows already beginning, the *Arbella* and the ten other ships that followed in relays reached the coast in its most pleasant season, with the whole summer ahead "to make a pitch," as Winthrop put it, and to build.

Nor were they like the Pilgrims oppressed with the circumstances that they had landed in territory to which they had no patent. The Puritans had arrived exactly on target, and were empowered to make the ordinances of which Cotton had spoken without interference from

London. They had accomplished the feat of bringing their charter with them, that their government might be here and here only. How they managed it no one knows. It was routine that all charters contain a stipulation that they remain in England; somehow the final form of theirs contained no such provision. The Puritans had friends in high places; they had acquaintance among clerks and copyists and knew which palms to grease. That is one assumption, but given their discretion no one can know. It is possible that God's providence was solely responsible.

Certainly Charles and Laud were not. When they grasped what had happened, when they learned what uses the Puritans were making in America of their freedom, they demanded that the charter be returned. Again they demanded it. There was anxiety on this score in Massachusetts, but at such a distance evasion was not difficult. Letters, one could explain, had been lost in transit. Finally a ship was built in England for the express purpose of going to America to seize the charter. This time God's providence really intervened; the ship broke apart in launching, and before anything else could be arranged, Charles and his archbishop were too preoccupied to give this annoyance further attention.

So the Bay Colony was free to institute what ordinances it would, found a commonwealth dedicated to God's will as His will was understood here, and for more than half a century governed itself like a sovereign, independent state.

Even so, and in spite of the happy landing in strawberry time, the beginning was not easy.

V

CITY IN THE WILDERNESS

When the *Mayflower* sailed home from the tragic first winter in Plymouth, not a settler had gone with her. Their numbers halved, their prospects of wresting a living from the soil uncertain, beset with grief and fear, every man, woman, and child had stayed the course. Widowers and orphans were absorbed into surviving families; Susanna White, widow of William and mother of Resolved and Peregrine, married the widower Edward Winslow.

The same could not be said of the Puritans who came in the great migration. After a hard look at the land even with the face of summer on it and an assessment of the labor required to make it habitable, some took the first opportunity to go home. After a bleak winter in Watertown, one of the organizers of the company, Sir Richard Saltonstall, decided that he was too old for pioneering and went back, sending in his place two sons.

Governor Winthrop, a man in his forties, was no younger; his friends had done their best to dissuade him from undertaking such a venture at his time of life. He had joined the enterprise late, having indeed restrained his eldest son and namesake from going with Endicott to Salem. He was now bowed with grief and care; grief for his son Henry, lately returned from the West Indies, who crossed the Atlantic safely only to drown on his first day ashore, care for his beloved wife Margaret, who was awaiting the birth of their youngest in England, care above all for the distressing problems of the new colony.

To the Pilgrims watching from Plymouth, mingling a cordial welcome with some justified anxiety as to what so massive a migration would do to their own claims, the newcomers had arrived with a substance beyond dreams. There was real wealth among their leaders and their backers in England; they had not spent years scratching out the leanest subsistence, did not have to bind themselves to impossible conditions to a company of adventurers to get the wherewith to travel;

they themselves were the company. They were many, fifteen hundred that first year, arriving in seventeen ships, for others followed Winthrop's fleet; the ships were generously provisioned and some even carried cattle, which the Pilgrims had managed to import a scant three years before.

Yet the colony was not so fortunate as it looked, nor was its provision adequate. In a day when a six weeks' crossing of the Atlantic was considered excellent time, passengers consumed an inordinate amount of the provision any ship could carry. Livestock was especially difficult to transport; human passengers adapted to the rolling of the ship more easily than cattle, which got thrown about, broke their legs, and had to be slaughtered. The newcomers had difficulty getting even their goats across alive. Prices were high in England that year; the cost of wheat meal and peas, added to the expense of shipping, had already been a heavy drain on the fortunes of the investors.

They had supposed that they could count on the plantation at Salem for supply. It was disappointing and frightening to learn that on the contrary Salem was eagerly looking to them for the same thing. The colony had suffered much from sickness, had lost eighty out of its three hundred, and there had been little planting.

Thus in spite of careful planning, the first winter was hard. Not as hard as it had been in Plymouth, but discouraging enough. When after a mild fall the bitter blast of winter came on Christmas Eve, the more humble settlers found their shelters cold comfort. Arriving in relays during the summer and early fall, faced with the immediate problem of finding suitable land and starting to build, they had had no opportunity to plant. Provision diminished alarmingly, and the very number of the settlers was against them. Men could hunt and fish, and until hard frosts set in, women and children took pleasure in scouting the shores at low tide to dig for clams. They found the clams, rare in England, very palatable, and the pious accounted them along with the now vanished strawberries of Cape Ann as manna in the wilderness provided by a gracious God.

When real winter came and hunger grew serious, some men broke a trail inland to Indian villages or down the coast to Plymouth to buy corn. Only Indian corn was available—Plymouth settlers had ill success with the English grains they had brought with them—and it offended the English stomachs of many newcomers. It was indigestible, perhaps poisonous; even a cow that had survived the voyage died after eating it.

That their stomachs rejected what the Indians, the Virginians, and the Plymouth settlers found nourishing was because they were falling ill. Sickness had begun during the summer; Lady Arbella had died in Salem just as the leaves were turning, and her heartbroken husband, absent in Charlestown at the time, did not long survive her. (He left his fortune to the colony.) The dread symptoms of scurvy became common; reproachfully, Winthrop remarked that they appeared first in those people who instead of thanking God for what they had, insisted on repining for what they had left behind in England.

But something must be done for a people homesick, scurvied, and hungry. Winthrop dispatched his supply ship the *Lyon* to England with instructions to his son John to load it with all possible speed and at whatever cost send it back; lemons must be included in the cargo. Captain Pierce made a speedy passage both ways through the winter gales, and in February, just as conditions were becoming desperate and a day of fasting and humiliation had been appointed, he triumphantly reappeared. The hunger for good English bread was gratified, and the lemons that cured the scurvy enabled queasy stomachs to accept and even relish the inevitable staple, Indian corn.

The Church-State

Winthrop had other problems than hunger on his mind. Where to make a permanent "sitting down"? What he wanted was a centralized community, a "city on a hill" that could be fortified. He was thwarted by the impulse of the settlers to scatter to wherever they could find sweet water and good land. While he variously considered Cambridge and Charlestown as suitable sites, Sir Richard Saltonstall was planting the servants he brought with him and the minister George Philips at Watertown. Other parties were trying Roxbury and Dorchester.

Winthrop's insistence on fortification derived from fear of the French and the Indians. News had come that Charles had granted land in the north to the one, and there was no end to rumors of impending hostility from the other. Though a principal attraction of this area had been the feebleness of the Indian tribes, strong nations who had escaped the Indian sickness lived to the south and west. One heard that the Narragansetts were on the march; a raid did take place at Ipswich on a sachem deemed friendly. One could not forget the appalling massacre in Virginia or that Plymouth, so generally successful in its Indian relations, had been frightened into stockading its whole village.

Nevertheless Winthrop abandoned this idea. Partly it was because of the friendly overtures of a local chief. More it was because of his sensible reflection that if the Indians were strong enough to attack, a fort would not save the white men, and if they were willing to treat for peace, a fort was unnecessary. Indeed, it would be more than a century before Massachusetts had serious cause to fear Indians on its own territory.

The French, being at peace with England, offered no immediate danger; for the time they could be forgotten.

It was necessary to draw up the ordinances of which John Cotton had spoken, indeed urgent now that the colonists were scattering at their own pleasure. During the *Arbella's* voyage, Winthrop had preached a layman's sermon on his concept of the matter: "Thus stands the case between God and us. . . . We are entered into a covenant with Him for this work. We have taken out a commission; the Lord hath given us leave to draw up our articles."

In August he took time from exploring the Bay and directing the building at his first choice of settlement, Charlestown, to call his assistants together and arrange that the four of them and he and his deputy governor serve as justices of the peace. In October he called a provisional General Court, which voted that the freemen choose the assistants and that the latter elect governor and deputy from their number.

In March 1631 ordinances were framed at the first regular meeting of General Court. The October rule was changed: the freemen would elect the governor and his deputy directly; only Church members would henceforth be accepted as freemen. This second provision was important to the future of the colony. In October, 109 freemen had been accepted on the same general principle as in England and early Plymouth; they were men of social standing, entitled to be addressed as master rather than goodman. They included some men who belonged to no congregation, among them two ancient settlers, Samuel Maverick of Noddles Island or East Boston, and William Blackstone, himself once a minister in England, who had left long ago to get away from the lords bishops. Now, almost before there was such a thing as a church in the sense of a physical structure, Massachusetts constituted itself a church-state. Ministers, to be sure, were debarred from holding public office, but they hardly needed the privilege to exert political power. It was they who would examine applicants for church membership.

The New Boston

After the first wintering in Charlestown, Winthrop transferred the seat of government to Boston. He was invited to do so by Blackstone, who called attention to its manifold fresh springs and excellent harbor. When the people came in and hastily threw together the wooden structures that would remain ramshackle for years to come, the oldest settler repented his generosity. A born hermit in his tastes, their numbers and their manners offended him, and he withdrew to Narragansett Bay.

Boston had its own minister, good John Wilson. He had done his first preaching in Charlestown, gathering his congregation under a great oak. He was a solid, stolid character, agile in body, able to climb a tree when occasion arose, to command attention from its branches, rugged enough to serve a forthcoming military expedition as chaplain. He was also apparently the least eloquent preacher Massachusetts ever had. For a time Boston did not see much of him. Having left his wife in England, he now went home to fetch her; she was reluctant and required long persuading. During his absence and until a more richly endowed assistant to him came, Boston made do as Plymouth had done so long with lay preachers.

Yet the Puritans of Massachusetts Bay did not want for ministers. Distinguished graduates of Cambridge and Oxford, "silenced" by Archbishop Laud, poured into the colony where their voices could be heard, and many brought whole congregations with them. Plymouth had been settled by a congregation; the Bay was settled by congregations, by children of Israel, each with its own Moses as leader, marching into the wilderness, choosing good land, raising the rooftrees for the buildings that would serve them for worship and town meeting. The little buildings were bleak: hard benches to sit on, no heating in winter except as some brought little footwarmers; no soft glory from stained-glass windows, no organ music. Nor did they crave such things. The Word of God expounded masterfully from the pulpit was all their pleasure.

The listeners were not saints only. Though Church membership was narrowly restricted to those people, gentle or simple (there was no explicit distinction here) who could demonstrate to the congregation their sincerity in covenanting with God, strangers were not denied the privilege of attending worship; in fact, their presence was obligatory. The strangers were many, for enclosures in England to provide sheep grazing and augment the wool industry were depriving yeomen and cotters of their livelihood, and many snatched at the opportunity to come where land was free. If they could not share the communion of the saints, they listened attentively to the sermons, for they were better than most had heard in England. Some rebelled against the Sabbath restrictions that kept them from bowling on the green or enjoying shuffleboard at the taverns. But they had good land and fair prospects, and few grumblers would willingly go home.

By 1640, when the tide began to turn, Massachusetts had drawn some fifteen thousand settlers. The first real success story among the English colonies in America, it was much talked of in England. Charles and Laud became alarmed at the extent of the exodus and made gestures toward suppressing it. Some ministers were obliged to go on shipboard disguised as common seamen. But restraining migration was no more successful than the attempts to repossess the absconding charter.

Even Plymouth reflected the Bay Colony's prosperity. Latecomers were never sufficiently supplied, especially in livestock. Plymouth began to breed its cattle to meet the demands in the Bay for young bulls and heifers. It profited largely from the enterprise, and wanting broader fields and wider grazing, its people moved out of the stockades to found new towns, new congregations, Duxbury, Marshfield, Kingston. Bradford, who had a sentimental regard for the status quo, rather deplored this expansion.

VI

COTTON, STONE, AND HOOKER

In the summer of 1633 Boston eagerly awaited the *Griffin,* which had left England in early July. If the "cruel Atlantic" could ever be clement, this was the season. One passenger, the helpmeet of John Cotton, must have boarded the ship with misgivings since she was big with child, and indeed in midocean she gave birth. If the circumstances were difficult, they were superior to those on the crowded *Mayflower* thirteen years earlier when Mrs. Stephen Hopkins had borne the lad she called Oceanus.

The godly of England, no less than the savages of America who were by definition godless, liked giving children names appropriate to circumstances. The Cotton baby was named Seaborn, but not immediately so baptized. This was not for want of a minister; there were three on the *Griffin,* two of them enormously famous in England; all three took turns in preaching to passengers and crew, and never was a voyage so constantly blessed with the Word of God. But the child's father was strict on Congregational technicalities. Until they could be met he would not administer the sacraments; only an ordained minister could do so, and his ordination in English Boston was no longer valid since he had no congregation with him.

If Mrs. Cotton made a protest, it was not recorded. She nursed her baby and prayed to God that it not be doomed by predestination. Any child, she well knew, was born to sin however virtuous its parents. The erring Adam was to the whole human race what the acorn was to the oak; Adam's sin passed from one generation to another as the defects in the acorn became the qualities of the tree. In the view of her eminent husband's equally eminent colleague Thomas Hooker, to God Almighty the natural man stank like carrion in the hedge, drawing "divils"—Hooker's pronunciation—as carrion drew vultures. If little Seaborn died before he could receive the grace of baptism, the divil would have him for all eternity. Mrs. Cotton strained her babe to her breast and her eyes to the horizon for the landfall.

Three Famous Preachers aboard One Ship

Besides John Cotton, the ministers were Thomas Hooker and Samuel Stone. Their names were a temptation to the punster, notably Cotton's future grandson and namesake, Cotton Mather, who would one day write the history of this voyage. New England was hereby provided, he would write, with Cotton for its weaving, a Stone for its building, and a Hooker with which to fish for the hearts of men.

All three were destined to great achievement. In England's old Boston, members of Cotton's congregation were urgently settling their affairs and preparing to follow. One of these was an ardent and gifted professor whom Cotton would welcome gladly to the new Boston only to wish later that she had stayed where she was; her name was Anne Hutchinson. Hooker's congregation had paid him an even greater compliment; it was already in America waiting for him at a place temporarily called Newtowne, and later Cambridge. Perhaps it was not in the formal sense his congregation, for it was long since he had been permitted to have one in England. It was made up of people who had heard him preach and had come to America to wait for him.

All three ministers were graduates of Cambridge. Hooker had as an undergraduate worked his way as a sizar. Such a necessity often humiliated scholars in class-conscious England; but not this serious youth, a "hard scholar," whose mind was on higher things, and to whom waiting table for a term was a small price to pay for the privilege of meeting the minds he met at Cambridge. If he had come already to the religion of his adult life, he would reflect that the Apostles had laid upon themselves the lowliest duties, and that humiliation was the soul's due preparation for admission to the kingdom of heaven.

When after rapid advancement at the university, he briefly took a "living" in Esher, he took a wife so lowly that without her marriage to a man of the cloth her designation might have been goodwife, not mistress. She was waiting woman to Hooker's patroness, Johanna Drake, who was stirred from her hypochondria by Hooker's vibrant preaching. The waiting woman's name was Susanna, no surname recorded until it became Hooker, and the first child of the union took the name of the benefactress, whose husband returned the compliment by naming the girl in his will.

When Hooker left Cambridge it was difficult for a known Puritan to get an opportunity to preach. He had gone to Chelmsford in 1626 not to preach but to lecture, and he had hardly entered on his duties before Charles I proscribed lecturing as well.

Nevertheless lecture he did, and on a people long used to "dumb reading" the effect was electric. "Come let us go hear what that bawling Hooker will say to us," once said "a profane person" to his companion, and when he listened, "the quick and powerful word of God in the mouth of his faithful Hooker pierced the soul of him. . . . He arrived at a true conversion." According to Mather, whose story this was, the man was one of those now awaiting Hooker in Newtowne. One of a group of fiddlers, hired by an ill wisher to distract the congregation by fiddling in the churchyard, eavesdropped at the door and was irresistibly drawn to repentance.

Mather wrote years later and from hearsay, but even more eloquent testimony came from a contemporary, the Vicar of Braintree: "If he be suspended . . . his genius will still haunt all the pulpits in ye country where any of his scholars may be admitted to preach. . . . Our peoples' palettes grow so out of taste that no food contenteth them but of Mr. Hooker's dressing. I have lived in Essex to see many changes and have seen the people idolizing many new ministers and lecturers, but this man surpasses them all. . . . If my Lord tender his own future peace . . . let him connive at Mr. Hooker's departure."

Lordships were prepared to connive, among them Archbishop Laud. Like the Separatists of Scrooby, Hooker took refuge in Holland, and like them he was disinclined to stay. There had already been negotiations in Massachusetts to bring him to America with Cotton; Hooker returned in time to take passage on the *Griffin*.

Though he came in secret, word got around, and Stone, in whose home Hooker was hiding, was questioned. At the moment Stone was enjoying an indulgence which not all Puritans, men or women, denied themselves; he was smoking a pipe. Hooker, who shared one conviction with James I, that tobacco was a "filthy weed," was reproving him when an ominous knock came at the door. Pipe in mouth, Stone went to answer it.

It was an officer of the law with an embarrassing query: Was Hooker there?

"What Hooker?" asked the smoker. "Do you mean that Hooker that lived once at Chelmsford? If it be he you look for, I saw him about an hour ago at such a house in town. You had best hasten thither after him."

The priestly conscience of Cotton Mather who reported this gossipy bit impelled him to rationalize Stone's equivocation by citing Athanasius; but Stone's answer had been true as far as it went, and Mather admired the "pleasant wit" that inspired it. Hooker for his part left Stone to his pipe while he sought securer concealment, and when the *Griffin* was ready at the Downs, both he and Cotton boarded it in disguise. Until the ship was well past Land's End and there was no further visiting between ship and shore, they left the preaching to Stone, who alone had formal leave for the voyage.

On September 4 the *Griffin* made Boston, and on the following Sunday its youngest passenger was safely baptized in Boston Church by John Wilson. The delay caused comment, and Cotton was moved to explain. Salt water, he said, would have been suitable for the rite; what was lacking was a "settled congregation," without which "a minister hath no power to give the seal."

In Boston he was settled for life in his congregation; Wilson remained its pastor; Cotton became its teacher. Perhaps the roles should have been reversed, for honest, earnest Wilson was a mumbling preacher. The day was to come, embarrassing to both pastors, when a communicant of forceful character, finding Wilson in the pulpit when she expected Cotton, gathered her cloak about her and swished out of meeting, followed by many of her friends.

It had been designed that Hooker also settle in Boston, but his congregation awaited him in Newtowne. Thither he and Stone repaired as pastor and teacher respectively, and there they did not long abide. In less than a year they and their flock were petitioning General Court for leave to remove to the Connecticut.

The Reasons for "Westering"

No one will ever know the full story of this congregation's impulse to go "westering" so soon after settlement. The reason it gave General Court was specious and was so received, for permission was withheld for two years. The people complained of "straitness," of want of land, "accommodations for their cattle," and it just didn't hold water. No part of the Bay Colony had yet approximated anything like metropolitan status. Boston itself was sparsely settled, with hastily built shelters whose untidy appearance dismayed each relay of immigrants. Newtowne across the Charles was well out of Boston; it was a difficult journey from one to the other. It was well wooded—getting firewood to treeless Boston was a problem and enriched those country folk who had barges to transport their superfluity; nor was there any lack of pasturage. However largely Hooker's congregation had invested in cattle bought from Plymouth, it was impossible that the good Middlesex pasturelands were already overgrazed. The reason for their petition had to be looked for elsewhere, especially when they refused an offer to take lands along the Merrimac, and stubbornly insisted on a removal of a hundred miles.

The true reason seems to have been incompatibility of outlook originating in Hooker and Cotton and extending to their congregations. The pastors were friends from Cambridge days, and remained friends, but that they differed in their bones on vital matters must have been revealed to Hooker at least during the eight weeks that they spent together in the cramped quarters of the *Griffin*. No less than Cotton he believed that strait is the way and few there be that find it, but he was no such purist on technicalities. Not impossibly, left to his own judgment, he would have baptized little Seaborn, congregation or no congregation.

There was no open quarrel. In spite of what Mather was to call a "choleric disposition," Hooker was discreet; "he had ordinarily as much government of his choler as a man has of a mastiff dog on a chain; he could let out his dog and pull in his dog as he pleased." Intent on peace, he leashed his mastiff while awaiting removal, but even so he was not altogether silent. After he left there was a report from a fellow pastor to John Wilson, again in England to induce his wife to join him in the wilderness: "There is great division of judgment in matters of religion against good ministers and people which moved Mr. Hooker to remove . . . that you are so strict in admission to your church that more than half are out of your church in all your congregations, and that Mr. Hooker before he went away preached against it."

John Cotton was not silent in the controversy; he preached against the "removal of the candlestick" on a text from Haggai, and snubbed discontent with the court's denial of the petition, saying that "the ultimate resolution . . . ought to be in the whole body of the people."

Two years later some of the arguments against removal had lost force. It had been contended that the congregation would be helpless against the Indians, more numerous and more powerful along the Connecticut than in Massachusetts. Now the Connecticut Indians had also been reduced by plague, this one recognized as smallpox. The argument that removal would seriously weaken the young colony was nullified by continuous waves of immigration in unprecedented numbers as Laud's persecutions continued in England. If land was not yet "straitened," it looked as if it soon would be.

In 1635, Thomas Shepard, another of Hooker's old friends at Cambridge, came with a congregation looking for a place to settle. Newtowne was "one of the neatest and best compacted towns in New England, having very fair structures, with many handsome contrived streets . . . well stored with cattle of all sorts, having many hundred acres of ground paled in with one general fence." Most newcomers had to content themselves for a season with sod-covered dugouts and tents of sailcloth or brushwood. That a whole village was available, ground already broken, fences set up, and its clapboarded dwellings more attractive than most in Boston, was a godsend such as no immigrants had been offered before. The Shepard congregation was eager to close the sale; General Court surrendered; and in June 1636 the congregation took to the road like a tribe of Israel bound for Canaan.

The "Old Connecticut Path"

"Road" was not quite the word. There was none, though there were some Indian trails. The migrants followed what was to be known as the "old Connecticut path" through the future sites of Framingham, Dudley, and Woodstock. The way lay through virgin forest, free of underbrush, barring recurrent tangles of thicket that had to be cleared with axes; cattle could be driven before them. They went on foot, except for the former serving woman of Mrs. Johanna Drake, who rode in a litter like a queen. This circumstance was not due to any insistence by Hooker on royal prerogative; she was ailing.

In two weeks they were on the east bank of the Connecticut River. Their scouts had recommended the west bank. After a pause to knock together rafts, they reached it, and there founded the "Connecticut towns," Hartford (named for Stone's birthplace), Wethersfield, Windsor.

That prior settlers already occupied two of these sites deterred them not at all. The Dutch of New Amsterdam had a fort at Hartford which they called the House of Good Hope. The Dutch claim was ignored; one argument before General Court had been the need of saving the river from the Dutch. Once settled in, they built a wall about Good Hope, cutting off its inmates from their own water supply and cornfields. The Dutch held out for some time, but except for an occasional broken head, resistance was bloodless; they surrendered to manifest destiny.

Windsor was occupied by friends; Plymouth had a trading post there. It was not much of a post, incapable of resistance when settlers came to ruin the hunting grounds by plowing the soil, cut the trees, and build fences. Governor Bradford protested in vain to Massachusetts General Court. The "unkindness," he wrote in his journal, was "not soon forgotten." The Indians were better treated; Stone and Elder William Goodwin were assigned to negotiate with them for the purchase of land about Hartford. The Indians obliged; that they had already sold the same land to the Dutch embarrassed them not at all. Land titles in the white man's sense did not exist among the American Indians, who when not actually on the warpath usually granted the nearest white settlers what they asked.

The Connecticut towns were not the first settlements in the area; Saybrook and New London had preceded them. But they became the nucleus of a colony that was to evolve independent of Massachusetts jurisdiction in spite of the express statement of General Court that they were to remain under it. By May 1637 they were holding their own General Court, and from the sermons Hooker preached in his meetinghouse, built about where the Old State House now stands, there would evolve a rather different concept of both church and state.

Details of the evolution are hard to come by. In spite of the vigor that had brought Hooker's congregation there, beginnings were rude. Either no one had leisure to keep journals such as John Winthrop's, which throw so clear a light on early Massachusetts, or pioneer homes lacked space to preserve them. Though the commanding role of Hooker was to inspire graphic memorials, a stained-glass window in the church which houses the heirs of his congregation, statues at the old and the new State House, no one can say that they are likenesses. Seldom has there been so little to go on in reconstructing the personality of so eminent a statesman. His course in old England is well charted; his achievement in New England can be followed only from bits and pieces. Some of his sermons survive in their entirety, but his most important work, the *Survey of the Sum of Church Discipline,* was lost on the "ghost ship" carrying it to England. Hooker made a start at rewriting it, but did not live long enough to complete it.

The Subtle Beginnings of Democracy

His most famous sermon, said to have inspired the Fundamental Orders of Connecticut, which in turn is said to have inspired the United States Constitution, exists only in a fragment, summarized in difficult shorthand by one of his parishioners.

It was delivered before Connecticut General Court May 31, 1638, and made these points: "That the choice of public magistrates belongs unto the people by God's own allowance," that election must be exercised by the people "not in accord with their humors but according to the will and law of God," that those who "have the power to appoint officers and magistrates have power also to set bounds and limitation" that "the foundation of authority is laid in the free consent of the people." And historians will never be done disputing whether these principles, none original with Hooker, and none fundamentally different from the principles governing Massachusetts theocracy, do or do not prove that Hooker was the first exponent of American democracy.

It is more fruitful to look from these fragments to the government that evolved in apparent response to Hooker's preaching. This does differ from that of the Bay Colony. It was hardly Jeffersonian democracy, but it was a move in that direction.

Massachusetts had made the franchise dependent on Church membership, which meant that both church and state government were conducted by an oligarchy of the elect. The authority of the latter was further limited by the fact that women members of the "visible congregation" had no vote either in Massachusetts or Connecticut.

To some extent this restriction carried over into Connecticut in that votes for higher officials could be cast only by property owners who subscribed to belief in the Trinity, were of good behavior, and that only these could serve as magistrates. People who met such qualifications were likely to be Church members, but it was not expressly so stated.

Qualifications for the vote in Connecticut town meetings were more liberal. Voters must be inhabitants of "honest conversation" who would take an oath that they were neither Jew, Quaker, nor atheist. They could vote for town officials and deputies to General Court. Excluded from the franchise were servants and apprentices.

If this was not democracy, it was a departure from the practice in Massachusetts, and for that matter another Connecticut town, New Haven, founded in 1638 on rigidly theocratic principles. Hooker could not have participated directly in laying this foundation, since here as in Massachusetts, no minister held civil office, but there was no restriction on his influence. The man who had worked his way as sizar at Cambridge and had married a serving woman, did not share the aversion to democracy that marked the founders of the Bay Colony, who liked to point out that democracy had nowhere been mentioned in the Old Testament.

This subtle liberalism of outlook carried over into his guidance of Church government, in his objection to the strict requirements for membership that he had found in Boston. And as he was more lenient in admitting the repentant sinner, he was more reluctant to expel. His Hartford ministry was peaceful; in fourteen years he only once censured and once excommunicated a member of his flock. Such dissensions as arose he dealt with in private conference and prayer.

This implied no lowering of standards. Of his most famous published sermon, "The Soul's Humiliation," Nathaniel Ward of Ipswich, "the simple cobbler of Agawam," wrote him, "Mr. Hooker, you make as good Christians before men are in Christ as ever they are after; would I were but as good a Christian now as you make men while they are but preparing for Christ."

In this long sermon (perhaps expanded for publication) based on the parable of the prodigal son, he described the state of unredeemed natural man as damnable beyond just expectation of mercy. "If the Lord will damn him He may, and if He will save him He may." The damnation derived not from incidental sins like adultery and drunkenness, but genetically, from Adam's fall. Even repentance would not save, though the soul's conviction of sin, opening "a little peephole into hell," was a necessary first step. Fulfilling the law was not enough: "You cleave to these poor beggarly duties and (alas) you will perish for hunger." Judas had done as much. "The divil slides into the heart unexpected and unseen because he comes under a color of duties exactly performed. . . . Mercy will never save you except mercy rule you too." Salvation came only from Christ, who came "not to call the righteous, that is men that look loftily in regard of what they do. . . . Christ came to call and save the poor broken-hearted sinners."

Strait was the way with Thomas Hooker, but more sinners found it through him than through John Cotton, and learned to delight in fulfilling God's ordinances, which though they could not save, were like a ferry to carry the sinner across the river "and land us at Heaven where our hopes are and our hearts should be."

In describing these ordinances he injected a touch of lyricism that may be more characteristic of his discourse than one can know. It sounds like personal experience, reminiscent of the time when thanks to Laud he had been in Holland without his Susanna. "As a wife deals with the letters of her husband that is in a far country; she finds many sweet inklings of his love, and she will read these letters often and daily. She would talk with her husband afar off and see him in the letters. Oh (saith she) thus and thus he thought when he wrote these lines, and then she thinks he speaks to her again. She reads these letters only because she would be with her husband a little and have a little parlee with him in his pen, though not in his presence. So these ordinances are but the Lord's love letters. . . . You do well to come and hear, but it is well that you may chat and parlee a little with Christ."

VII

THE REBELS

Hooker was neither the first nor the last to be impelled by scruples of conscience to leave Massachusetts Bay. Even while he was discreetly pressing his congregation's petition, he was playing a part in another removal; hardly was he settled on the Connecticut than he was recalled to participate in a third. In these other removals there was a difference—they were expulsions. Nor was there doubt about the issues involved, for neither party had practiced Hooker's discretion. For the peace of what was still a precarious colony in spite of the Bay's phenomenal success in attracting immigrants, they had to go.

Insofar as age brings discretion, there was another difference in the first of the exiles. When Hooker reached America he had already passed his mid-forties; the brilliant immigrant who had arrived nearly three years earlier was only in his mid-twenties; in later life, when he negotiated with potentates for the life of the colony he was about to found, he would manifest a discretion he had not brought with him. However, it is improbable that the wisdom of Solomon would have deterred young Roger Williams from his quarrel with the Bay Colony; the issues were fundamental.

His arrival in February 1631 had turned a day of fasting into one of thanksgiving. This was not due to his presence on the *Lyon* but to its cargo of provision. But when the colonists had sucked the lemons and enjoyed a square meal, they turned their attention to the passengers. Williams and his young wife Mary were warmly received, and the former was offered the highest honor at their disposal. He was invited to become teacher in Boston Church. Its pastor, Wilson, had boarded the *Lyon* to return to England to induce his wife to join him in the wilderness.

In Wilson's absence, Williams would have full charge of the congregation and on his return remain its second in command. If the church was hardly better than a barn, the prospects made for a magnificent opportunity. It was offered the youth, and his reply was a blunt no. Why, asked the startled magistrates, and Williams said that he "durst not officiate to an unseparated people."

Governor Winthrop had met Williams in England; he had recognized his piety and his gifts, but he had not known that the young man was a Separatist. Boston Church was not Separatist; through Cotton Mather's time it would declare itself "the little daughter" of the English Church, the true Church, purified of its corruptions. Its congregation had no intention of obliging the prejudices of this arrogant newcomer and so missed an opportunity to hear a round of such sermons as it would never have from John Wilson. For all the independence of both church and colony, what was practiced was not yet preached. People who like Williams brought up a subject best left unspoken could expect censure.

When Salem, the most "separated" church in the Bay Colony, called him, Williams accepted. But Boston took umbrage; the slight and the subversive reasoning that inspired it could not be overlooked. Williams retreated to the one colony of avowed Separatists—he went to Plymouth.

Even now, more than a decade after settlement, Plymouth lacked the means to support a pastor. The prosperity created by the demands of the Bay settlers for corn and livestock was just beginning. Plymouth permitted the young man to preach, but it could not support him in such style as Boston could afford; he had to "dig" for his keep.

Young Roger Williams

Between sermons he traded with the Indians. Endowed with a natural gift for language (he would presently compose a useful handbook of Indian speech), he learned their ways and became their friend for life. As he acquired facility in their tongue he preached to them, and became the first apostle to the Indians. They in turn came to love and trust him; he might have made converts in droves but for his own strict standards of the signs of true conversion.

It was his friendship with them that drove him from Plymouth. It was not that its leaders objected to such friendship, without which they could not have survived, but Williams, aware of the discontent of the Indians with patents awarded in England that infringed on their hunting grounds, sided with them against the whites. It was the scandal caused by his formulating his convictions into a treatise denouncing as immoral the King's patent that made it expedient for him to return to Salem. "He is to be pitied and prayed for," remarked Governor Bradford. "I hope that he belongs to ye Lord and that He will show him mercy."

In Salem he had good friends, almost too good a friend in fiery John Endicott. But he also had enemies, and magistrates of the Bay were ill pleased at his return. True, he was not now Salem's minister; he merely occupied the pulpit when invited, and when the meetinghouse was closed to him, preached at his home. But at either place he was a troublemaker, inciting one listener to action so subversive that it scared Boston.

Governor Winthrop dealt first with the dangerous treatise, unpublished, but circulating in the manuscript written for the edification of Bradford, and known from Williams' sermons. Were it to reach London it would be a powerful weapon in the hands of the Bay Colony's enemies. King Charles was not altogether unfriendly to a settlement that whatever its oddities in religious practice had found its footing so rapidly in contrast to the dismal early record of the Crown Colony of Virginia. But let him hear that a colonist was not only denouncing a royal patent as sinful, but equating the grantor with the kings mentioned in Revelation as receiving devils and committing abominations, and his sufferance would be at an end. Fortunately he never did hear of it. Winthrop had some success in reasoning with Williams and this crisis passed.

Another arose at once. *Lèse-majesté* was committed in Salem. In apparent response to Williams' influence, John Endicott turned on the royal standard and slashed it with his sword, his object being to remove the cross. Even Salem was roused. The militia refused to drill under the multilated colors. It would require a more stringent censorship than Winthrop could impose to prevent reports of the incident from reaching England. Even Salem had men who refused to attend meeting and read the service from the Book of Common Prayer in their homes.

Disturbingly enough, Endicott's gesture roused a sympathetic response in some magistrates. In many respects the founders of the colony were good Jews. The analogy of their present experience with that of the tribes of Israel following Moses into the wilderness had irresistible appeal. If they disregarded Talmudic law in observing the Sabbath on Sunday instead of Saturday, they followed it in beginning its observance at sundown and circumscribing it as strictly with taboos in blue laws inspired by the Pentateuch. Nathaniel Ward had been codifying Mosaic law to apply it to Massachusetts. His code was never adopted, partly because too many local exceptions had to be made, partly because Ward returned to England before he completed it, but the intent was there.

Puritans had a very Jewish reaction to what they considered Romish emblems, even the cross. Years after Endicott's day, Samuel Sewall would comment on the burning of the cross in Quebec with almost blasphemous glee:

> The baudy bloudy cross at length
> Was forc'd to taste the flame.
> The cheating savior to the fire
> Savory food became.

Thus the mutilation of the standard presented the magistrates with two problems: what to do if London heard of it; and, regardless of London, whether Endicott's act was sanctified by conscience.

Hooker had reached the colony by this time. He too studied the problem and made a pronouncement of Caesar-unto-Caesar common sense: "Not that I am a friend to the cross as an idol . . . or that any carnal fear takes me aside and makes me unwilling to give way to the evidence of the truth because of the sad consequences that may be supposed to flow from it. I bless the Lord my conscience accuseth me of no such thing, but as yet I am not able to see the sinfulness of this banner in a civil use."

Endicott was debarred from civil office for a year. The punishment was made no more severe on the grounds that "he did it out of tenderness of conscience and not of any evil intent."

Trials of a "Heretic"

In April 1635, before the Endicott affair was settled, Williams was called before General Court to answer for his own conduct, and again in July and October. He was not held responsible for Endicott's conduct; the docket was full enough without this. He had been preaching against the new resident's oath on the grounds that "a magistrate ought not to tender an oath to an unregenerate man." He had also attacked the magistrates for punishing offenses against the first four Commandments, saying that civil authority had no jurisdiction over one's duty to God. He denounced prayer with an unregenerate sinner even to the extent of giving grace after meals in his presence.

One court session had been held in the Newtowne meetinghouse, and Hooker there undertook to reason with Williams about his errors. "If it be unlawful to call an unregenerate person to take an oath or to pray, as being actions of God's worship, then it is unlawful for your unregenerate child to pray for a blessing on his own meat. If it be unlawful for him to pray . . . it is unlawful for him to eat it (for it is sanctified by prayer and without prayer unsanctified). . . . If it be unlawful for him to eat it, it is unlawful for you to call him to eat it, for it is unlawful for you to call upon him to sin."

To this *reductio ad absurdum* Williams found no reply; but neither did he surrender.

By this time Bay officials had word of the creation of a royal commission empowered to invalidate the patent and take over the government of Massachusetts, and that a ship was under construction to carry the commission across the Atlantic. They could not know that by God's providence the ship would never sail and that the mounting crisis in England would divert attention from the Bay. They knew only that in times so parlous they could not put up with so articulate a rebel on their own doorstep.

Reluctantly they condemned him to exile. They were no fools; most magistrates had been educated at Cambridge, and they knew genius when they saw it. Williams also had a gift of making friends with those who most deplored his ideas. John Winthrop was to remain a friend of sorts for life, and in the colony only John Cotton was to evince real bitterness against him, and that mostly later and for special cause. If the hotheaded young man were given a chance to grow up, to correct his errors, he would contribute to the colony.

In July General Court gave him time to reflect and repent; only in October, when Williams remained intractable, was sentence passed. He was given six weeks to get out.

Perversely he remained until January. He had bought a house in Salem and wanted to remain in it; his health was poor. Perhaps he believed that magistrates so slow to act didn't really mean it, and was fortified in this impression by a new friend who promised to have great influence. The younger Henry Vane had just arrived, and so enchanted the people of the Bay with his youthful ardor and patrician bearing that they were about to elect him governor.

Flight to Rhode Island

Williams dallied until he heard that he was about to be seized and shipped back to England on the *Griffin*. Then only, and in the worst month of the year, did he take flight into the wilderness; he spent an uncomfortable winter in the "filthy, smoky huts" of good Indian friends, and in the spring began the settlement of what was to be Rhode Island. Winthrop had privately recommended the area as safely beyond the jurisdiction of both the Bay and Plymouth.

Williams, who did not believe in the principle of the covenant, set up no church-state but a colony dedicated to freedom of conscience. It was the first such colony in America, barring Maryland, whose freedom was more narrowly restricted. It was not that Williams approved every sect that came his way. When Quakers took refuge with him, he endured them, but endeavored by preaching and the writing of tracts to show them their errors. Nor was his way easy. In the eyes of the settlers of Connecticut and Massachusetts, Rhode Island remained a vacuum for them to fill. Their incursions and their attempts to extend the jurisdiction of the parent colonies forced the man who had denounced the King's patent to cross the ocean twice to secure a patent of his own, first from Cromwell's Protectorate, then from Charles II. Even refugees from persecution in the Bay were often graceless, trying to force him to conform to their own views.

But no disorders in Rhode Island, no threats from the powerful Bay, no arguments from John Cotton, who made a career of denouncing Roger Williams, dissuaded him from putting into action his conviction that it was not for civil government to command private conscience. The civil magistrate, he wrote, "as he is bound to preserve the civil peace and quiet of the place and the people under him, he is bound to suffer no man to break the civil peace by laying hands of violence upon any, though as vile as the Samaritans for not receiving of the Lord Jesus Christ."

What was the proper term for his own faith? Briefly, when "Anabaptists," as Baptists were then called, came to him and he accepted baptism, he seemed to be one of them. But not for long. What he called himself was "Seeker." His friendship with the Baptists led to his denouncing his old friend John Endicott, who happened to be governor of the Bay when Baptists from Providence crossed the Massachusetts line to comfort a sick friend and were cruelly flogged. He warned theocracy itself: "Oh remember whither your principles and conscience must in time and opportunity force you! 'Tis but wordly policy and compliance with men and times (God's mercy overruling) that holds your hands from the murdering of thousands and ten thousands, were your power and command as great as once the bloody Roman emperor's was."

Williams' subversive little colony rose and grew and enjoyed homely happiness in spite of its proximity to the Bay. Massachusetts people had hard names for it: "Rogues' Island," "the latrine of New England." They could not, however, deny that the latrine had a function; where else could they cast their offal?

Anne Hutchinson

Williams was still in Massachusetts when the second rebel reached it. She was Anne Hutchinson, wife of William, whom she had persuaded to follow John Cotton, in whom she had heard "the voice of the beloved." No one, least of all her devoted husband, misconstrued such a remark. Everyone who read his Bible knew that it derived from the Song of Songs, and everyone (except perhaps Solomon) knew that the passage referred to no carnal love but to that of the Church for its Savior.

The conduct of Anne, which was to cause a scandal that would make Williams' departure seem a model of discretion, could not be ascribed to youth. When in 1634 she reached America, she was forty-three, the mother of many children including a grown son Edward, who in spite of the notoriety of his mother would presently take his place in General Court. The headlong enthusiasm of Anne could not be attributed to the instability of adolescence; it might be accounted for by the stresses of the menopause. Anne did not know that she was approaching the "change of life," supposed indeed that she was still fertile, but a recent and plausible theory holds that what she and all Massachusetts would take for a late pregnancy was really a pathological aberration of the grand climacteric.

Whatever her incipient handicaps, she arrived in full health and vigor. The first sight of Boston dismayed her. It had been named for the English Boston in compliment to John Cotton, but except that both were seaports, there was no resemblance. The new Boston, its houses made largely of unseasoned greenwood that began to go to pieces almost as soon as they were built, covered with unpainted clapboarding, roofed untidily with thatch (until recurrent fires caused the city fathers to order less flammable roofing), set higgledy-piggledy on miry ways where pigs rooted, was no city set on a hill. As for its meetinghouse, how could her beloved Cotton, who had so long occupied the pulpit of beautiful St. Botoph's, become eloquent in this cheerless structure?

So appalled was Anne at the looks of the place that she was tempted to climb back aboard the *Griffin* and go home. Her dismay, however, was only the usual first reaction of the newcomer; she would get over it. Besides, there would soon be no England to go home to; she had heard on the authority of Thomas Hooker that it was doomed. Her husband set to building a capacious home near the spring on School Street, obliquely across from Governor Winthrop's place, and Anne looked about for ways to make herself useful.

She found her scope among the women. Long before Massachusetts had been thought of, Virginia had discovered that women were as necessary to a new colony as men. Without a family to work for, the men of Jamestown had been an aimless lot, hoping only to make a fortune and go home, neglecting planting and building while they waited on the next supply ship. Plymouth in its turn had discovered that the lot of women in a new settlement was desperately hard; of those who came on the *Mayflower*, only a quarter had survived their first winter. The women of Boston had survived their first winters, but they were still in need. New England was far better supplied with university-bred ministers than with doctors, and the nursing profession existed only in the presence of able-bodied women willing to help a neighbor through a crisis.

In her native Lincolnshire Anne had often functioned as a doctor without diploma and as a nurse. She had a great lore of medicinal herbs, understood the course of most children's diseases, and there was little that she who had borne so many didn't know about midwifery. Rich in knowledge and unstinting in her services, Anne became the best-loved woman in Boston. Her husband, too, won honorable position; he was elected to General Court.

Then Anne began to serve the women in their spiritual needs. Attendance at Sabbath meeting was required of everyone, but not everyone could always make it. Excuse must be made for illness, and women were also often kept home by the afflictions of their children. When William had completed the spacious house on School Street, Anne began to hold meetings in it for the purpose of giving women who had missed the most recent sermon a proper summary.

She herself apparently never missed a meeting (except once willfully); not only that, but according to a statement she made when her zeal passed seemly bounds, she managed to hear every minister in the colony. It is improbable that she got about quite that much, but she no doubt did hear a great many. The lecture, invented in England when Puritans were forbidden to preach on the Sabbath, had been carried to New England. Delivered on various weekdays, it was possible for the zealous to hear any number of preachers without neglecting their own. Sermons were popular here, even with those beyond the pale of the elect; they were the only public entertainment, the only reliable source of news. Riding from one community to another to attend lectures became so popular that in the interest of getting people to attend to business, General Court presently restricted the days on which lectures could be given. In the meantime Anne had attended many and could relay to her followers not only the substance of the sermons of John Cotton, her kinsman John Wheelwright, but Thomas Hooker, young John Eliot of Roxbury, and perhaps even Roger Williams.

No one found fault with her doing so, not even the pastor she liked least, John Wilson. Women were not allowed to speak in Sabbath meeting, had no voice in the conducting of congregational affairs, but there was no restriction on their taking part in "praying companies." Such groups were later to become important when the indifference of the congregation would impel ministers to seek an "ingathering of souls" through revival meetings. In these vital early days there was little apparent indifference; if less than a fifth of most parishes could claim Church membership, that was due to standards of admission set deliberately high. The visible Church was by design exclusive, and there was no present inclination to admit the rabble to full communion.

The Silenced Prophetess

Anne's praying company soon deviated from ordinary practice. Husbands followed their wives to the meetings, and many were enormously impressed. Anne's "prophecies," as they came to be called, are not on record, but they must have been characterized by a simplicity and plain speaking not often found in the university-bred preachers, some of whom liked to parade a learning that was over the heads of ruder members of their congregations. Such listeners preferred Anne's discourse to that of the "black coated men" from the "niniversity" and said so. She also attracted a man fully able to follow the most erudite pastors, even when they embellished their sermons with Latin and Greek. Young Henry Vane, who had charmed Massachusetts into electing him governor (most injudiciously, for he was barely in his twenties and wholly lacking in the experience necessary to cope with Massachusetts politics), became her faithful attendant.

Even so there was no objection to the meetings. Trouble came only when Anne herself began to play politics within the congregation, when she conspired to rid Boston Church of John Wilson. She did worse; thanks to her attendance at lectures she began to pronounce upon the qualifications of ministers throughout the colony, distinguishing between those who were "sealed" with her conception of grace, and those who were not. Her list of the sealed was brief: John Cotton and John Wheelwright. She did not make this position so public as her opinion of John Wilson, but in her campaign against him she had most of Boston on her side.

The ousting of an unpopular minister would become common in New England; the congregation that could elect could also expel. But so early there was no precedent this side of Plymouth. Roger Williams was a special case, and his Salem congregation had deserted him only under pressure from General Court. Even if it had been otherwise, it was not for a woman to initiate such action, except as she might work discreetly behind scenes through her husband. There had been no discretion in Anne; it was she, not Wilson, who was expelled.

Long before a bleak November day in 1637 when Anne faced her accusers, many things had happened. Her most distinguished supporter, young Henry Vane, had gone back to England, but had he remained he would have been powerless to help her. His recent meetings with General Court had been so stormy that at one of them he had burst into tears. He was governor no more; at a stormy election held in Newtowne in May, Winthrop had been chosen to replace him.

Her brother-in-law John Wheelwright had gone to exile in New Hampshire. A conclave of ministers had met to examine his errors; Hooker had been called from Connecticut to moderate the meeting. When some eighty errors had been identified, General Court had warned him out. Anne also had been examined, but she continued to prophesy.

There had been war, the Pequot War in Connecticut, set off by the murder of John Oldham, formerly of Plymouth, and some others. Oldham was small loss, but the incident had been atrocious and suggested that the most powerful Indians in New England were preparing to oust the whites from their hunting grounds. Massachusetts and Connecticut militia had joined to hunt down the Pequots; the nature of their success was also atrocious. The major battle took the form of surrounding an encampment at night and burning them alive, men, women, and children. What captives they took they sold into West Indian slavery.

Atrocity is in the eye of the beholder. Thomas Shepard, the "soul ravishing minister" whose congregation had bought out Thomas Hooker's in Newtowne, called it a "divine slaughter." No one repented of the destruction of the Pequots any more than the Hebrew invaders of Canaan repented what by God's will they had done to the Canaanites. Roger Williams had a different point of view, but though Winthrop for one appreciated Williams' work in neutralizing his friends the Narragansetts, Williams didn't count.

Boston, infatuated with its prophetess, had contributed less than its share to the campaign. Thanks to the "Indian sickness" that preceded the great migration, Boston had no reason to fear the Indians. Its militia had refused to march to Connecticut when it learned that Wilson had been appointed as chaplain. The men refused to follow a man with whom Anne was now in open conflict. She had recently walked out of Boston meeting when she found Wilson in the pulpit when she expected John Cotton.

Even a community committed to religious toleration, as Massachusetts was not, might have found it necessary to take a firm hand with a prophetess whose precept and example inspired such conduct. For several days in early November Anne faced her accusers. They were this time not only the ministers but the Great and General Court. They met not in Boston, the usual place of assembly, but in Newtowne. The body would not risk an interruption of its deliberations by Anne's followers. To make doubly sure that there be no trouble, her known supporters had been disarmed.

It was cold in Thomas Shepard's meetinghouse, and Anne shivered when she stood before the court. She had lately been unwell and suspected that she was in an early stage of a troublesome pregnancy. Perhaps she was; but more probably, as recent research suggests, she was at a painful point of the grand climacteric. Even in the days of obstetricians, women sometimes confuse one with the other, and Anne, who knew everything about pregnancies, had less occasion to study the menopause. Constant childbearing wore out so many women that few of them got to it.

All the eyes fixed on her were cold with the exception of John Cotton's. John Winthrop considered that she had been meddling with what women, given their weaker intellect, had no business to meddle with. But her pallor was observed, and most of these men knew about "female troubles." A chair was brought her, and sinking into it, Anne began her recital.

She began very well. Her account of her conversion was such as any applicant for Church membership might have made. Its sincerity was touching and would have won her the right hand of fellowship from the most exacting congregation. Humbly she added that if the magistrates forbade her to conduct meetings in her home, she would desist. Was this the woman who had subverted Boston? John Winthrop knew well enough that she was, but her compliance, and the skill with which she parried some of his statements, made it difficult to demonstrate.

Others than he knew what serpentine wisdom lay under this dovelike gentleness. Magistrates like Joseph Dudley and John Endicott would not let their wrath be turned by soft answers, and most of the eight ministers present had already put her through a catechism with damning results. Her beloved pastor John Cotton was doing his best to save her. It took courage, for he had undergone examination with Wheelwright, and though he had passed it, a misstep now might yet condemn him to the same fate. He was no youth like Roger Williams to take on the wilderness. He was in his fifties, small of stature, mild of manner, and a born scholar who considered that day lost when he couldn't spend twelve hours in his study. Nevertheless he defended Anne until she herself made it impossible.

How, someone asked her, did she know that the Holy Spirit had directed her? "By an immediate revelation," Anne said, and added, "By the voice of His own Spirit to my soul."

She was undone. She was testifying to something very like the "inner light" of the Quakers. And having done so much, she proceeded to other heresies, and convinced the court that she was an Arminian. She followed Roger Williams into exile, and during her first summer in Rhode Island she vindicated her enemies when her "pregnancy" resulted in a monstrous birth.

The event must have sapped her extraordinary energies, for little was heard of her until yet another disaster rejoiced her enemies. In New York, whither she had moved her family after the death of her faithful William, she was killed in an Indian raid.

With the silencing of Anne Hutchinson, the women of the Bay were silenced. Until nearly the end of the century they were reduced to walk-on parts in the drama of the colony. No doubt their husbands heard from them, but with rare exceptions, historians do not. Presently Quaker women would make a sensation, but only in pantomime. There were the two girls who walked naked into Sabbath meeting; they must have spoken, for it is known that it was their purpose to demonstrate the nakedness of the human soul, but what eloquence they commanded was not recorded. A follower of Anne Hutchinson, Mary Dyer, got herself hanged on Boston Common, insisted on it, returning from Providence for the purpose after she had been expelled with a warning. If she spoke from the foot of the gallows, the embarrassed officials, reluctant to enforce their own decree but seeing no way out of it, did not record it. In effect Mary Dyer passed speechless into glory.

Anne Bradstreet and the Muses

One contemporary of Anne Hutchinson was heard from, Anne Bradstreet, wife of the good Simon, who had made the trip on the *Arbella* in 1630 with John Winthrop's company. She was then eighteen, but already an old married lady of two years standing, unhappy because the Lord had given her no children. In America, first at Newtowne, then at Ipswich, she became fruitful in more senses than one. She not only bore her husband children but composed verse, very good verse, a volume of which got printed in England in 1650 (and in an expanded edition in 1678) under the title *The Tenth Muse Lately Sprung Up in America.*

> Now goes the plowman to his merry toil,
> He might unloose his winter locked soyl. . . .
> The Pleiades their influence now give
> And all that seem'd as dead afresh doth live.
> The croaking frogs whom nipping winter kill'd
> Like birds now chirp and hop about the field.
> The nightingale, the blackbird and the thrush
> Now tune their lays on sprays of every bush.

As a naturalist she was inexpert, confusing frogs with hoptoads, and she had certainly heard no nightingale in Ipswich. She wrote from memory (an excuse later American poets who harked back to nightingales did not have) or perhaps she took the twilight song of the hermit thrush for the English bird. New England was not unlike Eden, with majestic virgin forest in whose depths no bird sang, but with a clamor of song in May about the little homes built in the clearings; but its Adams lacked leisure to give the unfamiliar fauna new names.

When Anne wrote of her husband, except for an allusion to the Song of Songs, her verse was not derivative:

> If ever two were one, then surely we,
> If ever man were lov'd by wife, then thee. . . .
> My love is such that rivers cannot quench.
> Nor aught but love from thee give recompense.

Of Simon's absence in England she wrote:

> Commend me to the man more lov'd than life;
> Show him the sorrows of his widow'd wife.
> My dumpish thoughts, my groans, my brackish tears,
> My sobs, my longing hopes, my doubting fears. . . .
> Tell him I would say more but cannot well;
> Oppressed minds abruptest tales do tell.
> Now pass with double speed, mark what I say,
> By all our loves conjure him not to stay.

In England Anne had been four years a contemporary of Shakespeare; she may even have read him. Her verse lacks the lovely sound of true Elizabethan music, but it was oddly un-Puritanical. (The messenger charged to convey her pleas to her husband was the pagan Phoebus.) Or better, Puritanical it was in a way that ignorant later generations do not think of Puritans. Husbands and wives clave unto each other in the Bay Colony as they did in societies less sternly committed to the glory of God, and they were not ashamed to say so.

VIII

THE SCHOOLS AND THE ROLE OF
THE ELECT

Williams coined a phrase to describe such crises as he and Anne Hutchinson had brought to Massachusetts: "these wonderful, searching disputing and dissenting times." What did he mean when he called them "wonderful"? Was it only the Elizabethan intensive of Juliet's phrase, "Well thou hast comforted me wondrous much," or did he intend a meaning more subtle, that a crisis was "wonderful" in the sense of the Chinese ideograph which is said to represent not only crisis but opportunity?

The danger had been clear and present. During the Hutchinson trial Winthrop had suggested an analogy between the explosive situation in Boston and the religious wars that were currently rendering the German states almost uninhabitable, and from which one might say they have never fully recovered. He demonstrated something more than his natural irritation with the woman who had brought discord to the congregation of which he was a member; he was capable of a breadth of vision beyond the hot and bother of a parochial dispute.

How meet such difficulties? Roger Williams' way in Providence Plantation was to suffer the dissenters, permit the tares to grow with the wheat, lest the wheat itself be uprooted, leaving them to God to separate at last. It was not that he had formulated a concept of religious liberty in the sense that he believed that many roads might be followed to reach the one God. He was sure that there were tares, and when opportunity arose to publish he would give nearly as much attention to exposing the errors of the Quakers as to defending himself against John Cotton. What he did not undertake was to suppress or expel.

It was a hard and dangerous way. In a time when those who held any religious convictions at all held to them intensely, sure that those who differed were hell-bent, tolerance did not bring peace. There was little in the early history of Rhode Island to encourage emulation elsewhere, though it would have been easier if its neighbors could have been persuaded to let it alone.

They Wouldn't Wait on God

Massachusetts did not wait on God to remove the tares. In the very act of creating what some would call theocracy, a state consecrated to the direct rule of God, Massachusetts leaders were reluctant to leave anything at all to God. Or perhaps more fairly they anticipated the dictum of their descendant poor Richard that God helps those who help themselves. They would not suffer dissenters; they would not wait on divinity to separate the tares from the wheat. They uprooted the tares and cast them into the fire, or at least into Rhode Island, whose troubles were fire enough. They undertook the construction of a monolithic state, a visible congregation that would move with one undivided accord.

They would not in the end succeed. Their adoption of congregational practice as opposed to the rule of a bishop or a presbyter, would eventually replace the aristocratic rule of the elect by the democracy they abhorred. But for half a century they would have their way, evolving a system which had some points of resemblance with a later government with which they would have had no sympathy at all, Soviet communism.

What if like Williams they had left the dissenters to God instead of suppressing them? Events were soon to demonstrate that their enemies in London were less potent than they looked. The charter was to remain inviolate through the lifetime of most of those who condemned Anne. When they lost it at last, it would not be because of the conspiracies of a Williams or a Hutchinson but because of their own rigidity, which presently led them to hang false prophets. Despised Rhode Island would never lose its charter, never know the humiliation that was to be visited upon proud Massachusetts.

Rigidity was to have another very serious consequence. After the thrust of first settlement, Massachusetts was to suffer a lamentable diminution of spirit. There had been creative vitality in the disputes over Anne; her followers had included not only many of the elect, but others who under the conditions imposed could not hope for Church membership. The enforcement of conformity, the suppression of disputes among believers (except when it came time to elect a new pastor or separate one congregation from another) eventually imposed lukewarmth of spirit and outright boredom. By the second generation ministers were complaining not of the prevalence of false prophets, but of congregations which seemed to care very little for their soul's salvation.

In the vigorous first decades decline was still a long way off. No one could anticipate it while there was still so much to be done, from the brute task of clearing the wilderness, raising houses and meetinghouses, to the great spiritual task of completing literally and metaphorically the building of a city on a hill.

At the very moment they were coping with Anne Hutchinson, ministers and magistrates were founding Harvard. As the first step in a concerted effort to ensure the education of their children, they began at the top with a college.

In proportion to its population, Massachusetts already had more university graduates than England, more indeed than it has ever had since. By 1640 the Bay alone had seventy-one, and there were 113 in New England at large. Most ministers had taken not only the first but the second university degree, usually at Cambridge. Nor was higher education limited to the ministry; John Winthrop had studied at Cambridge, and even such magistrates as had not were products of the English grammar schools, where they had learned to construe a Latin text and to cherish the books that they brought across the Atlantic with them.

But if there was no dearth of learned men now, what of the future? England had sent its finest, most highly trained ministers to America, but many were already well along in middle age, and even such young men as John Eliot would not live forever. New England needed leaders of disciplined intellect as much as it needed cod and cattle and Indian corn, and it needed them in continuous supply. Each town was a congregation, and each congregation needed a pastor versed in philosophy and able to read his Bible not only in the vernacular but in Latin, Greek, Hebrew, and Aramaic. Without such trained leadership any congregation might become the victim of an enthusiast like Anne Hutchinson, who knew her English Bible so well that she had sometimes forced her accusers to change the subject rather than answer her, but lacked the classical grounding that would have forfended her many errors. Future leaders must be given this grounding, but how?

Much later in other colonies the affluent would send their sons to

England for a gentleman's education. While Laud remained in power that was impolitic here; besides, so costly a measure was beyond the present means of most. Promising scholars must not be denied their opportunity to train for the ministry because their parents could not send him to the English Cambridge. An American Cambridge must be provided.

The Need for a School

Between the Williams and the Hutchinson expulsions, and under the presidency of a friend of them both, young Governor Vane, in October 1636 General Court took the first step by appropriating £400 "toward a school or college, whereof £200 to be paid the next year and £200 when the work is finished." It was not the intent to subsidize the college wholly—raising the wherewithal for upkeep was to be the perennial problem of presidents and overseers—but General Court enabled the founding.

The following November, when Anne was facing her accusers, the site was chosen. Salem had applied for the honor with an offer of three hundred oceanfront acres. Newtowne's offer was more modest, a house and an acre lot, and the court chose Newtowne. It may be that the Salem site was too far away for close supervision. Newtowne, aside from being nearer Boston, had the advantage of the newly settled Thomas Shepard, who in a year had become the best loved pastor in the Bay. Thanks to the loving kindness of his personality, his sermons which spoke more of God's love than of His wrath, he had achieved the feat of keeping his entire congregation out of the Hutchinson heresy.

Proximity to such a pastor would benefit unstable young men. The pastor, now in his early thirties, well remembered the temptations of his youth. His first two years at Emmanuel College, Cambridge, had been antic. "I drank so much one day that I was dead drunk, and that upon a Saturday night. . . . In shame and confusion I went out into the fields and there spent that Sabbath lying hid in the cornfields, where the Lord, who might justly have cut me off in the midst of my sin, did visit me with much sadness of heart and troubled my soul." His conversion dated from a sermon he heard soon after that dismal waking in the corn. No effort would be spared to protect undergraduates from shame and confusion, but when mischance occurred, a "soul ravishing" sermon by an understanding pastor would be available.

Nathaniel Eaton and John Harvard

In the summer of 1638 the new college admitted the class of 1642; a year later it closed its doors. The overseers had made an injudicious choice of master. Their mistake was understandable, for Nathaniel Eaton looked eminently qualified; after taking his master's degree at Cambridge he had studied in the Netherlands under the Puritan theologian William Ames. He was well connected; his brother Theophilus stopped in Boston only on his way with John Davenport to found New Haven.

But Eaton was a mistake. His temper was hasty; Shepard once had to rush in from the parsonage next door to deter him from his apparent intention of beating an assistant to death. The students rebelled against the food Mrs. Eaton was dispensing at the commons: "goat's dung in their hasty pudding" (she denied it), "bread made of heated sour meal," no beer for as much as a week and a half (she admitted these charges). The short supply of beer was a grave fault, given the Englishman's aversion to water.

Eaton was also negligent in his administration of funds. The school had received its first substantial private donation soon after it opened, from a new arrival, John Harvard, who bequeathed it a library of four hundred volumes and an estate of £777/17/2; he also left the college his name, for thus General Court acknowledged the benefaction. If it had been intended to name it for the English Cambridge, that matter was taken care of when Newtowne changed its name. Harvard got the library, but somehow not quite half the funds.

Eaton lost his job and went to Virginia. Until he could be replaced, the students scattered to their homes, keeping up their studies as best they could with their pastors or their parents.

In August 1640 they returned to the instruction of a new master, Henry Dunster. The date was unfortunate. Civil war had broken out in England; the massive emigration to New England came to an abrupt end and then went into reverse as some Puritans went home to join the contest between Parliament and King. The most prosperous of

American colonies entered a depression that continued until Massachusetts found its destiny in shipbuilding and in trade with the West Indies. That took time; in the meantime there were slim pickings to support a school that had nearly died aborning.

But this time the overseers had chosen well. Dunster rose to the emergency. Singlehanded at first, he instructed such members of the class of 1642 as he succeeded in recalling and four new freshmen. Under him they studied the Three Philosophies and the Learned Tongues. In spite of hard times he raised about £1000 to complete the drafty E-shaped building called Old College. The money came from what was left of Harvard's bequest, donations, sometimes as little as a shilling or two, from local well-wishers and gifts from England. The commencement for the class of 1642 was held in the new building.

Harvard was on its way. Students paid a tuition of £1/6/8 and the fees for their board in the commons in whatever their parents could spare in the way of beef, mutton, corn, dairy products, boots and shoes, and lumber. When the New England Confederation was formed in 1644 to provide the colonies with protection that could no longer be expected from the mother country, it acted favorably on the plea of Thomas Shepard that each New England family contribute a peck of wheat or a shilling to support the teaching staff and the less affluent scholars. Such humble beginnings laid the foundation of the charter member of the future Ivy League. By 1654 the student body of nearly sixty hailed not only from New England, but from Bermuda, Virginia, New Amsterdam, and England. The English universities already accepted the Harvard degree as equivalent to theirs.

Grammar Schools and "Dunce Schools"

In the meantime Massachusetts had founded some half a dozen grammar schools to prepare students for college. In 1640 the Bay had not only the famous Boston Latin, founded at about the same time as Harvard, but similar schools in Cambridge, Roxbury, and Ipswich. Their beginnings were obscure and not every town could afford the luxury. Where there was no school, boys who had ambitious parents got their learning at home, in the minister's study, or with whatever citizen had the knowledge and leisure to guide them. Schools became more general after 1647 when General Court passed the Massachusetts School Act, requiring every town of fifty families to set up an elementary school, and every town of a hundred to set up a grammar school.

Some girls attended the elementary classes and the "dame schools," for even a female should learn to read her Bible, but classical education in the grammar school was for boys only. Few were so frivolous as to suppose that women needed Latin and Greek; such studies were a prerogative of princesses, and Massachusetts had no princesses. There were some alert little girls, who by keeping their ears open and stealing a look into their brothers' texts, or by having parents who let them share their brothers' recitations, did pick up Latin, but the accomplishment was subordinate to their proper study of spinning and weaving, and milking and churning.

A Presbyterian Protests

Civil war in England imposed an embarrassment on Massachusetts quite aside from stagnation and depression. Whose side were they on? At first glance Parliament's, but sympathy was not unanimous. The fate of King Charles was shocking, and until the rise of the Independents, most of whom favored the English form of Congregationalism, Parliament was prevailingly Presbyterian. Such a Parliament might be as inimical to the New England Way as King Charles; it might well impose presbyters on the colonies as His Majesty would have imposed bishops. Neutrality looked to be the way of wisdom.

It was in this difficult period that Massachusetts achieved virtual independence. Neutrality was maintained to such an extent that once Governor Winthrop prevented a ship flying Parliament's colors from taking a Royalist craft in Boston Harbor. And lest Parliament have designs on the New England Way, the structure of the Congregational Church was formally proclaimed in the Cambridge Platform of 1648.

A newcomer inspired the platform. He was Dr. Robert Child, perhaps the most scholarly and brilliant immigrant who ever reached New England, barring that heir of the Renaissance, the younger John Winthrop, whose friend he was. The younger Winthrop, now resident in Connecticut, had been prospecting New England for minerals. In 1641, having found black lead in the Taconic Range, and bog iron in the Saugus and Taunton meadows, he went to England to raise capital for mining and the founding of ironworks. He hoped to counteract the depression by industrializing New England, and in a measure he succeeded; the ironworks that he founded on the Saugus River, complete with bloomery and slitting mills, became big industry for its day and remained in operation for most of the century. Dr. Child was one of those whom he persuaded to invest.

Child's education surpassed even the high standards of Massachusetts. He not only had his master's degree from Cambridge, but in 1638 had become a doctor of medicine at the University of Padua, after some preliminary study in Holland. He was interested in all science, as was the younger Winthrop, whom he met in a first visit to New England soon after receiving his doctorate. In 1645 he returned, apparently with the intent of settling, bringing with him a quantity of vines to enable Winthrop to establish vineyards that might rival the French. He also set to prospecting unsuccessfully for iron in southern New Hampshire.

Such a man, particularly one with money to spend in these impecunious times, should have become a leader. One might expect him to become governor, like the second Winthrop in Connecticut. But as it happened he couldn't even vote; as a Presbyterian he didn't qualify for Church membership.

In 1646 he joined a group of men similarly handicapped in presenting a remonstrance to General Court. It challenged the Bay's independence of Parliament, charged that lacking a settled "body of laws" it was in danger of arbitrary government, and pleaded, "We therefore desire that civil liberty and freedom be given to all truly English" regardless of religious affiliation. The petitioners asked that members of the Church of England (now not Anglican but Presbyterian) be admitted to the congregations, and added a threat: "if this were not done we . . . shall be necessitated to apply our humble desires to the honorable house of Parliament."

The substance of the remonstrance was reasonable; its tone was not. Bay leaders needed no reminder that they were acting as members of a free state; they proposed to keep it that way. They had no doctrinal differences with the Presbyterians, but they would not admit to Church membership a sect which subscribed to less exacting standards and which might take advantage of such privilege to insinuate their own presbyteries. The threatened appeal to Parliament spoke to their fears; General Court was furiously aroused and took a strong hand with the remonstrants.

It was already rumored that Dr. Child, who had once visited Rome, was a Jesuit. Now in a "Declaration Concerning a Remonstrance," General Court invited the petitioners to go look at Rhode Island to see what religious toleration had done. As for the vote, when had that been one of the rights of Englishmen? The charge that Massachusetts was acting as if it were independent, being true, had to be handled with discretion and was not discussed in the "Declaration." But there was a remarkable obiter dictum: "Our allegiance binds us not to the laws of England any longer than while we live in England, for the laws of the Parliament of England reach no further, nor do the King's writs under the great seal."

Massachusetts recognized no right of petition; for perpetrating this one, Dr. Child was fined £50 and other signers lesser amounts. When he prepared to sail home on the *Supply,* his chests were searched, and John Cotton came to the dock to preach to his fellow passengers: "When the terrors of the Almighty shall beset the vessel wherein they are [and] dangers shall threaten them . . . I will not give the counsel [which] was taken concerning Jonah, to take such a person and cast him into the sea. God forbid; but I would advise [them] to cast such a petition into the sea."

The *Supply* did have a rough passage, and Child's fellow passengers did seize the remonstrance as a Jonah and cast it overboard. The ship then safely reached England, and later so did Edward Winslow of Plymouth, whom the Bay Colony engaged as an agent to defend it before Parliament.

The Cambridge Platform

In the meantime Massachusetts was goaded into setting its house in order. Lest it be charged again with arbitrary government, it adopted in 1648 the *Book of the General Laws and Liberties.* In the same year ministers of the Bay and of Plymouth and Connecticut assembled in a synod (the term was later replaced because of its Presbyterian connota-

tions with that of association of ministers) to codify the New England Way in the Cambridge Platform.

Until now the growth of Church polity had been almost a historical accident. Not all magistrates or ministers arriving in the Great Migration had approved the system they found in operation in Salem, which so much resembled that of "Brownist" Plymouth. Winthrop had been dubious at first; a few ministers after protest had gone home. The majority, however, were either already inclined to non-separating Congregationalism or had no firm convictions one way or the other. They found the establishment of autonomous congregations suitable to circumstances. Autonomy was not absolute; each church owed fellowship to the others, and "synods" had been called as problems arose, like that presented by the conduct of Anne Hutchinson.

Dr. Child's challenge could not be ignored. It was time to make an explicit formulation of polity. It was characteristic of theocracy that the authority to do so had to come from General Court; it was petitioned to this end, and the date of the synod set for September 1646. Delegates from Connecticut, Massachusetts, and even Separatist Plymouth (but not, of course, Rhode Island) met long enough to appoint a committee, but it was two years before action resulted. New England was visited by a "plague," not the terrible Black Death which perennially struck England, but a nameless disorder fatal to those who resorted to bleeding or "used cooling drinks" for the fever. When it passed in 1648 and nearly fifty congregations sent delegates to Cambridge, there was one lamentable absence—Thomas Hooker had died.

Through the Cambridge Platform they achieved a system of checks and balances. Within each congregation, the officers, including the minister, were to be elected by the brethren, who became thenceforth subject to their leadership. Under Christ there would be no conflict between them; they would "sweetly agree together . . . after the manner of a mixt administration, so as no church act can be consummated or perfected without the consent of both."

Autonomous though the individual congregations were, the Platform ratified a custom in operation ever since the settlement of the Bay, the fellowship between churches in councils to be called to advise each other in times of pressing difficulty. Such groups would function

in "debating and determining matters of religion according to the Word
. . . and publish the same to the churches whom it concerneth . . . to
the correction of errors and heresies and the establishing of truth and
peace . . . which is the end of a synod."

All details of Church government were minutely provided for: how
members were to be received into the congregation, how disciplined, and
if necessity arose, how dismissed or excommunicated; election and ordaining of deacons, elders, ministers; financial support (devolving on the
entire community, member or not); the relation to civil government
(the magistrates had power to dissolve a congregation they found to
be heretical).

The Cambridge Platform pointed out the way that would be followed
for two centuries, and in most fundamentals today. There were to be
modifications: new rules of membership would come within a generation
in the adoption of the Half Way Covenant, and later be modified still
more in the "Stoddardean" system of western Massachusetts. The office
of elder would be forgotten. Synods would in Massachusetts become
ministers' associations, and in Connecticut for a century or more the
consociation, which somewhat resembled a presbytery. Circumstances already in operation but as yet dimly apprehended would bring about a
democratization of the churches by obliterating the aristocratic distinction between the elect of the "visible congregation" and the parish
at large by giving both a voice in church government.

Yet the essence of the Way, the combination of interchurch fellowship and local autonomy, would survive and does yet. As an example
of the latter, when some three centuries later the Congregational
Church united with other faiths, individual congregations abstained.

IX

DAYS OF HUMILIATION

Harvard was into its fourth decade in 1678 when a fifteen-year-old boy took his first degree. Three years later he took his master's from Harvard's president, who was his father, Increase Mather. By that time the boy had mastered a tendency to stammer in order to demonstrate publicly in eloquent Latin the thesis that had won him his degree: proof that the Hebrew vowels were of divine origin. A few months later, with proud solemnity, he was installed as assistant in his father's pastorate in Boston's North Church, and became at once a powerful force for righteousness among the young people of the congregation.

Ministers were lamenting that religion was declining in New England, that the vital faith that had brought the founders to build a city of God in the wilderness had long been spent.

It was true. There were children of the elect who, brought for baptism the first Sabbath after birth, squalled at receiving the sacrament and displayed commensurate ungrace ever after. They became boys who smuggled their dogs into meeting, scrabbled about in the gallery to which they were relegated, and between dogs and boys created an uproar that sent the tithing man tromping up the ladder to quell them.

They became girls who conspired to wear bright ribbons to meeting under their sober hoods, hitched about to ogle the young men, including the minister if he were as young and personable as Cotton Mather, and gave in sometimes to a hysteria vented in unseemly giggles. Being suppressed by their elders they fell asleep while the minister still labored toward his tenthlies.

Youthful misconduct was not always incurable. Some children grew in grace and eventually sought membership, reading their confessions and renouncing their sins before the congregation. But many did not. Troublesome boys grew into young men who frequented the taverns and coffee houses, from which came derision that sometimes amounted to blasphemy.

So many of the children of the elect were indifferent to their privilege of formally joining the visible body of the Church that adjustments had to be made. In 1662, after painful debate, a synod of ministerial associations adopted what was called the Half Way Covenant. It contained a kind of grandfather clause: grandchildren of the elect who had rebelled against the impiety of unregenerate parents just as the latter had rebelled against the strict piety of theirs, could be admitted to membership but without the privilege of partaking in Holy Communion. A lamentable necessity, diluting the aristocratic spirit of election, introducing something like democracy, a term disliked since it was nowhere mentioned in the Pentateuch; yet a necessity it was, else the visible Church and with it the voters at town meeting might have diminished beyond reason.

But if the antique zeal had fallen off, it had not vanished. There were still exponents of the heroic tradition that had brought the founders to America. There were ministers who begat only ministers or ministers' wives. This was true of the immediate forebears of Cotton Mather, who at eighteen had expounded the divine origin of the Hebrew vowels. His maternal grandfather was the great John Cotton; his distinguished father, Increase, was the son of Richard Mather, all of whose children had either become or married ministers. Cotton's brother Nathaniel had died untimely before achieving ordination, but it had been a holy dying, and now angels and archangels attended the way of young Cotton.

Cotton Mather

Impossible to imagine this babe howling at his baptism, though since he had been born in February quite likely ice had to be broken in the font. He pored over his father's Bible as soon as he was capable of taking it into his hands, presently learned to read it in Greek, in Hebrew, and in Latin as easily as he had learned to read it in English. His omnivorous appetite for language, ancient or modern, suggested the speaking in tongues after the outpouring of the Spirit on Pentecost. No language that struck him as worthy of his attention remained unknown to Cotton

Mather, and he could pun in all of them, one detail not mentioned in the Book of Acts.

With precocity in learning came precocious grace. He fasted almost in infancy, and at all ages he lived in prayer. In his journal (the favorite form of composition of the devout) he kept a record of what he called ejaculatory prayers, brief expressions evoked by the passing moment. No occasion was too humble, not even the satisfaction of his coarser needs, to evoke an ejaculatory prayer from Cotton Mather. He had no false modesty before God.

He was born to the ministry, particularly a Boston ministry. Boston was still a country town, whose homes, some of weathered clapboarding, some of elegant brick, stood in gardens and orchards, with hogs still rooting in the miry streets. But it had its metropolitan amenities. A country pastor labored in the fields as long and hard as his parishioners. The pastor of so well-found a church as Boston's North could devote his full time to his studies and his parish duties. With the younger Mather one of the more solemnly edifying of these was accompanying a repentant criminal to the gallows.

Nor was the criminal unappreciative. In 1686 "a passionate fellow," James Morgan, ran a neighbor through the bowels with his sword, and clung to the twenty-three-year-old pastor who accompanied him to the place of execution. When within sight of it they were separated by the necessity of picking their way through miry ground, Morgan was in panic. "I beseech you, Sir, speak to me. Do me all the good you can. My time grows very short. Your discourse fits me for my death more than anything."

"Poor man," said Mather, "thou art now going to knock at the door of heaven and to beg and cry, 'Lord, Lord, open to me.' The only way for thee to speed is to open the door of thy own soul now unto the Lord Jesus Christ. . . . The voice, the sweet voice of the Lord Jesus Christ (who was once hanged on a tree to take away the sting and curse of even such a death as yours). . . . Are you willing?"

"I hope I am."

So the two talked together and the young pastor's preaching was all of mercy. (It would be otherwise at another gallows, and Mather's unmercy there would not be forgiven him; but that day of wrath was still six years away.)

To the unrepentant he preached God's wrath. "There have been angry men among us, who have sat over their cups railing at such or such a minister of God and hoping ere long to see the death of him. In a little while they themselves have died miserably. . . . A town in the country enriched with two eminent ministers did one year pass a town vote that they could not allow their ministers above £30 apiece that year for their salary; and behold, the God who will not be mocked immediately caused the town to lose £300 in that specie of their cattle by one disaster. . . .

"I have known a weary mother says she hopes this is the last child she shall ever have; and multiplied and unhappy miscarriages ever after have given 'em cause to remind what they said with bitterness of soul. . . . There was a sailor in a boat bound hither from the northward who being dissuaded from taking a pipe of tobacco because they had a barrel of powder aboard, replied, 'I will take it though the devil carry me away alive.' The fire somehow came at the powder, which tore the boat to pieces. . . . All the men were to admiration preserved except that one sailor whom they long after found in the woods with his body torn to pieces. Who *carried him away*, think you?"

And so through a roster of one who cursed his eyes and so went blind, one who "clothed himself with curses like as with a garment" and so got a cancer on his lips that spread to his bowels, a man who refused salvation, saying "No, I will burn before I turn," and fell into the fire and burned indeed.

God's Thunder

Young Mather's sermons were not dull. Quite possibly the congregation at Old North hung on the words of the ardent young minister more than on those of his more stable father. The fascination of the son was his unpredictability. One afternoon, finding his congregation cowering under the crash of a thunderstorm, he threw aside his prepared sermon and took the thunder as his text. It was a grand discourse, calculated to divert the attention of his congregation from their immediate terror to the manifold studies of the young pastor: Biblical, historical, scientific.

Biblical: though God distributed the "producing of thunders among His Angels, in the thunder itself His own voice spoke as it would in

Doomsday." What if this were indeed "that great and thundering day"? Would his parishioners' hearts "leap and spring within you were you sure that in the very next thunders our precious Lord would make His descent unto us?" Historical: the ignorant Greeks mistook the thunder for the voice of Jove. Scientific: in the Cartesian theory thunder is caused by "weighty clouds clashing and hurling upon one other." His own theory: "the vegetable matter protruded by the subterraneous fire and exhaled also by the force of the sun in the vapors that makes our showers a mixed matter of niter and sulphur does also ascend into the atmosphere and there it goes off with fierce explosions."

Some may have puzzled over a possible inconsistency: thunder as the voice of God, and thunder as the product of natural forces. Mather, who added to his religious fervor a passionate interest in science which would make him a fellow of the Royal Society of London, perceived no inconsistency. In his peroration he added another. Early in his lecture a messenger had brought him "tidings that a thunder-clap had fallen upon his own house; and that no person had been hurt, yet the house had been much torn, and filled with the lightnings."

The news inspired several reflections. "Suppose we should be slain by thunder, we shall but in that thunder of heaven have a great voice from heaven, saying to us, 'Come up hither.'" These were brave and devout words. But later something impelled him to a remark that must have caused his enemies to nudge each other and his friends to exchange uneasy glances. "Whatever the witch advocates may make of it, it is a scriptural and rational assertion that in the thunder there is oftimes by the permission of God the agency of the devil. . . . He has vast power . . . and armies that can make thunders in the air. . . . A great man has therefore noted it that thunders break oftener on churches more than any other houses, because the demons have a peculiar spite at houses that are set apart for the peculiar service of God."

It was well that this passage came at the close of his sermon, for his contention that God consented to evil, and that ominous phrase "witch advocates" was bound to send the minds of his listeners down distracting lanes of thought. The year was 1694 and Massachusetts was still in shock from the aftermath of the calamitous witch hunt of 1692. Why revert to what was better forgotten, thought even some of his friends, thought in particular Robert Calef, who was about to declare himself an enemy.

"He won't let it rest; good," thought some others, including an elderly woman who sought him out to inform him privately that a second and more dreadful witchcraft was in the making as God's judgment on those who had "wilfully smothered" the first. And Cotton, who retained a lively interest in the subject, would take her seriously.

Did his congregation include the likes of Martha Cory, who combined a display of piety with an outspokenness not recorded against any other Massachusetts woman since Anne Hutchinson? Though she lived in prayer she was capable of unseemly expression like the blasphemy of disbelieving in witchcraft itself, and laughing in open court at the torments her own sorcery visibly inflicted on young girls. A mind such as hers, hearing this exposition of a God who licensed evil, might have gone back to the earlier sermon in which Mather described God's vengeance on the wife who had cried out for relief from incessant childbearing. Was God really so petty, so blind to the lot of the women?

But Martha herself could not reflect thus. She was unable to be present, except possibly as a little yellow bird in the beams, the guise in which crazed little girls had identified her on the last Sabbath she had been permitted to attend meeting. Martha had been hanged two years ago, almost to the day, and some of the "witch advocates" of whom Mather had spoken so scornfully, those who had dared come to the defense of such as she, had been hanged with her.

A Series of Calamities

The witchcraft had been the climax of a long series of disasters with which God, or perhaps by His permission the devil, had been overwhelming New England. None of the colonies had gone unscathed, but it was as if the full force of divine displeasure had been reserved for Massachusetts, mother of them all.

The most general calamity had been King Philip's War in 1676. From the chieftain's point of view this had represented a desperate attempt to drive the white men back into the sea before they reduced the Indians to beggary in their own land. In the view of the white men the war was the last stand of Satan against the forces of light. And indeed the

Indians wrought fiendishly, wreaking havoc even in Roger Williams' Rhode Island and in Plymouth, where there had long been friendship with the Indians, and wiping out whole villages along the Connecticut.

The white men, in forces hurriedly summoned from all the colonies, had wrought even more havoc in their turn, massacring Indians rounded up in the Rhode Island swamps, selling their children into captivity, and finally displaying in Plymouth the head of King Philip and in Boston his right hand. If the white man's destruction was the more thorough, it was in the name of righteousness.

At the same time, counting their dead, surveying the charred ruins of prosperous little villages, the godly asked themselves what sin unrepented of had led God to visit this upon them. "We have one enemy more pernicious to us than all the rest, and that is our own backsliding heart," Mather was to write (at the time he was in his Harvard childhood), "and that has plunged the whole country into so wonderful a degeneracy." There were days of fasting and prayer, soul searchings, and legislative action to expel offenses to God.

Perhaps Connecticut and Rhode Island repented most effectively, for the later calamities were visited on Massachusetts alone. Before Massachusetts had recovered from the contest in the great swamps, action was taken in London that would in the end afflict the Bay Colony more than anything King Philip could do. The Massachusetts charter was voided. For once it was a blessing that communication with England was so difficult. Massachusetts had time to catch its breath before it learned its fate, and it was not until 1686 that it underwent the humiliation of receiving its first royal governor. The mills of the Crown ground slow, but they ground exceedingly small, for this man, Sir Edmund Andros, was to be the most hated man in Massachusetts this side of George III.

The wonder was that all this had not taken place decades earlier. It had been no part of the plan of British authority that the founders of the Bay Colony take their charter with them and govern themselves under it like an independent sovereignty. Civil war in England had indefinitely postponed demands for the return of the charter, and even after the Restoration, the ministers of Charles II were long too busy to give attention to what was going on in the colony.

Given a larger grasp of diplomacy, Massachusetts might still have postponed the day of reckoning. But its leaders were slow and ungracious about acknowledging their fealty to Charles II. (After all, he might not last.) Regicides taking refuge in the colony were not surrendered. And by bad timing, the Restoration had coincided with an extreme exhibition of theocratic severity: in 1662 Massachusetts had hanged four Quakers. It was not that England was fond of its Quakers; it always had a quantity of them in its prisons. But prison was one thing and hanging another. The temerity of the hangings called attention to something worse: the Bay suppressed not only the Quakers but the Church of England. It didn't, to be sure, hang its adherents, and it would claim that as "the little daughter" of England in America it "hath always retained a dutiful respect to the Church of God in England." The fact remained that dutiful or not it recognized no bishops, spurned the Book of Common Prayer, and permitted no Anglican a place, not even so much as a barn, to worship according to his own liturgy.

Sir Edmund Andros—The King's Governor

In 1684, moving with majestic deliberation, British authorities decided that this had gone on long enough; the charter was voided, and two years later the last elected governor was superseded by a Crown appointee. Sir Edmund Andros had served with success in New York, lately taken from the Dutch. Odd that the latter after conquest should assent equally to foreign rule and that Englishmen would resist government by another Englishman with fire and fury. Andros' administration was to be stormy and brief.

Technically, more than Massachusetts was involved; all the New England colonies were to be administered under Andros. But only the Massachusetts charter had been voided; when Andros went to Hartford to demand the surrender of the Connecticut charter, its legislature, by the neat Yankee trick of hiding the document, evaded the demand and was not troubled further. Rhode Island was not molested at all. Andros might in time have gotten around to it, but events in the Bay Colony prevented. In 1689 he was seized, imprisoned on Castle Island, and then shipped back to England.

Whatever tact Andros may have displayed with the Dutch, he lost the last traces of it when in Massachusetts he faced a stubborn and stiff-necked people who wanted no part of him and apparently identified him with the anti-Christ.

He roused the Boston ministry by demanding and then taking the Old South meetinghouse for the performance of Anglican services. Faced with the need of revenue, for General Court had thoughtfully prepared for his coming by rescinding every tax law on the books, he imposed by fiat poll and property taxes, and thus came in collision with nearly every town in Massachusetts. In Ipswich a hitherto obscure country parson named John Wise came to town meeting to raise a cry later to become famous, that taxation without representation was tyranny. Wise was thrust into prison for such misconduct, and when he demanded his privileges as an Englishman under the Magna Carta, Andros told him, "Mr. Wise, you have no more privileges left you than not to be sold for slaves."

Even those, who having no vote, had always been taxed without representation, were stirred by Andros' claim that all land titles had been invalidated with the voiding of the old charter, that "the calf had died in the old cow's belly." If the very land were not theirs, what had they? Had God utterly forsaken Massachusetts?

The First American Revolution

But God saved them. The intuition that the new regime might not last had not been groundless; true, it had outlasted Charles II, but his successor, James II, was giving old England as much dissatisfaction as Andros was giving its "little daughter." When in 1689 news came that England had risen, bloodlessly expelled James and his papist associates and installed the firmly Protestant Mary and her husband William of Orange in his place, Massachusetts knew what to do with Andros.

It was the first American Revolution. Andros reported the part ministers played in it, John Wise among others, and Thomas Shepard of Lynn coming to Boston at the head of a pack of ravening wolves, Andros' description of his congregation. And Cotton Mather composed its Declaration, and read it from the gallery of the Town House.

It was, however, only a halfway revolution. While the French held Canada and perennially stirred up the Indians "to the eastward," no responsible citizen would consider it possible to live without the protection of old England. It had been hard enough during the waning days of Cromwell's Protectorate, when the New England colonies had had to unite for their mutual defense. Massachusetts already had an agent in England, dispatched to renew the old charter. At a delicate point in these negotiations Increase Mather heard of what had happened in Boston and summoned all his tact to conceal his dismay and put a proper patriotic face on it. "Your Majesties may have heard of the great favor Massachusetts hath done you." But it was not deemed so great a favor as to induce Majesty to restore the old independence. When Mather returned in 1692 he bore a new charter. It confirmed many liberties, including the land titles; but it also confirmed the humiliation of the Massachusetts electorate. Henceforth they could not choose their governors; these would be appointed by the Crown.

The blow was softened by the choice of the first, Sir William Phips. He was no stranger, being born in Maine, and had in early manhood lived in Boston where he learned his letters and the trade of shipbuilder. There also he had listened to the sermons of Increase Mather and had been smitten "with a deep sense of my miserable condition who had lived until then in the world and had done nothing for God." Having grown up in an unchurched frontier community, he had not even been baptized. Soon after being knighted in 1690 he presented himself before the congregation of the Old North. "I would be a knight of order too." He made his confession before Cotton, the elder Mather being in England, was baptized and received into Communion. Hence the new governor was not only a native son but a Congregationalist.

He returned from a mission to England on the same ship as Increase Mather in the spring of 1692 and took office. But there were Indian troubles to draw him "to the eastward," and it was some months before he learned that in his absence Massachusetts had again become a disaster area. Witchcraft had broken out in Salem Village, and before he could look into it, was threatening to overwhelm the entire colony.

Witchcraft in Salem

It had begun among country people so obscure and in a hamlet so remote that one would not have supposed it would interest the colony at large, let alone engulf it. It was like a brush fire, easily contained when it is first discovered, but if not controlled capable of generating fire storms that can lay to waste a country stricken by drought.

There had been a long drought of God's grace in Massachusetts. When "witches" were identified, men and women and particularly their ministers eagerly seized on this evidence that two decades of suffering and humiliation were the direct work of Satan.

Witches had been known before without provoking a general witch hunt. One Glover had been hanged in Boston just four years earlier, when anxieties had been no less but there had been Andros to serve as scapegoat. Now Andros had gone, but under the new charter who knew when his like might come again. Almost reassuring to learn that the real culprit was Satan, working through his human agents. As one revelation after another threw fresh light on this fact, people engaged in a holy war to send the devil packing after Andros.

As was proper, the ministers took the lead. Proof of witchraft had first been discovered in the household of one of them, Samuel Parris of Salem Village, about six miles out of Salem. Parris was no minister to rank with the Mathers; he had left his studies at Harvard to go into business, and only when that failed did he look about for a pulpit. In this he was not unlike those younger sons of the British gentry who took a church "living" not for the glory of God but because a living was exactly what they needed. However, Parris had some merit. He preached against sin and for virtue most effectively. When two little girls in his household, his eight-year-old daughter Betty and his eleven-year-old niece Abigail Williams fell into fits, he acted sensibly; he got them to a doctor. It was only when the doctor found himself unable to help and the affliction spread among other girls in the neighborhood that he restored to standard Congregational practice in a crisis, and called the North Shore association of ministers to advise him. The doctor's diagnosis that the girls were under the evil eye had made this necessary.

It was these ministers from Salem, Beverly, and roundabout, all learned men and graduates of Harvard, who, questioning the girls, elicited the names of the witches tormenting them. They were what one might expect, a female tramp, a woman who used ill health as an excuse for not attending Sabbath meeting, and a slave in the Parris household named Tituba.

This was the brush fire, and it seemed safely under control. The accused were of small consequence and the invalid relieved the community of further trouble by dying in jail. But Tituba released the fire storm. Like the others she had first declared her innocence, but Parris, now aware that all the afflicted had sought Tituba's company (apparently she told fortunes) wouldn't take a denial from her. In a private interview he whipped the truth out of her (a circumstance Tituba dared report only much later) until she "confessed." Yes, she had attended the witches' Sabbaths and had seen the others there, also a woman with a hood whom she did not know and a "tall man of Boston." The latter kept by him a book of those committed to Satan, and in it she had counted nine names.

And so the trembling slave, seeking only to oblige, hoping only not to be beaten again, achieved a spectacular revenge upon the whole Bay Colony. After her testimony the magistrates knew that their labors had only begun. At the best they had only a third of Satan's agents; they still had to find a tall man of Boston, a woman with a hood, and four others.

Working with the girls as detectives, since the afflicted usually recognized their persecutors, exacting in time other "confessions" which they never accepted until the confessor named accomplices, they soon had a roster of witches whose numbers and identities astounded them. The most pious members of Salem Village were in the conspiracy: Martha Cory, who prayed so often that it bothered her husband; Rebecca Nurse, whose seventy years and whose deafness did not disqualify her from the errands of Satan; her sisters Sarah Cloyce and Mary Esty. The tall man of Boston was discovered to be John Alden, whose parents John and Priscilla had helped found godly little Plymouth. When affliction broke out in Andover, the girls were dispatched to pick the witches from a lineup, and they picked nearly everyone they saw.

Heresies were exposed. Philip English, a proud merchant of Salem who eschewed Congregational meeting because he hankered after papist Anglican rites, was accused with his wife. Quakers, or people with Quaker affiliations, were brought in: Elizabeth, wife of John Procter; Susanna Martin, who for three decades had been the chief figure in Amesbury wonder tales. Even a judge was accused, Nathaniel Saltonstall, who left the bench in protest when Chief Justice William

Stoughton refused to accept the jury's finding that the charges against Rebecca Nurse had not been proved.

By the time Governor Phips came back from his Indian campaigns he heard it whispered that the girls had cried out against his lady wife. The charge was not pressed, nor was that against Saltonstall. Several of the accused, including English and Alden, had fled the colony. But eighteen had been hanged and Martha Cory's husband Giles pressed to death for refusing to testify.

A reaction was setting in. Rebecca Nurse's whole neighborhood had signed a memorial in her defense. John Procter had denounced the accusation of his wife, and when he too was accused, old friends in Ipswich, John Wise among them, had put their names to a document testifying that they knew nothing but good of this man.

One confessor, Samuel Wardwell, had recanted his confession, declaring that he had made it only under torture. It was an act of high courage. The magistrates were not hanging confessors, whose testimony they needed to corroborate that of the girls'. They hanged only those who pleaded innocent, as they hanged John Procter and then the recanting Wardwell.

Perilous to become what Cotton Mather was to call a "witch advocate." Yet in spite of Procter's fate more and more were risking that peril. Husbands in Andover who had "broken charity" with wives accused by the girls and insisted that they confess, came to their senses and petitioned General Court to stop the madness. "We know of no one who can think himself safe if the accusations of children and others who are under diabolical influence shall be received against persons of good fame."

In October General Court took action. Though the witchcraft had been largely confined to Essex County, for six months it had been nearly impossible to attend to anything else. A stop was put to the trials. When in January they were resumed, as they had to be since the jails were overflowing, they operated on a new basis. Hitherto the accused had been convicted on what was called "spectral evidence." Had the girls claimed that Rebecca Nurse for one had come to them in the flesh to pinch and choke them, she could easily have proved her innocence. But against their charge that she had sent her spirit to do so, she was helpless. Not even her most loyal sons and daughters (and all were loyal, for Rebecca was greatly loved) could prove in court where her spirit had been at the hours specified. Only the girls could see it, and thus on the dreams and hallucinations of hysterical children Rebecca and her kind had been convicted, and being convicted, hanged.

When spectral evidence was thrown out of court in January, a strange thing happened. The judges found that Massachusetts, so recently overrun with witches as with a plague of locusts, now had none. Or very few. They did convict some confessors.

But Governor Phips, returned from Indian fighting to find worse troubles at home, would not honor the death warrants of these confessors. Investigating, he found some of them deranged, some "simplish at best," and affronted the judges by reprieving them all. The witch hunt was over.

It was to have far-reaching consequences in law. English jurists were impressed by Massachusetts experience with spectral evidence and remembered that precedent when witches were brought to trial. The part played by the confessors led to a ruling that a confession that was unsupported by other testimony could not be admitted as evidence.

The "Church Watch" Dangers

The witchcraft had brought Doomsday to Massachusetts, "that great and thundering day" of Cotton Mather's sermon. No mortal storm, not even King Philip, had been so demoralizing. Farms were abandoned, fields unplanted because their owners were in prison awaiting trial, in flight, or else too distraught to attend to worldly concerns. As in the great and general Doomsday the graves opened and the dead came out to testify before the bar of justice. They were invisible to the judges, but the clairvoyant maidens saw them and served as their interpreters and put the testimony of the dead on record with that of the living.

This Doomsday had brought out the worst in the conduct of the churches under theocracy; at long last it would bring out the best.

It made a travesty of such customs as the "church watch," a kind of honor system by which members of the congregation were obligated to observe each other and report irreligious "carriage." It was a practice of venerable, even divine origin; if these people read their Book of Acts correctly, it had been instituted in the primitive churches under the guidance of the apostles. The intent was holy, for it was necessary to expose hypocrites who crept into the congregation. The practice had perilous possibilities which disregarded another Biblical precept, that it is easier to detect the mote in a brother's eye than the beam in one's own. Normally people of good sense probably exercised this duty with a grain of salt. Now times were anything but normal, and perhaps seldom had been so in Salem Village, torn by contention and suspicion long before the witchcraft.

Under the stress of the witch hunt the "church watch" became a vicious parody of itself. Not only the girls but their supposedly sane elders rushed to court to report events that illumined the homeliest details of country life. Wagons falling into holes which had not been there a moment earlier; cattle, obviously possessed, swimming into the sea until they drowned. The "poppets" a woman had made (she said) to amuse her children. (Everyone knew that a poppet, assigned a name and stuck with pins, was a deadly weapon.) The "shovelboard" games that the light minded enjoyed in the tavern kept by Bridget Bishop and the familiar "red paragon bodice" that her shape injudiciously wore when she sent it to torment her victims. The ability of a witch to come through miry ways in a storm without muddying her skirt. "I scorn to be drabbled," she would say. The suspiciously long prayers of Martha Cory who remained at the hearth for this purpose long after her husband Giles wanted her in bed.

Excess in prayer was an eccentric charge to bring against a witch. Giles' blundering, bewildered account could even be construed as defense and hence suspicious conduct. Giles himself was presently accused. He too may have had second thoughts about Martha's prayers; this time he would not testify at all. The legal recourse against "standing mute" was to extort testimony by pressing the culprit under weights. Giles, remaining stubbornly silent, was pressed to death.

But the practice of "church watch" could include testimony of good conduct. Some thirty of Rebecca Nurse's neighbors, at the risk of their lives, put their names and marks to a statement that they knew nothing of her but virtue and Christian charity. Former Ipswich neighbors of John Procter signed a similar statement and their pastor, John Wise, contested the belief that God would not permit Satan to lay hands on the innocent by calling attention to Job, who had been sorely tried by the adversary under God's express permission.

Wise, who was to be heard from in another context, was touching on the great problem of theology—how it was that God, as omnipotent as He was good, permitted evil in the world. The Puritan theory was that every human misfortune manifested God's displeasure at wrong-doing. Rebecca Nurse had given touching expression to this conviction when, warned by compassionate neighbors that the girls had "cried out" on her, she exclaimed, "Alas, what sin unrepented of hath God found in me that He brings such affliction upon me in my old age?"

The pettiest expression had been uttered by the learned Cotton Mather with his reference to the woman cursed with miscarriages after she craved relief from childbearing. It was as if he conceived God as a celestial snooper, making a perpetual church watch, at the ready to forget a lifetime of good conduct in order to pounce on a momentary weakness. At least he applied this theory to himself; when he had a toothache he solemnly considered what sins he had been committing with his teeth.

The Burden on Women and Children

The attitude of ministers and magistrates toward women and girls was remarkable. Apparently in their eyes witchcraft was essentially a female occupation; men were rarely accused except as they defended a woman, or like old George Jacobs slandered the afflicted girls, for whom his epithet was "bitch witches." The great majority of both accusers and accused were female, the former very young, the latter mature. The circumstance threw a strange light on the lot of women under what were still pioneer conditions.

Certainly they bore the heaviest burden, in marriage almost constantly pregnant and often bringing forth their babes in sorrow only to bury them. But some, "natural breeders," as the downright country phrase put it, brought mighty endowments to this task, bore their children alive, reared them to manhood and womanhood, and when in their later years they were excused from the curse of Eve wished that they had it all to do over again, and consoled themselves with their grandchildren.

Others, and these were many, fainted under the task. Mrs. Cotton Mather was already old before her time while her husband still enjoyed lusty youth. She would give up at last, having borne nine children, only one of which survived her, and Mather would promptly seek (and presently bury) another helpmeet. God commonly gave the men as many wives as the patriarchs of Israel, with the difference that He required them to bury Leah before they took Rachel.

In the prosecution it was the hearty matriarchs, Rebecca Nurse and her sisters being notable examples, who fell suspect, and those who fainted under their burdens who joined the girls as accusers. One of these was the elder Ann Putnam, who had buried several children before she succeeded in raising her gifted namesake to the age of hysteria.

Of the afflicted girls the prosecution would hear no evil. They were turning court and every Sabbath meeting to pandemonium with their antics, they if anyone were exponents of diabolism, but they were deemed innocent as angels. The magistrates could not be blamed for their credulity; belief in witchcraft was almost an article of faith. They were not to be blamed for their failure to understand the nature of hysteria; in their day no one did.

What could be charged against them, especially the ministers, was the hysteria itself. It was a symptom of a defect in Congregational practice which would not be rectified for more than a century. Sermons must have been preached on the text, "Suffer little children . . . and forbid them not, for of such is the kingdom of heaven," but in their time who understood that text?

They loved their children, hurried them to meeting on the first Sabbath after birth to snatch them from the devil by baptism. They taught them the catechism, prayed over them, brought them to hear God's Word. But they ill understood the effects on the young of concepts like predestination, the unpardonable sin, and of a jealously watchful God ever on the lookout for the least misdemeanor.

Two possible effects upon the young were illustrated by the children in the Parris household. Little Betty apparently fell ill under an unbearable sense of sinning against she hardly knew what, but unpardonably in any case. Her tough-minded cousin Abigail, on the contrary, took damnation as something predestined to someone else, and exhibited zestful relish in the prospect. Tender little Betty was of no service to the prosecution; mercifully she was early sent away from the contagion. The likes of Abigail, juvenile emblem of everything that was harsh and self-righteous in Puritanism, became the mainstay of the witch hunt.

Repentance

But even while the worst was being manifested, the best was coming to light, and when reaction became irresistible, the trials were stopped, and good people looked back at what had been allowed to go on with the same aghast incredulity that they looked at wreckage left in the tree-tops by a disastrous flood. In its waning days theocracy achieved a virtue that it had professed but imperfectly practiced in the days of its pride: it learned humility.

Laymen learned it first. In 1697 Judge Samuel Sewall and after him the entire witch jury arose in meeting to confess that they had been in error in judgment upon many of the witches and took on themselves "the blame and shame of it." The jury added, "We fear we have been instruments with others, though ignorantly and unwillingly, to bring upon ourselves the guilt of innocent blood."

The ministers were searching their souls. Even Parris, whom Salem Village had cast out, acknowledged at least the possibility of error. John Hale of Beverly wrote a whole book in the spirit of atonement. Cotton Mather, who believed in the devil and his witches as firmly as he believed in God and His angels, wondered "whether they did not kill some of their own side in the noise and smoke of this dreadful war."

Repentance went so far that in 1710, thanks largely to the efforts of John Wise, General Court reversed the judgment against many of the witches, and a year later compensated the families of many who had suffered in the prosecution. The heirs of Wise's parishioner John Procter got the highest award, £150.

And though witch trials continued in old England and on the Continent, Massachusetts had seen the last of them.

X

"A FURIOUS MAN CALLED JOHN WISE"

Cotton Mather, kept in Boston by pastoral duties, had been unable to observe the witchcraft at first hand. It was a matter of regret to him, for of all God's providences, none interested him more than this. He had already written a book on the subject, a study of the malefactions of Boston's witch Glover. Now that it seemed to him that in Salem was being enacted as grand a drama of the contest between the almighty righteousness and evil as that recorded by Milton in *Paradise Lost,* a book from which he sometimes quoted, it was a sore trial not to have had a hand in it.

Early in the outbreak he had offered to take any six of the afflicted girls into his home for observation and treatment. It was a pity his offer had not been accepted, for Mather was something of a psychiatrist. He had an abiding interest in medicine, having pursued what medical studies were available at Harvard at the time when he supposed that his stammering would disqualify him from preaching. He had some practical experience of hysteria; he had studied the children afflicted by Glover and had wrought a cure. His therapy was not analysis but prayer.

He could surely have done as well with the afflicted maidens of Salem Village (any young girl exposed to the charm of the personable younger Mather quickly achieved what psychologists call a transference), and more important, these girls, removed from the hysterical surmises and gossipings of their own neighborhood, would soon have run out of material for further accusations. Many lives might have been spared had Mather's invitation been accepted.

But the magistrates were less interested in therapy than in prosecution. Or rather they reasoned that prosecution was the real therapy. When all the witches were hanged, the girls, being tormented no longer, would recover of themselves. The magistrates came to each session confident that this time they would get at the root of the matter by exposing the last witch. Until they reached that end they needed the girls, whose visions were their most dependable evidence.

Mather did have opportunity to interview some of the witches, many of whom were brought to Boston jail. Two interested him especially, John Willard, a constable, accused soon after he angrily declined to arrest any more good neighbors, and John Procter, whose fighting spirit and whose championship by John Wise had drawn the attention of both Mathers. It was in response to appeals from these men that Mather took the trouble to ride out from Boston to attend their hanging on August 19.

This hanging was unusual in that men outnumbered the women four to one. The men were Procter, Willard, the profanely outspoken George Jacobs, and the minister George Burroughs; the woman was Martha Carrier. The presence of a minister at the gallows was of special interest; Increase Mather had gone to Salem to satisfy himself that Burroughs receive fair trial and had reported, "Had I been one of the judges, I could not have acquitted him."

Now there was a near miscarriage of justice. All witches were given an opportunity to make a statement; Burroughs' was so moving that it brought tears to the eyes of the spectators. Then he repeated the Lord's Prayer. This had been one test of witchcraft, for no one pledged to the devil could repeat these holy words without faltering. Burroughs repeated them and he did not falter. A murmuring arose from the crowd, and as the minister stepped on the ladder there was a surge forward, as if to snatch him from the hands of the sheriff.

Cotton Mather, standing by his horse, saw the peril and averted it. He swung himself into the saddle, rode forward, and wheeled about to address the crowd. There was no impiety in hanging a minister, he assured them; a minister, in fact, Burroughs was not, for though he had preached in Salem Village, he had never been ordained. The devil was never more dangerous than when he appeared as an angel of light.

The hanging was allowed to go on, but Mather never lived down his part in it. Some knew how tenderly he had prayed with murderers whom he had accompanied to the scaffold. Had he then no charity at all for a man who, "ordained" or not, had faithfully preached to Salem Village until its spites had driven him out? The difference was, as Mather could have told them, that the murderer had acknowledged and repented his crime, whereas Burroughs had not.

He did not have opportunity to explain, and it oddly came about that when reaction set in full tide, the younger Mather was blamed as if the whole tragedy were of his own conniving. Thanks to such circumstance he never achieved the status to which his birth and talents entitled him; he was not to realize his dearest ambition of succeeding his father as president of Harvard.

This train of events was set in motion that August day on Gallows Hill; it might not have come to a climax but for what Mather did afterward. At a time when all Massachusetts had had enough of the witchcraft and many were ashamed of their part in it, he was constitutionally incapable of letting the subject drop.

Wonders and More Wonders of the Invisible World

Late in the trials he composed an official history of the witchcraft; he had been asked. The prosecutors, disturbed by the reaction, were anxious to have an authoritative record of the painstaking procedure they had followed. Cotton Mather, to whom newsprint was more fragrant than roses, and who was never happier than when parishioners suggested that "some poor sermon of mine" be put between covers, snatched at the assignment and wrote that learned treatise, *Wonders of the Invisible World*.

It was an able document for which historians are grateful, but there were two things wrong with it. One was the spirit of credulity in which Mather wrote, his entire absence of critical sense. Beyond the erudite prologues on the nature of devils and the prevalence of witches in contemporary England and Sweden, it might have been dictated by one of the afflicted girls. It was noteworthy that he described the trials of only five witches, avoiding such controversial cases as Rebecca Nurse and John Procter. He did include George Burroughs; one gathered from his account that the "small black minister's" diabolism had been most consistently exhibited in athletic prodigies of strength.

Its other defect was its timing, though this was due to Governor Phips, who would not permit publication until 1693. No one took opinion polls then; quite likely there were many who agreed with the old woman who spoke to Mather of the "willful smothering of the witchcraft." One such was Chief Justice William Stoughton, who left the bench in a rage when Phips reprieved those whom his court had condemned. But there was no question that the majority of the best educated and most influential people in the colony had turned in revulsion against the conduct of the trials. Mather's book, admitting to no defects in the prosecution, by implication countenancing the use of spectral evidence, gave them offense and roused their fears as to what the eminent young clergyman would do next.

What he did was discover witchcraft in Boston; in fact he had already done so. It had happened in the summer of the hangings when young Mercy Short was carried screaming from one of his sermons and whom he discovered to be possessed. Sarah Good was responsible. Boston prison, where she awaited hanging, was attracting as many visitors as a zoo. The witch begged Mercy for tobacco for her pipe, and being refused, cursed the girl, whose fits began after.

Mather worked with her and by prayer expelled her demons. He also wrote a book about her, *A Brand Pluck'd from the Burning,* but though he doubtless circulated the manuscript, he did not publish, and even deterred other visitors to Mercy from reporting names that she denounced in her delirium. One was his own, a circumstance that he took as the devil's acknowledgment of his own good work. (Odd that such reasoning did not occur to him when his colleague Burroughs was accused.) He was obeyed, and Mercy's prophecies led to no prosecution.

In the fall of 1693, long after the trials were over and such of the accused as survived had been delivered from their jails, he found fresh proof of witchcraft in the fits of Margaret Rule. This case could not be hushed up, for the antics of the girl, who practiced levitation and all manner of wonders, became the chief spectator sport of Boston. Sometimes Mather was able to pray with her in privacy, but more often he operated before a cloud of witnesses, one of them a Boston merchant named Robert Calef. This time it was Calef who wrote the book; his avowed purpose was to prevent a "bigotted zeal [from] stirring up a blind and most bloody rage" by such credulity as Mather's, and his very title was satiric, *More Wonders of the Invisible World.*

He did not publish until 1700, but the manuscript had circulated widely long before then. He presented the girl as an attention-grabbing hussy and created for Mather a ridiculous image that the poor man never lived down. It may well have been Calef's derision that cost him the presidency of Harvard.

The Brattle Street Church

Publication of *More Wonders* was only one of Calef's subversive activities. He also played a role in a newly gathered church in Boston, whose strange ways affronted both Mathers. Their inability to control this congregation very nearly impelled them to abandon the Congregational Way which Mather had recently and eloquently expounded in his masterpiece, *Magnalia Christi Americana.*

The Brattle Street Church had opened its doors in December 1699 after delays occasioned by the reluctance of the other three Congregational churches in Boston to consent to a fourth. (Bad enough that they already had other rival congregations: Anglican King's Chapel, and a church for what had been anathema to the founders, the Baptists.)

The reluctance was normal. Everywhere in New England congregations jealously held to their members and contested the appeals of those who claimed that their distance from the meetinghouse, such as Salem Village from Salem, or the necessity of crossing rivers in all weathers prevented their attending service in the parent church with due regularity.

The reluctance had been manifest from the earliest times. John Winthrop had deplored the scattering of congregations about the Bay instead of their uniting to build one "city upon a hill." Bradford had regretted the expansion of little Plymouth into Duxbury and Marshfield. The Massachusetts legislature had opposed the removal of Thomas Hooker's congregation to Connecticut. But deplorable or not, the tendency had been irresistible. Hooker's congregation did remove, and after years of stormy town meetings one community after another had been permitted to gather a separate congregation out of which often grew a second town. The visible congregation of Boston had been thrice divided; now a fourth was consented to.

Here there were other reasons for reluctance. The claim of the advocates of a new meetinghouse on the grounds that they lacked convenient seating places in the old may have been valid. What lacked validity was a proposal to make unseemly innovations in the new church. These were not doctrinal; Brattle Street would hold to original sin, predestination, and election. But its prospective members rebelled against the rigid requirements for membership that denied the sacraments to so eminent a Bostonian as Thomas Brattle because he would not publicly present proof of his conversion; and they were demanding what the Mathers called "dumb reading" of the Scriptures. They wanted them read without commentary.

To ministers of the old school, unexplicated readings were no different from the "superstitious" ritual of the Anglicans. Why else had Harvard been founded if not to give ministers the learning to expound to the laity to full significance of a Biblical text? (Cotton Mather, it sometimes seemed to these more restless auditors, could not even read "Jesus wept" without citing every authority of antiquity from Herodotus on.)

The new congregation had an even more startling innovation; they proposed that ministers should be elected not by "male communicants" alone but that "every baptised adult person who contributes to the maintenance should have a vote." This was direct disobedience to Paul's charge that women be silent in meeting. So encouraged, women would be demanding a voice in town meeting next.

Once gathered, the new congregation put these innovations into effect and drew fire from the Mathers. Cotton accused them of "causing much temptation and inequity" in Boston, and of undermining the whole Congregational Way. His father denounced "dumb readings," saying that the proper expounding of one chapter would "edify the congregation more than the bare reading of twenty." This, retorted Brattle Street, did not "savor of modesty. . . . Alas, Sir, the Scripture wants nothing of ours to make it perfect."

Under the Congregational Way, in which each church was answerable only to the rule of Christ and so was a law unto itself, it was difficult to discipline such deviationalism. At first the Mathers resorted to denunciatory pamphlets and saw to it that Boston printers would not accept work from the offenders, who had to send to New York to get their replies in print. But when the unrepentant Fourth Church remained impervious to reason and flourished and grew, they looked about them for a surer means of bringing it under control.

Fellowship between churches was maintained by informally organized regional associations of ministers, called not at stated periods, but whenever an emergency impelled a local minister to seek counsel from colleagues. Parris had followed accepted practice when he summoned the ministers of the North Shore to advise him on the witchcraft. The power of an association was purely advisory; now in a situation which to the Mathers threatened to rival the witchcraft itself, they sought to extend its power. They wanted what would have been much like a presbytery, an association meeting at specified intervals and empowered to outlaw a congregation that ignored its counsel.

In 1705 delegates from five associations ratified a series of such proposals presented by Cotton Mather. But ratification was not implementation. Only nine delegates had attended the convention. Most ministers remained dubious about imposing what seemed to be Presbyterian formality on the autonomous churches. Their misgivings found a compelling voice. It came not from fashionable Brattle Street, but from a country town so inconsiderable that one would not expect it to be listened to at all. It came from Chebacco, recently split off from Ipswich and eventually to be known as Essex. The voice was that of John Wise.

The Fighting Pastor

No one in his college class (Harvard, 1669) would have nominated him as the one most likely to succeed against men of such distinction as the Mathers. Far from possessing illustrious lineage, he was the first son of an indentured servant to be admitted to Harvard. His father had long since served out his term, and was respected in Roxbury where he was a maltster of middling means. He sometimes paid his son's college fees in malt.

Nor was young Wise an infant prodigy. He must have done well at Roxbury grammar school or he would not have qualified at Harvard, but he made it not at the tender age that Cotton was to enter it a few years later, but at the ripe age of seventeen. There were advantages in doing so. Where sensitive little Cotton was at first to be bedeviled by hazing, Wise was able to give rather better than he got. He was a tall youth of powerful build and athletic prowess. Even after he achieved the dignity of the ministry he was reported to have accepted a challenge from a wrestler and to have thrown the challenger.

Harvard was nothing if not class conscious, ranking its scholars by social status. Wise, whose status was of the lowliest, was sought out by his betters. Several of them invited him to a turkey dinner that came to the attention of Middlesex County Court, the turkey having been stolen.

Wise was called to the ministry immediately after graduation. Before he came to his permanent pastorate in Chebacco, he had put in four years as minister in Branford, Connecticut, had served in the war against King Philip, and had preached three years in a town nearly destroyed by the Indians, Hatfield, Massachusetts.

Whether by accident or his own predilection, each of these congregations had been newly gathered after secession from a parent church. The contest between Chebacco and Ipswich was not entirely resolved until after Wise settled there. Repeatedly Chebacco had appealed to Ipswich town meeting, and being ignored, to General Court, only to be referred back to Ipswich. Aside from the usual prejudice against a new church, there had been two difficulties. Chebacco did not propose to go on paying rates to the support of the Ipswich ministry after it had one of its own. Ipswich, though finally willing to allow Chebacco to hold meetings in a private home, would not consent to the erection of a meetinghouse. Nevertheless, just before Wise's arrival, one had been built. It was the product of the energy and enterprise of the women. No one had thought of applying the ban to them. They got together, enlisted the help of a hired hand and some men from Gloucester and Manchester who were outside Ipswich jurisdiction, and raised their meetinghouse.

Ipswich authority was wroth. Warrants were issued for the arrest of all who had aided the mutinous women, and again the case went before General Court. This time it received a sympathetic hearing. Chebacco was empowered to have both meetinghouse and minister; soon after John Wise came, it was also excused from supporting the Ipswich church.

A fighting parish had achieved a fighting pastor. Chebacco still being under Ipswich town meeting, Wise played a vigorous part in its quarrel with Governor Andros. When the latter was expelled and Phips, not yet governor, was sent with an expedition against the French in Quebec, Wise went with him as chaplain. Home again in Chebacco in time to observe and deplore the witch hunt, Wise rallied his congregation to the defense of the Procters.

A man so active in public affairs would not remain silent when the Congregational Way itself was imperiled. Yet he did not act promptly, either because he heard late of the Mathers' proposals or did not until after long reflection take in their full significance. It was not until 1710 that he delivered his first broadside, and until 1717 that he delivered his second. That one was mortal so far as the Mathers' Presbyterian impulses were concerned. Wise's dicta were to become as important as the Cambridge Platform itself, not only then but for more than a century to come.

The "Mad Book" and the Congregational "Magna Carta"

It was not his first book, *The Churches' Quarrel Espoused,* published in 1710 and again in 1715, that was to become something like the Magna Carta of the Congregational Way. He had cast part of his argument in satire, a literary form of small appeal to plain-speaking New England ministers. Calling attention to the fact that Mathers' proposals had been adopted on November 5, which was Gunpowder Day, he arraigned them in a mock trial as conspirators in a popish plot. "Zeal and Conscience, those two solicitors for the Crown [would] at the Grand Court of Oyer and Terminer implead and prosecute . . . [the proposals] as traitors to the Prince of Peace, and felons to those churches, Christ's loyal subjects."

He arraigned the proposals rather than their advocates, and serious as his purpose was, his form was humorous. Aside from Cotton Mather's puns, humor was not generally accepted as a prerogative of the pulpit. "A Satanick insult," was the punster's first reaction. Later Mather added, "A furious man called John Wise . . . has lately published a foolish libel against us for presbyterianizing too much in our care to repair some deficiencies in our churches. And some of our people, who are not only tenacious of their liberties, but also more suspicious than they have any cause to be . . . are too much led into temptation by such invectives."

Even young Joseph Green, whose compassion and good sense in his ministry at Salem Village had repaired some of the damage done by his predecessor Samuel Parris, called it a "mad book."

But from Mather's own statement, the book had influence; and those already "led into temptation" by it became a receptive audience in 1717 when Wise published his more important book, *A Vindication of the Government of New England Churches.* The argument of this book was not only to shape the course of the Congregational Way for more than a century to come, but to bear on concepts of civil government. Republished just before the outbreak of the American Revolution, one remarkable statement must have inspired many ministers to hearten their parishioners in the conflict against George III. "The Prince who strives to subvert the Fundamental Laws of the Society is the traitor and the rebel, and not the people who endeavor to preserve and defend their own."

Here Wise paraphrased a German author whose work he had lately pondered, Baron Samuel Pufendorf. He was also recalling Charles I, James II, and his contest with that "traitor and rebel" who had once interfered with his own liberty, Governor Andros, and very possibly the intransigent magistrates who during the witchcraft had done to death men like John Procter.

He traced the Way back to its origins in the primitive Christian churches of the Apostles, and described the extinction of ancient liberties by prelates who found it "no pleasant thing to flesh and blood to engage in the conduct and oversight of Christ's volunteers; to bear with their manners; to exercise patience toward them in all their infirmities; and in all their weaknesses to continue a high valuation for them as the flock of God, which He hath purchased with His own blood; all this requires abundance of self denial; and if it is so, then it's no wonder that many of their prelates were willing gradually to extricate themselves out of this uneasy condition, and embrace all opportunities of introducing another order into the churches that might tend more to the exaltation of their own power and dignity." So came the bishops.

So also eventually came Luther, "who turned the horses' noses into a direct way from Babylon toward the city of God, and held on in a good round trot through thick and thin, not caring to bespatter others in this high fog as he himself was finely bespattered by others."

Luther had effected a "glorious reformation," but, and here Wise quoted Increase Mather, it was still "very imperfect. . . . These churches in New England, as to their order and discipline, have surpassed all churches of the reformation. And under the head of discipline, it seems to me that Christ, the Captain of Salvation, has given out His Word to these churches . . . and His word of command is: As you were, make good the old front; or place yourself in that regimental order which the primitive churches were in whilst they marched under My banners and encountered the devil in their heathen persecutors for the first three hundred years. . . . The churches in New England and the primitive churches are eminently parallel in their government."

By natural transition Wise turned to civil government. No one who had shared the difficulties of the separation of the Chebacco congregation from Ipswich could miss the significance of the Way in conditioning New England government. He spoke of man, "the favorite animal on earth," in a state of nature, of his essential equality "till man has resigned himself with all his rights for the sake of a civil state; and then his personal liberty and equality is to be cherished and preserved to the highest degree as will consent with all just distinctions amongst men of honor and shall be agreeable with the public good."

He reasoned from concepts that John Locke would make familiar to a later generation, and anticipated the *contrat civile* of Rousseau. In this he abandoned Scriptural precedent, beyond remarking that the Jews had changed their government five times, a fact which demonstrated that God had prescribed no one form. Not having read Locke, his inspiration was Pufendorf; even more it was his personal experience: the father who had come to America as an indentured servant and risen to an honorable place in the community, his own work with the deacons and laymen of his congregation, and perhaps his observation of leaders as conspicuous as the Mathers. "How very uncertain we are of the real goodness of those we esteem good men; and also how impossible it is to secure the entail of it to successors."

Without apology he defended the concept deplored by the founders of the Bay: democracy. "Possibly the fairest [government] in the world is that which has a regular monarchy (in distinction to what is despotic) settled upon a noble democracy as its basis. . . . A democracy was the noble government which beat out in all the bad weather of ten bloody persecutions under the management of antiquity. And this is our constitution, and why can't we be pleased?"

He discussed the Congregational election of ministers ("Here is no back stairs for cousins and favorites to climb up to high seats without desert; it is merit and intrinsic worth sets the value"), the Cambridge Platform, the use of ministerial associations. He quoted Thomas Hooker at length, and every chance he got he quoted Mather against Mather.

So doing was the "Satanic insult"; it left the Mathers virtually speechless. To reply that Increase had changed his mind on the points cited might be accurate, but it was not politic. To reply that Wise had misconstrued them put the burden of proof on the Mathers. Increase might once have been capable of it, but he was aging. Cotton's talents lay in narration and the collection of magpie details (it is a real pity that he was born too early to try his hand at novel writing) rather than logic. He had already judged that the best reply to the earlier treatise was contemptuous silence; this one he denounced in his journal as a "cursed libel." Publicly, Wise went unanswered, and his views prevailed.

They had done so before he wrote. The Mathers' proposals failed less because a country pastor denounced them than because of a passive resistance almost universal among local congregations. The proposals could not take effect until they were implemented by action of the ministerial associations, which did not so act. They preferred the status quo. Wise had not so much defeated the Mathers as clarified and justified the thinking of those who had already done so. His most important influence was not on the immediate present, but on the future.

Cotton Mather outlived this adversary by three years (and his father by five), and though his later life was marked by sadness and humiliation, it was not altogether a time of defeat. No less than Wise, he faced into the future, and there were many points on which the men agreed.

New Ways of Singing

Like Wise, Mather worked to enable his congregation to make a more joyful noise unto the Lord. Congregational singing had fallen into strange ways in New England. Though a Bay psalm book had been published soon after first settlement, it had no notes. It became the duty of a deacon to "set the tune," to "line out" the psalm verse by verse, the people following his lead. All singing was *a capella;* even the Brattle Street Church was not yet modern enough to accept the offer of an organ. The singing was also male. Women might sing at their own devotions, in their sequestered "praying companies," but in meeting they kept the silence enjoined on them by St. Paul.

The result, according to auditors with some musical knowledge, was awful. Each man became a soloist, vigorously raising his voice without reference to tune or tempo, indulging in quavers and crotchets according to his own fancy and without regard to what his neighbor was doing. It was a glorious pandemonium (a relief at least from passive enduring of the parson's tenthlies), and with each singer coming raggedly to his separate conclusion, the wonder was that the deacon knew when to line out the next verse.

Just possibly it was less dreadful than advertised. Slave songs, Negro spirituals, were evolving in a system not unlike the deacon's lining out, and they were often beautiful. It may be that musicians of a generation that has come to appreciate cacophony and atonality might find merit in what John Adams was to call "all the drawling, quavering discord in the world."

By Mather's time singing masters were coming to Boston and teaching part-singing "by notes." Mather knew something of notes; in youth it was by learning to sing that he had controlled his stammering. Now he took the side of the singing masters and made some impression on his congregation at the Old North, and the movement spread. But in New England at large many doggedly held to the old style; some congregations were divided into those who sang by note and those who held to ruggedly individualistic vocalisms. It was half a century after Mather's death that John Adams commented on the "quavering discords."

The Long Shadow of a Giant

Another innovation defended by Mather required courage. When in 1721 Boston was devastated by a smallpox epidemic, it was he who urged on the local doctors a precaution that had had some success in

Europe, inoculation. In this situation it was the doctors who held back, partly on the grounds that inoculation itself was dangerous, partly on the grounds that it was flying in the face of God's providence; not they but the ministers recommended making use of the latest discoveries of science. Mather saw no Biblical reason why God should not help those who helped themselves (nor did Wise), had his household successfully inoculated, and was physically attacked for his pains; his house was bombed. The "granado," as he called it, did not go off, and he could read the attached message: "Cotton Mather, you Dog, Dam you; I'll inoculate you with this with a Pox to you."

He had long since become a fellow of the Royal Society of London and made contributions to its publications. They were more quaint than scientific, but he was keeping abreast of scientific developments, reading Newton, and as a result published one pamphlet which suggested the future heresies of those who called themselves Deists. It was not surprising that in his old age he was given an opportunity to link hands with the future by attracting a visit from a former Bostonian now indulging in a propensity for scientific experiment in Philadelphia.

Actually it was not Mather's science but his morality, his recent "Essay to Do Good," that drew the young man. No more than Mather did the youth see "do goodism" as a reproach; he was founding self-improvement societies in Philadelphia, and like Mather he was keeping a journal. In it he recorded no dreams, no visions of jeweled angels coming to prophesy his future; instead he kept in it a moral report card, making weekly note of his departure from the virtues he had set himself to achieve. If one week he found he had failed in chastity, he did not, as Mather would have done had occasion—heaven forbid —arisen, beat his breast and humble himself in the dust; he merely recorded the demerit on his personal gig sheet and hoped next week to do better.

The meeting between Mather and young Benjamin Franklin was cordial, and the latter never forgot it. Mather did not live long enough after to appreciate its significance, what a long step into the future the younger man represented. The latter was to be many things, even, in spite of his free-thinking, uninhibited later career, something of a Puritan. Much later another youth, a Russian, would be impressed by Franklin's moral report card and adopt a similar device in his own journal. If to Cotton Mather can be attributed any part of the Slavic Puritanism that was to characterize Leo Tolstoy in sinful youth and saintly old age, he cast a long shadow indeed, and the visionary angel who spoke to him of great deeds knew what he was talking about.

XI

THE GREAT AWAKENING

In 1702, at the height of the Brattle Street controversy, Cotton Mather was in a position to gratify his ambition of becoming college president. The Connecticut Assembly had granted a charter to the trustees of what was called a "collegiate school" and Mather was invited to assist in the founding of Yale as its first rector.

He had every reason for sympathy with the project. In establishing a college, the Connecticut ministers were not only interested in giving their youth a means of completing their education more conveniently and less expensively than by making the long journey to Cambridge, but in combating the libertarian tendencies that had lately beset Harvard. They deplored as much as Mather the innovations that Brattle Street was threatening to introduce into the hallowed Way, and they wanted to protect future ministers from such contagion.

But Mather's affections, his wistful hopes, still centered on Harvard. Though it had once had a president whose Anabaptist tendencies had to be curbed, though some of its fellows championed Brattle Street, it was Harvard still, now well along into its sixth decade and not for a moment to be compared to a brushwood enterprise of dubious future. Besides, Mather was Boston-bred, and what Bostonian would exchange the amenities (and the printshops) of the "city built on a hill" for what he called the wilderness?

In a surge of early Boston provincialism he declined the honor with thanks. From a practical view he was justified. To have directed Yale in its first stormy decades would have taxed the wisdom of Solomon and the diplomacy of the younger John Winthrop. Mather's strong points were not wisdom and diplomacy; in staying with Boston and the Old North he spared himself much grief.

The trouble was that for many years the new college couldn't settle down. The trustees were divided as to its proper location, and so was Connecticut; rival claimants divided the "collegiate school," like all Gaul, into three parts. There was Saybrook, which had few students but kept a stranglehold on a library bequest of 1250 volumes; New Haven, which had a plot on which to build, and a tutor (unpopular) named Samuel Johnson; and Wethersfield, to whose Harvard-bred tutor, the gifted Elisha Williams, New Haven students repaired when they had enough of Johnson. Hartford also had academic hopes. In 1718, the year in which the college received its name from Governor Eli Yale, there were two commencements, an authorized one in New Haven and a counterfeit in Wethersfield. Saybrook citizens compounded the confusion by overturning the oxcarts when the library was removed to New Haven and making off with a quantity of books.

The situation was not unlike that of a congregation trying to set up a separate meetinghouse against the will of the parent church. The tumults attending the founding of Yale were very much in the tradition of the Congregational Way. Cotton Mather, watching from afar the difficulties attending the birth of his "godchild," sorrowfully remarked that the infant college was "in danger of being strangled in the birth by a dissension . . . as to where it should be nourished in the wilderness."

Yet the dissension did not prevent those who attended the wandering college from getting an education. In 1716 a class of ten was entered that included a thirteen-year-old lad who was to become a distinguished alumnus. He and his classmates began at New Haven under Johnson, seceded in a body to Williams in Wethersfield, obeyed an order from General Assembly in 1718 to return to New Haven, went back to Wethersfield, and back again to New Haven, where in 1720 Jonathan Edwards took his first degree.

The Boyhood of Jonathan Edwards

He had his early training from two remarkable parents. Esther, his mother, belonged by birth and family connection to New England aristocracy. Her father was the great Solomon Stoddard, who as pastor in the frontier community of Northampton was nearly as famous as the Boston Mathers. Her mother had been the wife of Eleazar

Mather, brother of Increase. When he died, Stoddard had stepped into his pulpit and married his widow.

The lineage of the father, Timothy, barring certain sensational components, was more obscure, but he had two degrees from Harvard, whence he had been called as pastor to East Windsor. Besides preaching and managing his farm as all country pastors must, Timothy Edwards kept school in his parsonage for children whose parents could afford the tuition. As teacher he was a perfectionist, especially with his ten daughters and his one son. His mind carried logical analysis to the most meticulous detail, and he was a demon for thoroughness. At seven young Jonathan was not only probably as advanced in Latin as Cotton Mather at the same age, but was hearing the recitations of his younger sisters. Under a training that brooked no inattention, no faltering of effort or halfway mastery of Latin accidence, one of the finest minds New England ever produced was being cut to gem-like brilliance. When the opportunity came for Yale, Jonathan was ready, nor would the college's wanderings distract him from his studies there.

East Windsor was an obscure country village. Timothy Edwards came to it just as Wise had come to Chebacco, when the congregation was newly gathered and still in contention with the parent church in Windsor. Persuading Windsor that members who lived on the eastern bank of the Connecticut could not cross the river to meeting in all weathers had not been easy. After all, reasoned the old guard, if the folk on the farther bank got a wetting on the way, if lives were risked in a stormy crossing in unsteady canoes, they should remember that it was all for the glory of God, who would sanctify their hardships to them. The country folk, taking a different view of God's will, had persisted, had first been given grudging permission to build their own meetinghouse, and at long last were excused from paying Windsor rates. The new congregation became a separate town which eventually took the name of South Windsor.

It had grown up helter-skelter along the best farmlands and so lacked the compactness of most New England communities. Thus "wilderness," the irreplaceable virgin forest, was close to every home, and its potential danger was on the mind of the adults. A palisade against Indian attacks stood near the meetinghouse, and though the local Indians of Jonathan's childhood were few and friendly, his parents could not forget that at the time of his birth, his mother's half sister had been killed in a raid on Deerfield. On the pastor's rare trips from home he worried about his family and sent back word that Jonathan was not to be allowed to roam the woods with the hired boy Tim.

As the boy grew toward the six-foot-one of his manhood, the prohibition was lifted. He was not always in the front parlor schoolroom. He shared Tim's chores of woodsplitting, weeding, milking, and when they were done, he explored the woodlands. He and some of his boy cousins (whose proximity made up for his lack of brothers) liked to build huts under the trees. Thanks to family devotions and his father's sermons, Jonathan had already acquired a lifelong interest in the ancient Feast of the Tabernacles. The boys called these huts "booths," and used them for prayer. Later, perhaps because there was no solitude in the sister-ridden house, Jonathan built a booth in a remote spot so that he could obey the Biblical injunction to pray in secret.

Prayer was not the only interest of the lively and inquiring young mind. He took an objective interest in the phenomena of nature. Rainbows obsessed him at one time. He was fascinated to discover that he could make his own by filling his mouth with water and spewing it into bright sunlight.

Then he turned to the study of spiders. Just before he entered Yale he completed a remarkable essay based on his investigations. Tirelessly he had studied the construction of webs, collected the little weavers and sorted them into their kinds, and when he was able to observe a thread of gossamer emerging from the tail of a captive spider, he knew something of Franklin's triumphant discovery with a kite. He would have distinguished himself in the laboratory had the "collegiate school" possessed one; but Yale, like Harvard, was designed as a "school for prophets," and the boy, speedily absorbed not only in Greek and Hebrew texts but in the English writings of John Locke and Isaac Newton, abandoned science for pure speculation.

His father's solicitude followed him to college, and there tried to correct one defect in the lad, the craving for solitude that held him aloof from human companionship. By no means would the elder Edwards have his austere son join undergraduates in their fussing about what they were fed in their commons, in the thieving of turkeys and hens to supplement their diet, in their indulgence in "unseasonable night-walking, breaking people's windows, playing at cards, cursing, swearing, and damning and using all manner of ill language"; but he did urge his son to visit friends and join conversations. There were limits to the youth's capacity for sociability, but at least he and his father remained the best of friends all their lives.

Conversion

He had entered Yale "unconverted" in spite of his prayers in the woods. He was at graduate school when in 1721 the spirit of Pentecost descended on him, and he turned to his father to report the event as spontaneously as a young girl tells her mother of her first love. "I walked alone in a solitary place in my father's pasture. . . . And as I was walking there and looked up at the sky and clouds, there came into my mind a sweet sense of the glorious majesty and grace of God. . . . I seemed to see them both in sweet conjunction, majesty and meekness joined together."

After such experience Jonathan was ready when he received his master's degree in 1722 to accept calls to his first pastorates, New York, then Bolton, Connecticut, and in 1727 to Northampton as assistant to his aging grandfather Stoddard.

Northampton gave every promise of being his permanent charge, for the life of grand old Solomon Stoddard was obviously running out and Edwards was called not only to assist but succeed him. Now in his mid-eighties, Stoddard still scorned to read his sermons, as Edwards did, but recited them from memory; but he was becoming inattentive to the carriage of his congregation and it was time to bring in young blood.

Northampton was an excellent situation for so young a man, and not only because of the prestige Stoddard had given it. Boston considered it the Far West, a frontier outpost, but Northampton's orientation was not primarily to Boston. It was too hard to get there over one hundred miles of track too rough to be dignified by the name of road. It was easy to get to Connecticut down the great river; Northampton and Springfield were a natural extension of the original

Connecticut towns, which had been wroth when Springfield was claimed by Massachusetts.

Now some eighty years old, the town enjoyed a modest but solid prosperity; its most substantial citizens like the Pomeroys, the Hawleys, and the Strongs were known as the "river gods" because they owned the rich bottom land. The plain but adequate houses of the two hundred families, unlike those of straggling East Windsor (easily accessible downstream), were compactly grouped. Schools were available. Four months in the year boys could attend public school, the schoolmaster paid by town rates supplemented by donations from some parents. Able scholars looked to Yale rather than Harvard. A number of front parlors were also open for the instruction of the daughters of those prosperous enough to afford the fees.

Thanks to Stoddard, who in his half century of service had made six hundred converts, the town was respectable. Edwards was grateful that it lacked the disreputable floating element that he had observed in his brief pastorate in New York; a few riverside wharfs for launching craft downstream with produce for Hartford did not make the place a port. There were taverns, and people frequented them more than he liked, but farm folk dropping in for a noggin between chores were very different from sailors spending entire shore leaves in such places.

A Match Made in Heaven

The twenty-three-year-old assistant pastor looked on Northampton, and though he saw need for improvement, it was good. Now that he was installed as his grandfather's heir apparent, he was ready for marriage. He returned to New Haven and fetched back the seventeen-year-old Sarah Pierpont as his bride. He had been waiting for her five years.

He had found her in the parsonage of her father, James Pierpont of New Haven, when she was a girl of twelve. Like his mother she was of royal descent in the New England sense, a great-granddaughter of Thomas Hooker. Her father was a contributor to the Yale Library, for whose possession Saybrook had so vigorously contested. There is a story that Sarah had never been accepted to full membership in her father's church because she could not testify to the exact date of her conversion. That was because she had never known a time when she had not lived in radiant faith; she was a product of what a later Connecticut minister would call "Christian nurture."

Young Edwards, then still "unconverted" in the strict technical sense, was dazzled by the child who so visibly lived in God. "There are certain seasons in which this Great Being . . . comes to her," he wrote, "and fills her with exceeding sweet delight, and that she hardly cares for anything except to meditate on Him. . . . She will sometimes go about from place to place singing sweetly, and seems to be always full of joy . . . and no one knows for what. She loves to be alone, walking in the fields and groves, and seems to have one invisible always with her."

It was a match made in heaven, two young people who preferred the society of God to that of all others. Their yearning for holy solitude did not prevent their appreciating each other. Edwards revered his wife, watched and recorded her mystical transports of ecstasy with awe and wonder. It must have been partly for this cause that this intellectual logician came to place a high value on emotion in religious experience. He would never neglect doctrine, but he recognized that without the quickening of spirit provided by the emotions the soundest doctrine could become a dead thing.

The young couple were fruitful and began to multiply at once. There were always small children underfoot at the parsonage, to say nothing of guests. Ministers traveling from one engagement to another, as happened often during the revivals for which Edwards became largely responsible, were always stopping in for bed and board, and even if they came at midnight, necessitating the tumbling of children from one trundlebed to another, Sarah's hospitality never failed. One very famous minister, then a bachelor—this was George Whitefield—envied Edwards' joy in his Sarah and took a wife soon after.

Turning the Young to Sanctity

During his first two years in Northampton, the junior pastor, alertly eyeing the congregation while his grandfather preached, was distressed by what he called "indecent carriage at meeting." It was especially marked among the young, whose attention was everywhere but on the sermon, who nudged each other, whispered, giggled, and sometimes laughed aloud.

The old pastor preached on, oblivious to such misconduct; nor did he seem to know that out of meeting the young indulged in the "lewd pleasures" that Edwards had deplored among Yale undergraduates whenever he looked up from his books. They frequented the taverns, they went "night-walking," got together "in conventions of both sexes for mirth and jollity which they call frolics," and some frolics lasted most of the night.

Was it for the junior pastor to call attention to these oversights? Tact was not an Edwards trait; what an Edwards saw amiss he forthwith corrected. About this time Jonathan's youngest sister Jerusha, the saint of the family, was getting jilted by a suitor who tired of being told what was for his own good. She would die at twenty before a more corrigible lover came her way. Jonathan was as given to speaking his mind regardless of consequences as his sister, but in this situation deference to his grandfather deterred him.

He looked in vain to the parents to curb their young. Church and town were beset with the jealous contentions of petty politics which distracted the saints of the visible congregation from the proper government of their young. Though Stoddard had in his long ministry produced no less than five notable harvests of souls, in late years religion had fallen on slack times.

But when Stoddard was gathered to his fathers and his grandson grasped the reins in his hands, there was a soul-shaking change; the young turned to sanctity. It did not begin entirely in response to his preaching but in response to reminders of their own mortality. A lusty youth taken with a pleurisy and dying of it in delirium had particularly afflicted them. No one dies alone in a country town, and no one there doubts for whom the bell tolls. Neighbors are tireless in their inquiries, and getting heavy news, walk away as bowed as if the dying were one of their own.

The frolics ended. A girl who Edwards never thought was "in any wise serious" came to him to report that "God had given her a new heart, truly broken and sanctified." The minister had unworthy misgivings about accepting just this sheep into his fold, for she was a very black sheep indeed, one of "the greatest company-keepers in the whole town," and he feared that receiving her would cause malicious tongues to wag. "Oh ye of little faith!" his Master might have said, He who had not scorned the woman taken in adultery. This conversion was the first in that quickening of spirit to be known as "the great awakening." "The news of it seemed to be almost like a flash of lightning upon the hearts of the young people of the town. . . . Many went to talk with her concerning what she had met with. . . . The noise amongst the dry bones waxed louder and louder; all other talk but about spiritual and eternal things was soon thrown by."

Old and young flocked to the deathbed of one Abigail Hutchinson. There was no notoriety attached to this girl, for though during conversion she had undergone an agonizing conviction of sin, her outward carriage had always been exemplary. Now, though her body was dying of famine, for her swollen throat would admit only liquids and finally not even that, her soul was rising into radiant life.

She suffered constantly, from pain, from hunger, and one might suppose from the streams of visitors who made clinical inquiries into the state of her soul under these trials: "whether she held her integrity still; whether she was not afraid of death. . . . Why she would be so confident."

"There is," replied the girl, "a dark entry that looks something dark, but on the other side there appears such a bright shining light that I cannot be afraid."

And on Monday, June 27, 1735, in "sweet composure of soul," she made her entry into the light.

From his pulpit Edwards was aware of a very small saint who lifted her eyes to his in rapt attention and sat sermon-long without wriggling. She must have looked like a little angel; from the Anglo-Saxon population one may deduce eyes of blue and a kind of Fra Angelico haloing of soft golden hair. This convert was all of four.

She was Phoebe Bartlet, a younger daughter of the William who owned twelve acres of meadowland on Pleasant Street. Between Sabbaths Phoebe enjoyed country pleasures like shucking corn in the barn with her sisters or joining them in a raid on a neighbor's plum tree. But ever since her eleven-year-old brother had converted her, she took none of these sports thoughtlessly. She stopped shucking to weep over her unconverted sisters. "Oh poor Nabby. Oh poor Eunice. Poor Amy!" She loved them dearly, and yet one day, if they persisted in disregarding her entreaties for them to prepare their souls for death, she would have to watch then writhe in hell.

The incident of the "plumbs" (Edwards' spelling) became a moral crisis. When the children charged into the kitchen with their juicy loot, their mother reproved them for the sin of not getting permission first. Phoebe was overwhelmed. First, rather like Adam with Eve, she blamed Eunice for leading her astray. Then she wept and retired into what her pastor called a "closet"—the clothes press perhaps?—to pray. For her the plums had taken on the deadly significance of the apples of Eden, and even when permission was obtained, she would not partake.

When she wasn't following her patient but sometimes baffled mother, plucking at her sleeve, asking her to leave her household chores long enough to take Eunice or Nabby aside to pray, she was begging her father to give one of his cows to a poor neighbor who had lost his, or to receive the stricken family into the Bartlet household.

She had her joys, counting the days to the next Sabbath, catechism, family prayers. One Biblical text released in her a flood of happy fantasy: "Behold I stand at the door and knock; if any man hear my voice I will come in and sup with him." Her mother heard her telling her playmates the delights of supping with God, and when it was her turn to lay the crockery on the table and get out the joint stools, she had her ear cocked for the knock of the divine guest.

Edwards was almost that when he visited their house. He was one reason she counted the days to the Sabbath. "She seems to love God's house and is eager to go thither." She loved it best when Edwards was in it, languished when he was afield, and when he returned ran about crying to all the world, "Mr. Edwards is back! Mr. Edwards is back!"

There was sanctity among the Edwards brood; during the revival the junior Sarah was accepted into Church membership at seven, and her baby sister Jerusha was to follow the example of her saintly aunt and namesake. But such extreme precocity had never come Edwards' way before, and he reported her saint's progress in the analysis he was then composing on the nature of conversion. Her raptures did not impair Phoebe's health; she lived to grow up and become spiritual grand-mother of a whole race of infant saints to be recorded in the Elsie Dinsmore and Pansy books.

Delirium of Damnation

Now and then a sect climaxes such a revival as Northampton had experienced with an announcement of Doomsday, and the faithful climb to a mountaintop to await it there. The impulse is understandable; it might be a sovereign manifestation of divine grace if it were gratified. No one, barring an occasional mystic, can long remain on the mountain peak of spiritual ecstasy. It subsides, and when it does, the slope is downward. How many of the literal-minded faithful, denied death and transfiguration, have had to descend again to the mockery of the world?

It is not on record that any in Northampton ascended Mount Tom to await apocalypse. For some, however, it came, and in dismaying fashion. There was a wave of suicides attempted and consummated, and even some of those who stayed their hands were obsessively tempted.

The first incident was unimportant. It did not succeed, and it was only Thomas Stebbins, a man of "weak mind." The second was of deep concern to all the town, especially the pastor; it was the husband of his Stoddard aunt.

Joseph Hawley was one of the "river gods," a prosperous merchant whose bonnets and silks were eagerly sought by the women. Though not college-bred, he was a man of culture, whose library contained not only innumerable volumes of sermons but classics in Latin and Greek.

When, in response to Edwards' preaching, this man fell into deep dejection of spirit, there seemed at first no cause for concern. "Broken-heartedness" as a consequence of conviction of sin was a normal stage in conversion. Everyone had to pass through it; with some it took a few days, some might suffer for weeks before they were visited with a sign of God's redeeming grace. When with Hawley the agony was prolonged all out of reason, like that of a woman unable to give birth, his reverend nephew was alarmed. There was a history of mental instability and melancholia in the Hawley family, and Edwards had other reason for knowing psychosis when he saw it and distinguishing it from the normal anguish of a soul in travail. There was a taint of it in his own family on his father's side. Its most tragic manifestations had taken place before he was born: an uncle who went berserk and killed his sister, an aunt who destroyed her son, and the grandmother whose husband had finally succeeded in divorcing not only because of her threats of physical violence but because of her promiscuity. Edwards must have known of this background, especially as it reappeared in a younger sister and two of her children.

In meeting, when in response to his preaching members of his congregation cried out for him to spare them, he did not. He stood erect before his parishioners, his eyes fixed not on them but on the bell rope, as impervious to entreaty as a surgeon who will not let pity for a patient deter him from completing an operation necessary to save life.

He was no sadist; whatever suffering was necessary on the part of the sinner, he was no man to relish it. Terrifying his congregation was not his chief objective; it would be a sorry commentary on God's heaven if the saints had to be stampeded into it like cattle. He preached God's mercy, but to reveal the full magnitude of that mercy, he must also preach God's wrath, and in doing so he could excel the descriptions in Dante's *Inferno*.

"How dismal will it be when you are under these racking torments to know assuredly that you never, never shall be delivered from them; to have no hope; when you shall wish that you might but be turned into nothing, but shall have no hope of it; when you shall wish that you might be turned into a toad or a serpent, but shall have no hope of it . . . when after you shall have worn out the age of the sun, moon, and stars in your dolorous groans and lamentations, without any rest day or night, or one minute's ease, yet you shall have no hope of ever being delivered; when after you shall have worn out a thousand more such ages, yet you shall have no hope but shall know that you are not one whit nearer to the end of your torments."

Joseph Hawley could not waken from the nightmare of such a vision. It was as if he had already entered into his eternity of suffering. Night after night he writhed sleepless on his bed. When morning came he went to his shop, but people who came to buy his clothes and ribbons, his butter, lard, spices, and tobacco (for after the manner of country stores he sold nearly everything) were frightened at his distraught manner. He seemed not to know his oldest customer or to be capable of finding his place in the ledger.

Edwards hurried to him, reasoned with him, gave him consoling texts, talked of God's mercy and grace equal to every need. But Hawley had retired to a private hell beyond the reach of logic. He knew only that he was damned. If damnation was eternal at least mortal life was not. One sunny May Sabbath morning after another night of eternal wakefulness, he rose up early and was presently found lying in a pool of blood with his throat cut.

The effect on the town was frightful. The merciful coroner softened the fact of suicide by recording that the man had died delirious. But other people not sure of salvation felt themselves also sinking into delirium. They heard voices: "Cut your own throat. Now is a good opportunity." Some managed to resist long enough to consult their pastor, who saved them; but others, "multitudes" according to Edwards, made the attempt.

Edwards himself was shaken. In a clinical analysis of this phenomenon which he made five years later when a second revival came, he made one concession to his surgical disregard of the patient's suffering. "I know of but one case when the truth ought to be withheld from sinners in distress, and that is in the case of melancholy; and it is not to be withheld from them as if the truth tends to do them hurt, but because if we speak the truth to them, sometimes they will be deceived and led into error by it through that strange disposition there is in them to take things wrong."

While Edwards reasoned thus, many members of his congregation turned in revulsion from a concept of Pentecost whose outpouring could result in morbid excess. Religion again fell into a slack season. But not for long. George Whitefield was on his way to America.

Enter George Whitefield

The revival of 1735 was not yet the Great Awakening. It had been a local event, confined to the Northampton neighborhood. It had, however, aroused wide interest. Thanks to Stoddard's eminence, Northampton was no obscure parish. When at a time that ministers throughout the colony were experiencing a lukewarm response from their congregations the new Northampton minister achieved so remarkable a harvest of souls, attention was paid even in Boston. It was in response to the inquiry of a Boston minister, Benjamin Colman, that Edwards had composed his account of the revival.

In the meantime word was coming in of the work of a marvelous evangelist in old England. He was George Whitefield, follower of John and Charles Wesley. The Boston papers were full of stories of miraculous conversions en masse; when it was learned that Whitefield was to cross the ocean in 1740 to bring all America to God, even such a hotbed of skepticism as Harvard looked eagerly to his arrival.

Odd that followers of the Congregational Way should look for salvation to an Englishman. Early in the century when the Society of the Propagation of the Gospel had been founded in London for the purpose of bringing the gospel to America, New England had taken umbrage. It was also true that as a follower of the Wesleys, Whitefield represented an alien denomination, the Methodists.

However, the Congregational Way was still a way rather than a conscious denomination. Its members abhorred the heresies of the Arminians, the Quakers, and to some extent the Baptists, but they had no doctrinal quarrel with the Methodists. Only when the new sect built the structure of the Methodist Episcopal Church, meaning that its congregations submitted themselves to bishops as the Presbyterians did to presbyters, would the New Englanders take issue, and that only on government.

Whitefield was partly American already. He had done some work with the Wesleys in Georgia. Moreover he sometimes referred to himself as a Congregational Methodist. In 1740, when he made his whirlwind tour of America, he was twenty-six.

Whitefield was everything that Edwards was not, and very little that Edwards was. Though the latter acknowledged the place of emotion in religion, his power lay in his intellect. He did not, like Cotton Mather, embellish his sermons with a parade of learning; his texts, his analogies were all derived from the Bible. He spoke quietly, with grave pauses, usually read his sermons, and when he lifted his eyes from the page looked not at his congregation, no matter what tumult prevailed among it, but at a distant point. In conducting a revival he very much resembled the surgeon to whom he compared himself, working impersonally to complete an operation without regard to the agonies of the patient.

Whitefield was an actor and a great one; David Garrick was said to have envied his delivery. Sensitive to atmosphere as Edwards never was, he established rapport with his listeners, often improvised in response to their reactions. A logician, a man of culture he was not, and reading his sermons in cold print it is difficult to imagine what the shouting was about. But the same sermons had irresistible effect when the impassioned young man, not notable for wisdom or even good sense, but utterly sincere, stood up to deliver them. When he got to Philadelphia Benjamin Franklin went to hear him, expecting to be diverted. Instead this most rational auditor, whose own faith was a rarefied Deism, found himself in tears and emptied his pockets into the collection plate.

In 1740 Whitefield spent a month in New England, and body and soul, New England was his. It remained his for tumultuous months after as other preachers, Edwards among them, followed his example by going from pulpit to pulpit to harvest the souls awakened not only by Whitefield's presence but by his reputation.

Harvard heard him, and sinful Harvard undergraduates dissolved in tears. In Boston he preached at one church after another, and when the overcrowding in one caused a panic that led to five deaths, he led his followers to Boston Common, where five thousand heard him. As many as eight thousand heard him when he preached in the fields. Whenever his coming was announced, whole households arose at three in the morning to be sure of a place in the meetinghouse; Boston shops closed at noon when an afternoon meeting impended.

Divine Possession or Moderation

The more extreme responses of his congregations, the pandemonium of screaming that often interrupted his discourse, the writhing of bodies on the floor of the tabernacles, must have made those whose memories went back so far wonder if the witchcraft had come again. Like demoniac possession (but of course this was not that) it commonly began among the young. In retrospect Edwards wrote that God "has taken the young people and has cast off the old and stiff-necked generation."

In the presence of Whitefield and in his wake, few even of the old remained stiff-necked. The Pentecostal outpourings led to speaking in tongues, caused the sober citizens of Northampton to march singing to meeting (Edwards was of two minds about the propriety of that), drowned out the efforts of the preacher in Ipswich in the independent efforts of his congregation: a man who cried tirelessly, "Come to Christ!" a woman denouncing the legal profession, an unlettered goodman launching into an elaborate discourse of his own.

Nothing could have been farther removed from the ancient sobriety of New England meeting, where congregations sat reverently silent at the feet of the minister, and the repentant who sought God's forgiveness and their fellows' consent to membership in the visible congregation read a statement carefully prepared in conference with the minister, or if they were women, stood with downcast eyes while the minister read it for them. Divine possession in which much of the congregation participated would have as strange an effect on the New England Way as had demoniac possession, which had after all been confined to a small number of girls. The old Way had its aristocratic aspect in its limitation by design of Church membership to a fraction of the population, to the "elect." What would be the long-range effect of Whitefield's repeated call to "whosoever will"?

In October Whitefield went from Boston to the Northampton area where he preached six sermons. He was charmed with the Edwards family, with whom he lodged. "A sweeter couple I have never seen. Their children dressed not in silks and satins, but plain, as becomes the children of those who in all things ought to be examples of Christian simplicity." He was not a little in love with Sarah. "I have put up to God that He would be pleased to send me a daughter of Abraham to be my wife," exactly such a daughter of Abraham as Sarah was.

Edwards, who had been unwell, kept in the background; his guest noted that like the congregation he wept. Edwards had been praying for such a leaven as Whitefield could work on the human spirit, for religion here as elsewhere had become lukewarm. He had recently induced the town to build a new meetinghouse, aided in the project by the collapse of the gallery in the old one. Luckily no one had been hurt, but his congregation saw the light. Otherwise his flock had lately shown a livelier interest in the world than in the kingdom of God. Young people hankered after "frolics" and "company keeping"; their parents returned to their political squabbles. Whitefield changed all that. When he left it was again given Edwards to speak with the tongue of angels; he preached the most famous of all his sermons to a shattered congregation in Enfield the following July.

After the first impact of Whitefield's delivery, the critical sense of such Boston ministers as Benjamin Colman had awakened to question his substance. Edwards recorded no such misgivings, but thanks to his experience of 1735, he was alert to excesses. It was not that he wanted any diminution of zeal, but he did not want it carried to the point where it would impel "self-murder," and he did not want his flock to become ridiculous.

Zeal was excellent, but not "indiscreet zeal." The impulsive "are for putting on the cupola and pinnacle before the lower parts of the building are ready; which tends . . . to hinder its ever being a complete structure. . . . Things must have a time to ripen." He was alarmed by the impulse of some to permit the uneducated to preach. "Opening a door for the admission of unlearned men to the work of the ministry . . . would . . . be especially prejudicial at such a day as this; because such persons for want of extensive knowledge are oftentimes forward to lead others into . . . impulses, vain imaginings, superstition."

Excesses must be curbed. "There ought to be a moderate restraint on the loudness of persons talking under high affections; for if there be not, it will grow natural and unavoidable for persons to be louder and louder without any increase of their inward sense; till it becomes natural to them at last to scream and halloo to almost everyone they see in the streets. . . . But this is certainly very improper and what has no tendency to promote religion. The man Christ Jesus, when He was upon earth, had doubtless as great a sense of the infinite greatness and importance of eternal things . . . but there is not the least appearance in His history of His taking any such course or manner of exhorting others."

Singing in the streets on the way to or from meeting was permissible, practiced with discretion. Prayer meeting? By all means, but Edwards, whose first converts had been adolescents, one a notorious "company keeper" and who kept a sharp eye on them, seemed to have a prescience of how easily religious fervor could pass into sexual excitement. He would not risk the fertility rites that in a later day would be alleged to take place on the fringe of camp meeting revivals, and so imposed a

Puritanic and wise precaution. Men and women, young and old, and children, should meet to pray and fast, but only in the absence of the opposite sex except when they came together in the meetinghouse under the watchful eye of their pastor. There was no age limit on prayer meetings. Remembering Phoebe, now in her teens, he denounced those who would spare children the knowledge of hell. "Why should we conceal the truth from them? Will those children who have been dealt tenderly with in this respect and lived and died insensible of their misery till they come to feel it in hell, ever thank parents and others for their tenderness in not letting them know their danger?"

Aided by Whitefield, he led his flock to a spiritual mountaintop. Most of his flock. There were always some holdouts; even at Harvard seven undergraduates were known to have resisted Whitefield's Pentecostal outpourings. But if some must be lost, surely the rest could be maintained on the heights. His Sarah, that born mystic, lived there; his young daughter Jerusha gave similar promise. Why not then all of those who so recently had cried out when the Holy Spirit came upon them?

But they could not; the slope again was downward. Northampton settled again to worldly affairs and looked back with more surprise than pleasure at its recent transports. For Edwards too, though in a different sense, the slope was inexorably downward.

The "Bad Books" Incident

He had come to Northampton expecting to settle there for life. It had been so with his grandfather Stoddard, it would be so with his father Timothy, who would die at eighty-nine in the sixty-fourth year of his ministry. Both had sometimes differed with their congregations, but not fatally.

But under the New England Way, the congregation that can call its minister can also cast him out. Less than a decade after the Great Awakening, Edwards was cast out. And what was bitterest about this providence was that the first trouble began among the newly redeemed young.

In 1744 he discovered that pornographic literature was circulating among the young, including the children of the river gods. He referred to it only as "the bad books," and for a long time local historians thought it might be Richardson's *Pamela*, a volume written with virtuous intent, but being a novel by definition bad, especially as it dealt with the manifold temptations of a poor serving maid. Since his term was plural, perhaps *Pamela* was involved, but recent research has identified the chief offender as a practical guide to midwifery.

Its primary appeal must have been to the boys. In the crowded household few girls, however well-bred, could have reached their teens without some observation of the midwife's art. There was no Victorian prudery among Puritan country folk; obstetrical matters were discussed in plain terms. Boys and girls heard them, and the former were also acquainted with practical midwifery so far as it concerned calving and sowing.

However, a complete handbook of human obstetrics had never come their way before, and it fascinated them. They devoured it by turns, hid it carefully until it could be passed to the next reader, and eventually one hiding place was discovered. The pastor was told, shown the book, and the pastor took action.

To this point Edwards had the cooperation of the parents. Far from objecting to his looking into the scandal, they formed a church committee to assist him. Trouble arose only from his manner of investigation. He denounced the infamy of the young from the pulpit and read a roster of those summoned to the parsonage for examination. What outraged the parents was not only the notoriety given their children before they could be judged, but that the list did not distinguish between those accused and those called only as witnesses; all were smeared with one brush.

It would be thus on Doomsday, Edwards may have reasoned, when just and unjust would be summoned together, neither knowing their fate until divine justice had spoken. True, parents would reason in their turn, but by what authority did the Reverend Jonathan Edwards take on himself the prerogatives of God Almighty? Some refused to send their children to the parsonage. Many young people who did obey the summons, infected by their parents' anger, came in a spirit of levity.

Such was true of some of the boys. The investigation was conducted on two levels; the girls were interrogated in an upper chamber, the boys on the first floor. The parsonage being crammed with its own young folk, the boys waited their turn in the yard. Looking out at them from a window, dedicated little Jerusha saw them playing leapfrog while they did so, and told her father. She missed an even greater indecorum which took place on the opposite side of the house. A ladder stood there, and a Pomeroy boy used it to climb up and peer through the second story window to see how the girls were making out.

The investigation went no farther. Parents refused to cooperate and the committee quit. The excitement died down, but not its long-range effect. The young whom Edwards had found so much more responsive than their parents were not so respectful as they had been. Among the parents there was a rankling which became evident in the trouble four years later.

A Majority against Edwards

Until 1749 and aside from the bad-books episode, Edwards' troubles with his parish had been nominal. He had to prod them into building a new meetinghouse, but few congregations went to such expense and trouble without prodding. He had difficulties over his salary, his "rates," but what country minister did not? In the poorest country parishes the minister was sometimes given little more than a parsonage and land on which he was expected to scratch out his living like everyone else. Most ministers got a salary, but it was said that often they had to put more time into collecting it than in preparing their sermons.

Northampton was not one of the poorer parishes, but even during the Great Awakening, Edwards was disputing his salary, demanding a fixed sum instead of an allotment computed yearly. In 1740 he was allowed £280 plus the perquisite of the "minister's wood spell"; in 1744 he was allowed £380. The allowance was not necessarily what he got. Such cash as came his way often came in depreciated currency, and many farmers were unable to pay in cash of any kind. Throughout New England they were more likely to pay in produce, "a piece of beef, a pail of soap, a loaf of bread, a few candles, two quarts of milk, a cheese and four pounds of butter." Aside from the problem of assessing the value of such commodities to apply them against the rates, a parsonage often became overstocked with superfluous perishables while wanting for necessities. A minister could trade excess butter for something more needful, but it was time-consuming and humiliating to have to do so. Some parishioners delayed even in supplying their share of cordwood; the parsonage went cold while Edwards administered reproof.

The dignity of the ministry required more than mere subsistence; the parson might attend to chores in a leather jerkin, but for the pulpit and his parish rounds he needed good black broadcloth. He needed a library, which must be kept up to date by ordering the latest sermons from Boston. Edwards was never to achieve such a library as that possessed by Cotton Mather. He had a growing family, increasing almost yearly; the children had to be educated, and good education was not free; they had illnesses, and Dr. Samuel Mather, kinsman of Cotton, had to be paid for attending them.

It was unfortunate that one of Edwards' disputes about his salary came when parents still smarted at his handling of the bad-books episode. Naturally they seized the opportunity to question the parsonage standard of living. Whitefield may have thought that the family lived in Christian simplicity, but they observed details that Whitefield had missed. Why did the minister need a beaver hat, ordered from Boston and costing three pounds? Why must his wife have a locket and chain costing eleven? Why above all did the saintly Sarah Pierpont Edwards, who had no lack of daughters to help her in cooking and churning and spinning, need a Negro handmaid, a slave by the pagan name of Venus, purchased for eighty pounds?

But the controversy that led to Edwards' dismission did not result from such cause. His congregation simmered down after the quarrel of 1744, raised his salary when it had to, put up with Venus, shrugged off the locket and the beaver hat. In 1748, when the seventeen-year-old Jerusha suddenly died and Edwards made a touching statement from the pulpit—"Her place here in the House of God you now see empty"—his congregation did not lack sympathy.

Less than a year later Edwards did that which antagonized all but his most loyal friends. He turned on his own grandfather, the revered Solomon Stoddard. He undertook to abolish by fiat the "Stoddardean way."

Stoddard had introduced his system in 1700, two years before the Brattle Street Church incurred the wrath of the Mathers by a similar practice. Stoddard had also been attacked, and his intransigence and the fact that other churches in Berkshire County followed his lead was another reason that the Mathers had demanded that the autonomous churches submit to something like Presbyterian control.

Stoddard's system carried the Half Way Covenant one step farther. Under this covenant, people whose parents had not been of the elect but whose grandparents were, could be received into the congregation without the privilege of the Lord's Table. Stoddard resolved that they should not be denied, that all who would, provided only that they were of seemly conduct, could partake in communion. It was his faith that the solemn experience of partaking in the sacrament would lead them to full conversion.

His own experience may have inspired this conviction. According to a story, somewhat suspect because it did not become current until after his death, he himself had been converted at the Lord's Table.

He had, so it was said, come to Northampton as an "unconverted minister." The term, used by Edwards himself, implied no defection in doctrine or lack of preparation, but only that the minister lacked the saving grace of "experimental piety." A congregation might be oblivious to such a lack, but not Stoddard's wife, who had been the wife of the Mather who had preceded him. She is supposed to have assembled a company of pious women to meet the emergency by prayer. They met regularly for this purpose on a weekday afternoon. One day Stoddard observing his wife put on bonnet and shawl to set forth at her accustomed hour, asked what her errand was, and she told him.

Her answer sent the young minister, who perhaps did not suppose himself to be "unconverted," into deep thought. Not long after, in the act of serving communion to his congregation, his soul was suddenly flooded with a sense of divine being that he had not known before. For the first time he experienced the emotional reality of conversion, and since it happened at the Lord's Table, he came to the belief that others should share this opportunity.

The new system, so much more democratic than the strict old way, under which salvation was almost a hereditary privilege, became immensely popular. By the time Edwards came to assist his grandfather, it was followed by most of the churches in the county. If the practice surprised the young man, if he had any question as to its validity, he held his peace. A neophyte does not begin by reforming his master.

When the parish became his sole charge, Edwards followed in the

Stoddard way so long as he had the privilege of reaping a recurrent harvest of souls. It was only after he observed that the fervor of revivalism was regularly followed by indifference that he questioned it, and even then he put in years of study before he spoke out. He ransacked both Testaments, studied the experience of the prophets and the practice of the Apostles. He came to a long pause over the example of Judas. Was it true, as many said, that even he had partaken of the Lord's Supper? No, he decided, it was not. Judas had been present at the Passover, but the Lord had dismissed him before He broke the bread and poured the wine.

It went against the grain to take public issue with the doctrine of his grandfather, but it was not in an Edwards to let sentiment interfere with the execution of duty. Shortly after the bad-books controversy, Edwards assumed the role of King Canute in directing the sea to reverse its tides. He put his convictions into his *Treatise of the Religious Affections,* published in 1746.

Nothing happened. His flock accepted the treatise placidly for the reason that few took the trouble to read it. Publication was all very well and brought prestige to the parish, but one needn't read what one had already heard world without end from the pulpit. But no one had, as a matter of fact, yet heard just this; indeed, when Edwards asked permission to preach his new doctrine, he was sternly restrained. That, however, came later.

The controversy came into the open only when Edwards imposed ancient conditions on a new applicant for Church membership. This was not until 1748, for so sluggish had the spirit become that none had come forward for several years. It was then that Edwards presented his ultimatum. He asked of the woman that she confess her faith before the congregation as Sir William Phips had done before Cotton Mather's Old North, when he asked to "become a knight of that order too," as little Ann Putnam, one of the "afflicted girls" of Salem Village had done in 1706, asking to "lie in the dust and be humbled for it, in that I was a cause . . . of so sad a calamity" to the kin of Rebecca Nurse.

Not that Edwards required so dramatic a confession. He suggested a very simple statement: "I hope I do truly find a heart to give myself wholly to God according to the tenor of that covenant of grace which was sealed in my baptism, and to walk in a way of that obedience to all the commandments of God as long as I live." It did not strike the woman applicant as an unreasonable request; she was willing to comply. It was the congregation that would not have it. Edwards was turning the clock back; he was presuming to take upon himself the right of judging who was regenerate.

The controversy raged until Edwards' dismissal in 1750. He was allowed to publish another statement (ignored by all but his friends), but not to incorporate it into a sermon unless another minister were present to make an immediate rebuttal; and Edwards would not agree until he could see an advance copy of the rebuttal. An association of ministers committed to the Stoddard way was called; only with great difficulty could Edwards get representation on it for two who agreed with him.

In the later and bitter stages the younger Joseph Hawley took an active part. He must have been still obsessed with the memory of that May morning when he found his father lying with his throat cut. Apparently he held Edwards responsible, for he had lately turned to Arminianism, which held the pleasanter doctrine that salvation came not by predestined election but by good works. Five years later Hawley would turn again and apologize to Edwards for conduct that he now called "irreverent, immodest, derisive, magisterial, and savoring of haughtiness and levity, and such as ill became me when arguing with you, Sir." But at this time the "irreverent, immodest" young man spoke for the majority and had his way.

A minority remained faithful to Edwards, one a kinsman of Phoebe Bartlet. Though they represented only twenty families they offered to secede from the congregation and set up Edwards in a separate parish. But the offer, which would have produced bitterness without end, Edwards had the wisdom to refuse. He withdrew to Stockbridge, where like Milton in a more tragic exile, he applied himself to his life's work; he justified the ways of God to man.

Productive Exile

The Stockbridge Indian mission was seventeen years old when Edwards settled there. It had been founded by the efforts of his kinsman and good friend Colonel John Stoddard; and David Brainerd, a prospective son-in-law, had been a recent missionary. Brainerd was the betrothed of Jerusha, who nursing him in the final stages of tuberculosis had contracted it herself. Edwards had composed a memorial to Brainerd; continuing his work must have seemed like God's providence.

It was also apparently God's will that Edwards be followed by Northampton enmities. The most influential of the twelve families of Stockbridge included connections of those who had ousted him, and they lost no time in making trouble for him here. Nevertheless the Edwards family settled into ruder quarters than they had before, and for seven years lived more happily than not, the younger children quickly picking up the Indian dialects.

Edwards coped with the language with more difficulty. He was no natural linguist in spite of the stern drilling he had had from his father in Latin accidence, or perhaps because of it. To become fluent in any language one must not be thinking always of grammar; one must be willing to make mistakes, even to be sometimes ridiculous. It might have been good policy to give the Indians who sat impassively before him in meeting a chance to laugh at him; it would have insured their attention. But Edwards would not risk bringing ridicule upon God's Word. He preached in English, with long pauses while an interpreter made what the pastor trusted was an accurate translation. He used his old sermons; when he preached a new one it was usually on strong drink. It was not that he had any prejudice against rum as such; his parsonage was suitably supplied, but the Indians were given to overindulgence. "Who can think that the great and holy God will take such as make beasts of themselves to Heaven?" he asked them. "Who can believe He will take such to live with glorious saints and angels forevermore?"

The Indians nodded solemnly, and seldom missed the next opportunity for a spree.

With the Indian lads who attended boarding school after a fashion, Edwards risked his Indian vocabulary. It was necessary to win their confidence and hear their complaints: not enough blankets, lumpy food, work six days a week with scant time for instruction. He relayed the complaints to the proper authorities, the Massachusetts General Court, and the Society for the Propagation of the Gospel in London, which had somehow got a finger in this pie. His suggestions were practical, and he expressed them incisively. To an English clergyman he expressed his opinion of the Society's missionaries: "almost universally High Church and great bigots, using all manner of methods to promote their own party and to encroach upon and root out the New England Churches."

When the French and Indian Wars broke out in 1754, the parsonage became a stockade. White settlers in the area had been murdered, and survivors thronged into the hastily constructed fort and consumed, as Edwards reported to General Court, eight hundred meals and seven gallons one quart of West Indian rum. There was panic in 1756 when Mrs. Edwards was visiting one married daughter in Northampton, and a second, Esther Burr, was in Stockbridge with her baby son, the famous Aaron Burr. The young mother was torn between her terror of the Indians and her duty to her father; duty won. "So I must tarry the proposed time," she confided to her journal, "and if the Indians get me, they get me."

The troubles passed, and the seven-year exile in Stockbridge was for Edwards immensely productive. Thanks to a backlog of sermons composed over nearly a quarter of a century and requiring only minor revamping to be made suitable to the local congregation, he was able to give his best energies to his greatest work.

Cramped as the household was, room had been set aside for a study. There were shelves for Edwards' books, his Northampton sermon booklets on which he now drew for his preaching, and surprisingly one novel, Richardson's *Pamela*. If the latter had been one of the "bad-books," Edwards after examining it had second thoughts.

Aside from the bookshelves, the study had room for one chair and a writing table, and here, when parish duties permitted, Edwards spent most of his time. His first task was to get the final word in his controversy with Northampton. When his *Reply to Solomon Williams* had been safely printed and Williams did not reply to the *Reply*, he turned to the work on which his reputation as the greatest of New England theologians was to be based.

His first work was *The Freedom of the Will*. He had been pondering the subject for years. It involved the concepts of predestination and election, the whole rationale of conversion, and the Arminian heresy. Did God, by definition omniscient and hence knowing from the beginning of time which soul was to be saved and which not, grant the individual any choice in his own salvation? Would the elect be saved whether they made any effort or not? Would those predestined to damnation be damned no matter what effort they made? Was there, in short, such a thing as the human will, and what part did it play in the cosmic drama?

In his own terms Edwards based his long, intricately reasoned statement on metaphysics. In a modern frame of reference it was also psychological, almost Freudian. Every man, he argued, had freedom to choose; but each man's choice was governed by inclinations deriving from motives which lay beyond his control. Such motives, predestined if you will, account for those souls who in the heat of revival remain aloof. If Edwards did not cite the seven Harvard students who resisted Whitefield, his theory accounted for them. Man's will accordingly was not active but passive.

Next he wrote *The Great Christian Doctrine of Original Sin*. He answered those who denounced the Calvinist doctrine of innate depravity —in Adam's fall we sinned all—on the excuse that what Adam did was his own personal responsibility and not chargeable to the whole human race. Edwards had noted that during revival those souls that were undergoing the agony of spiritual rebirth had in the moment of conviction of sin and the certainty of damnation cried out, "It is just! It is just!" Now he examined the foundation of this justice. "A tree, grown great and a hundred years old is one plant with the little sprout that first came out of the ground from whence it grew." So the human race, now some fifty-five hundred years old by rabbinical reckoning, had grown from the sprout of Adam, and until redeemed by God's grace, shared his defect.

Relentlessly Edwards pursued these lines of reasoning, and his books, many published after his death, were to bring a revival of theological inquiry which would eventually result in the founding of a whole series of schools of theology—the Hartford Seminary, Union College in New York, the apostate Divinity School at Harvard, and as antidote to it the Andover Seminary.

His reasoning did not go unchallenged, though so long as his premises were accepted, no one could refute it. His system was as perfectly constructed as the "wonderful one-hoss shay" in the poem with which an irreverent son of Calvinism was to satirize the faith of his fathers. There was no weak spot in Edwards' logic. If his theological system never exploded and disappeared as dramatically as the deacon's chaise did, it would fall apart when men no longer accepted his premises.

Before he could write his intended masterpiece, *The History of Redemption,* he was called in 1757 to succeed his son-in-law, the first Aaron Burr, recently deceased, as president of New Jersey College, the later Princeton. Earnestly Edwards pressed his disqualifications for the office upon the trustees: he was low-spirited, lacking in alertness, unacquainted with any Greek classics but the New Testament. But his *Freedom of the Will* had brought him fame, and the trustees would not be denied.

Edwards packed up his books, journeyed to Princeton, and died there at once. There was smallpox about, and he who like Cotton Mather did not believe that God's providence forbade a man to help himself, got inoculated as a precaution. Vaccination had yet to be invented; inoculation, which meant undergoing the disease after careful preparation and under medical supervision, was a sometimes desperate expedient. Edwards had not recently been well; he and his daughter Esther did not survive the inoculation.

Sarah was on her way to him from Stockbridge; she arrived too late. Her piety did not fail her. God "has made me adore His goodness that we had him so long. My God lives, and He has my heart." She had an important task, the rearing of the two orphaned Burr children, but on her way to Philadelphia to join them, she was fatally stricken with dysentery.

XII

THE BLACK REGIMENT

Cotton Mather wouldn't have believed his ears. A minister duly ordained and consecrated was directing a substantial part of his congregation to break the Sabbath. At the conclusion of a morning sermon he not only gave his female listeners leave to absent themselves from the afternoon service but told them to apply the time to spinning.

Mather could take comfort that this took place not in Boston but in Litchfield, Connecticut. The pastor, one Judah Champion, had preceded this extraordinary announcement by reading a letter describing the suffering and need of Revolutionary soldiers in Canada. Confronted by Mather's outraged ghost, Champion might have replied that the God of the Jews did not forbid rescuing an ox from the pit on the Sabbath and that the God of the Christians had said that the Sabbath was made for man, not man for the Sabbath. Such sophistry might be expected from a pastor probably not Harvard-bred but given inferior instruction at Yale, and thus knowing no better than to take Hebrew and Greek subtleties at face value.

If Mather had looked about Boston or into country towns like Ipswich and Newport (the latter in Rhode Island where holiness could not be expected) he would have seen similar goings on, though not necessarily on the Sabbath. On church lawns, in parsonages, women were engaged in daylong spinning bees. "Mr. Otis's black regiment," reported a critic, the Tory Peter Oliver, "were also set to preach up manufacture instead of Gospel—they preached about it and about it until the women and children both within doors and without set their spinning wheels a-whirling in defiance of Great Britain."

In the meetinghouses, Oliver added, "the preachers take their turns and spin out their prayers and sermons to a long thread of politics." It was true. Before ever the Declaration of Independence was put on paper, every phrase of Mr. Jefferson's "inalienable rights" had been expounded from New England pulpits, barring perhaps the questionable

reference to "pursuit of happiness." The way the ministers put that
tenet, and Jefferson too, until his committee decided that so blunt a
wording would lack appeal to idealists in Europe, was "property."

Aside from the Sabbath-breaking, Mather would not find the situation entirely unfamiliar. Less than a century had passed since he himself
in ringing tones had read an earlier declaration to all Boston from the
gallery of the Town House. He would recall precedent for the ministers
in places as far away as New Hampshire and Vermont, who hearing
of Lexington, threw aside their sermons, picked up their muskets, mustered every able-bodied male they could reach on short notice, and led
them down the road to Massachusetts. He would remember how the
expulsion of Andros had drawn from Lynn a reverend descendant of
the "heavenly-minded" Thomas Shepard at the head of his congregation, which to the scared royal governor resembled so many wolves.

A craving for independence was no novelty in Massachusetts. During the heydey of theocracy it had been exercised, if not *de jure,* at
least *de facto.* That the colony didn't make a forthright declaration
after it got rid of Andros was only because it needed England's protection against the French. The latter, possessing Canada, infiltrating the
West, and arming the Indians against Englishmen, had for a century
and a half bottled up the English settlers within the Appalachians.

Now the French were conquered and the colonies could get along
without England. Not that they took so cold-blooded a resolution. They
might well have remained indefinitely content with the status quo but
for London's insistence that they who had already paid for the French
and Indian Wars in blood, now pay for it again in treasure. English
navigation acts, based on the philosophy that colonies should be managed
to profit the mother country, had never been popular; they had made
some colonists, including pillars of the Congregational Church, adept in
tax evasion and smuggling. Now that the acts were to be enforced with
new stringency, multiplied, supplemented with the Stamp Act, levies on
tea, and other tryannical impositions, something more than evasion
was called for. The first spinning bees were born of a resolve to defeat
such measures with an intercolonial non-importation agreement and by
setting up local manufactures.

When more overt confrontation became necessary, New England

congregations were ready for it. Their ministers, though not always with such end expressly in mind, had long been preparing them. The substance of the Declaration already existed in a hundred sermons; more than that, ever since the fervors and tumults of the Great Awakening, forces had been in operation that would shape something unforeseen by the old theocrats, the bills of rights that were to be attached to state constitutions, and at long last to that of the United States of America.

Old Lights and New

That taxation without representation was tyranny was a concept familiar to New England long before the time of James Otis. John Wise had given it political expression in his defiance of Governor Andros. Since the Great Awakening it had found another application in combination with a demand for true religious freedom.

Religious toleration had been imposed by the Massachusetts charter of 1691. When the religious ferment of the 1740's impelled many people to withdraw from the congregations to set up Baptist and Quaker groups, nothing could be done to prevent them, odious as was their practice to followers of the old order. But toleration was not yet freedom. Massachusetts, Connecticut, and New Hampshire all had "establishments"; dissenting congregations had to pay taxes for the support of the authorized church. The Baptists were loud in their protests and eventually in Massachusetts obtained relief.

There were also Congregationalists who had set up separate meetinghouses but could not obtain dismission from the parent church, including exemption from paying rates to their former affiliation. Formerly most such separations had been prompted by geographical convenience. Since the Awakening many were due to a division of the faithful into "Old Lights" and "New Lights."

The latter, who also sometimes called themselves Separatists, were those who after the anguish and glory of conversion looked on the old congregation with fresh insight and found that the salt had lost its savor. In their eyes good deacons and the laity at large followed mechanically and without vision the old path; the very ministers were "unconverted," had no knowledge of the vital travail of new birth. Those who shared such vision craved to withdraw under the guidance of a "converted minister."

The antagonism of many Old Lights was not merely a response to the challenge to their claim to sanctity, but to their recognition that these "converted ministers" were often "unlarned men." This circumstance indeed gave many New Lights to pause before they broke away. Nothing was more firmly entrenched in the Way than the conviction that only the most highly educated men were fit for the ministry. There had been exceptions before this time; Samuel Parris of Salem Village had not completed his studies at Harvard. But he who had led his parishioners and much of the colony into the terrible delusion of the witchcraft was no man to cite as an example. In general the ministry were the intellectual elite, sometimes the scientists of the community, and God had so ordained it. The New Lights, who often elected ministers with no better than a grammar school education and sometimes even less, were little better than the Quakers, who would listen to the simplest plowman if he spoke from the Inner Light.

An occasional Old Light pastor expressed sympathy with the sincerity of the deviants, even acknowledged that they were possibly right, but few congregations, few towns, were inclined to encourage the movement. People who persisted in separate evangelistic meetings could not be excused from their obligation to support the authorized church. This was especially the case in Connecticut, where some Separatists made eloquent protest.

"The Word of the Lord was like a Fire shut up in my bones," wrote Solomon Paine of Canterbury in 1752, "and the Cry of the poor Innocents, who are some of them shut up in Prisons, and others with their little Children crying for Milk and could get none, for the Collector had taken their Cow for the Minister; and the very grey-headed stript of their necessary Household-stuff; and poor weakly Women, theirs taken away even to their Warming-Pan. Men's Oxen taken out of their teams; Horses stript of their Tacking. . . . And when they have nothing but a family of small children, to prison with the Head of the Family, and all to support the Minister. . . . In Love and Pity to my dear Country People, I yielded to the Conviction to give them one public Warning more." Nor was Solomon Paine's protest the only one.

As time went on, the older churches, firm on their foundations from the day of Cotton, had cause to fear that what they imposed on the New Lights would be imposed on them. The Society for the Propagation of the Gospel, whose missionaries Jonathan Edwards had despised, was making ominous headway in founding Anglican churches. There were grounds for fearing that an episcopy would be established on American shores among those whose ancestors had made the journey expressly to get away from the bishops. Even Virginia, whose gentry had been Anglican from the first, had no craving for a bishopric. None had ever been established, and local church wardens had enjoyed much the same autonomy as the New England congregations. What Virginia apprehended with uneasiness, New England apprehended with passion.

It was unfortunate for George III that the passage of the Townsend Acts coincided with much vehement preaching on this subject. On the eve of the Battle of Lexington, good Congregationalists were further aroused by Parliament's passage of the Quebec Act of 1774, which by sanctioning Catholicism in the conquered province seemed to threaten its extension elsewhere. The spirit of old John Endicott was still alive, and this time people would not stop with cutting the cross from the English standard.

Preaching against Tyranny

It was no coincidence that a new edition of Wise's *Vindication* came out at this time. James Otis and Samuel Adams, who had their doctrine of natural rights and the civil contract out of John Locke, didn't need it, but the ministers did. Some who all their lives had preached obedience to authority felt reluctant to countenance defiance. It was reassuring to read in the work of the country parson whose philosophy had reinforced the foundation of the Way, that when tyranny threatened, it was not he who resisted it but the tyrant who was the rebel.

There were misgivings still. The learned Ebenezer Parkman of Westborough, who had reached his three-score-and-ten before the crisis came, went through the same travail of spirit during the labor pains attending the birth of the nation that he must have undergone during his own spiritual rebirth. The present governor of Massachusetts was no Andros but that sterling son of New England, Thomas Hutchinson. He was also a descendant of the subversive Anne, but no one held that against him now, and when Samuel Adams and Joseph Hawley connived at the publication of "incriminating" Hutchinson correspondence, Parkman prayed that the man was innocent. Indeed, could he have read the letters out of the context of outrage generated in the newspapers he would have found small guilt in them.

Since unanimity was unlikely among Congregationalists, there were some ministers and laymen who like most Anglicans remained loyal to the King and deplored rumors that the fiery Bostonians were talking of independence. This was especially true in the western part of the colony, where Boston newspapers penetrated rarely and where there was a tendency to resent Boston's pretensions to leadership. Hatfield, close to Jonathan Edwards' Northampton, went so far in 1768 as to denounce in town meeting Boston's recent activities against the King as "unconstitutional, illegal, and wholly unjustifiable." Then up from Connecticut came a new young pastor, Joseph Lyman, and by preaching Sunday after Sunday on the virtues of liberty and the duty of resistance to tyranny, so won over his congregation that it placed a prominent Tory under house arrest. But like other conversions, this one was impermanent. Before the Revolution was over, men from Hatfield and its environs would mill about Northampton courthouse shouting, "Hurray for King George!" and remark apropos of the persuasions of Samuel Adams and Joseph Hawley that they would take care "how they were catched again."

These were exceptions. More commonly the minister who out of habit or loyalty persisted in praying in public for the King was expelled by his congregation. Such ministers were few and were more than balanced by some so patriotic that they let the town store powder under the pulpit, on Election Day preached fiery resistance, and urged on recruiting at musters. When things got really rough, when it transpired that the dispute with England called for something more than the outpouring of minutemen at Lexington (after which most returned to their farming), ministers went to the diversified fronts as chaplains, and what probably entailed severer sacrifice, some contributed much of their small salaries to the relief of the ill-clad, ill-fed, and seldom paid Continental Army.

Ministers Turned Politicians

Ministers were entering the political arena. A profession that was credited with inspiring the Fundamental Orders of Connecticut had never wanted for political influence, but even in the church-states, church and state had been kept apart to the extent that a pastor was debarred from public office. In the extralegal bodies engendered by the Revolution, that distinction was gradually blurred. Ministers were said to have been involved in the cabals of Boston's Sons of Liberty; they became members of the Committees of Correspondence and Safety. They would serve as delegates to conventions called to draw up state constitutions.

Boston's Brattle Street Church had an active patriot in the person of Samuel Cooper. He was the confidential correspondent of Benjamin Franklin, was recommended to Washington as a thoroughly reliable patriot, and was one of the several ghost-writers employed to enable John Hancock to give a resounding oration on what had become Boston's holy day of obligation, the anniversary of the Boston Massacre. Hancock had a magnificent public presence, but he didn't excel at composition. Often Sam Adams, and once Cooper did that for him.

When the French came to the aid of the Americans, it was Cooper who took the lead in providing their officers with a home away from home. War, like politics, creates strange bedfellows. Little more than a decade ago the colonists had bent every nerve to help the mother country expel the French from the New World. And here was a Congregational minister encouraging his flock to welcome and befriend the late enemy, who was still papist. Boston would never again be quite so provincial.

The Disagreeable Surprise of George Washington

A distinguished Virginian, making his first visit to Massachusetts in the summer of 1775, had an opportunity to survey the extent to which the Bible Commonwealth still adhered to the ideals of its founders. George Washington was disagreeably surprised to find that it had apparently departed from them.

He brought with him some natural but sentimental preconceptions. The descendants of Puritan theocrats might be straitlaced, but they would be of godly and upright carriage. They would also, to judge by Sam Adams and the stand of the "embattled farmers" at Concord and Lexington, be imbued with selfless patriotism. What he found was that Massachusetts men could curse in oaths as round and frequent as any Virginian; that the minutemen, considering their duty done at Lexington, had gone home and had small inclination to abandon mowing and haying at the behest of an outlander, even one appointed by the Continental Congress to rally them against the British.

Most shocking of all was the way town meeting democracy had infected the military; it would also have shocked the founders of the Bay Colony, who had not planned that the Congregational polity of electing church officers be expanded into grass roots democracy. Yet it had been going on under their noses in town meeting, where votes originally limited to church members had gradually been extended to other parishioners, and it had long since infiltrated the militia, which had adopted the practice of electing its own officers.

Washington was not one to oppose democracy on the high ground that it had not been mentioned in the Pentateuch. New England town meeting was none of his business, but the militia was. It was the base on which he must build an army, and its informal practice appalled one who had served in youth with the British regulars. Its men not only clung to their right to elect their officers, but often refused to re-enlist until they saw how the election would go. Officers so chosen often had no proper conception of the dignity of hierarchy. They shambled about as dirty and unkempt as their men. Washington caught one of them acting as body servant to one of his subordinates; he was shaving him, presumably for pay.

It was fortunate that no one intercepted the letters describing Washington's first impressions of Massachusetts; nothing Governor Hutchinson had written was half so incriminating. Had their contents been common knowledge he might never have been allowed to stay to discipline recruits and militia into the Continental Army, lead them through the vicissitudes of a long war, and so become the father of his country.

The minutemen were not to be blamed for assuming that participating in a skirmish completed their obligation. At the outset every war looks to be a short one; a similar impression would prevail at the outbreak of the Civil War. But wars begun blithely to the sound of fife and drum have a way of dragging on unendurably.

Massachusetts got off more lightly than many colonies, for after the defeat at Bunker Hill (it was called a "moral victory") the British had to evacuate Boston, including the Old South Meetinghouse, which they had profaned by using it as a riding school. But it was Washington who had to evacuate New York; the Continental Congress had to flee when the British approached Philadelphia, and the sacred Liberty Bell had to be hidden by pious German patriots. The grim privation of the winter at Valley Forge lay ahead. Even the wonderful victory at Yorktown, when Cornwallis surrendered over five long years after the Declaration, was not at the time conclusive.

What the Preachers Didn't Foresee

Had the preachers foreseen what they were getting their flocks into, they might not have let gunpowder be stored in the pulpits from which they spiritedly preached resistance to George III. It was not only a matter of suffering and want, of young men killed or maimed, of women and children trying to farm it without their menfolk, of malnourished soldiers paid in the currency "not worth a continental"; of officers won over to spit and polish by Washington's Prussian drill sergeant, Baron von Steuben, unable to keep body and soul together on what Congress paid them; it was worse than this. New England youths, reared in strictest piety, were meeting young men who knew nothing of the Way, and imbibing from them strange, unsettling ideas. Boston had small cause to fear the papistry of the French; the danger came from the rationalism and Deism of many French officers. When the veterans came home at last, some would look at what went on in the old meetinghouse with fresh and skeptical eyes. Eventually their skepticism would rend the congregations asunder.

But what the veterans questioned first was not the ancient pieties but contemporary social justice. They came home to attack the very foundation of what was now the sovereign state of Massachusetts, and again bring consternation to George Washington. They were to teach him what he had taught the minutemen of Lexington, that his duty was still unfulfilled, that he must come out of retirement as a country gentleman to head a constitutional convention and become first president of "a more perfect union."

The Plight of the Veterans

The first to realize the plight of the New England veterans and to anticipate their revolt was the man who had conspired with Samuel Adams to oust Thomas Hutchinson from the governor's chair as a few decades earlier he had conspired to oust Jonathan Edwards from the Northampton pulpit. His conduct had deeply grieved the royal governor, who would have valued the friendship of the younger Joseph Hawley, and the conflict of loyalties placed such a strain on the latter that he succumbed to the melancholia that had undone his father and had to let young John Adams attend the Continental Congress in his stead.

He remained in Northampton, where like his father he brooded on the unpardonable sin, though with a difference. His sin was against earthly majesty rather than the eternal goodness, and his obsession was not the damnation so vividly described by Edwards, but the vengeance of George III. It was his delusion that his name headed the list of rebels that could never expect pardon. There was such a list, but it was restricted to two, Adams and Hancock. British George, himself subject to manic-depressive seizures and so equipped to sympathize with the torments of Joseph Hawley, had probably never heard of this rebel.

Hawley had clearheaded remissions when he was able to attend to business. At such times he forgot his guilt and robustly urged his townsmen to enlist in the war against King George. He was in full possession of his faculties in 1780 when Northampton town meeting, of which he was moderator, voted on the new Massachusetts constitution. It was to replace the hated charter of 1691 and had been ably designed by John Adams; it is still substantially in effect 185 years later in spite of perennial demands for a new constitutional convention. The portions which Hawley denounced have, however, long since been amended.

What most aroused him was the imposition of taxation without representation. Franchise was now limited to men of property, but every man from sixteen on must pay a poll tax. Thus penniless veterans who "have gone for us into the greatest perils . . . in the present war to rescue us from slavery" were disenfranchised. "Shall they now be treated like villains or African slaves? God forbid!"

He carried town meeting with him in this protest, though with some difficulty. The "river gods," of whom he was an eccentric representative, saw the property restriction as a natural and desirable substitute to the old limitation of the vote to church members. Church membership had never been expressly limited to the propertied class, but in fact that was what it often amounted to. The Puritans tended to equate worldly success with election, as one of the visible signs of God's grace. That had never prevented them from denying both church membership and the vote to men of substance who did not otherwise qualify, but such exceptions were rare. In town meeting Hawley had opposition, but its voters were not river gods only; he carried his point and was elected to represent Northampton at General Court.

But Hawley did not serve. The new constitution required a loyalty oath of legislators; each must certify himself as a Christian, and this Hawley would not do. A Christian he was; he had long since renounced the Arminian tenets that he held at the time of Edwards' expulsion. In health he never failed to conduct family prayers in his home on Pudding Lane or attend Sabbath meeting. But he would not take an oath which seemed to him a violation of his soul's privacy, and so, rather unfortunately, his town was without representation at a formative period of state history.

It was well that he was in Northampton in 1782 when a mob attempted to disrupt a Court session. The rioters were led by one Samuel Ely of Connecticut, a preacher apparently of the undisciplined New Light species, and the animus against the Court was directed at the sentencing of debtors to prison and other operations of the new constitution. The attack was beaten off by veterans annoyed by hearing Ely's followers hurrah for King George. Hawley witnessed the event,

and talking with the veterans he had an alarmed and accurate prescience of the future.

He knew that the veterans would not always defend the Court in
a state that had rewarded them ill. As a class they were penniless,
likely themselves to become poor debtors. Their pay had come in
securities so worthless that not even the tax collector would accept
them, and which many had sold to speculators at a fraction of face
value. Urgently Hawley warned state officials of the danger. "You
cannot hear them speak of the matter but in rage and flame. . . .
They are a fierce lot of men, and the government will find that these
people, unless they are speedily satisfied . . . will become outrageous,
and the numbers who will side with them will be irresistible. . . .
Were they the common enemy we could bear it, but they are our
equals, our acquaintance, our brethren . . . we cannot fight them."

His warning was heeded; something was done, but not enough.
Good church members whose estates had not suffered from the war
could still hold, perhaps unconsciously, to the old Puritan belief that
prosperity was a sign of God's pleasure, that reverses were God's will
and should be accepted without complaint. Some people complacently
watched mortgage foreclosures which would forward their own pursuit of happiness by enabling them to enlarge their own estates at
small cost. The Congregational Churches were still a long way from
seeing the necessity of a social action committee.

Five years after Hawley's warning, at a time when he had lapsed
permanently into the shadows of his affliction, anarchy came to Massachusetts. The veterans marched on the county courts as they had
once marched on the British at Lexington and with a more immediate
sense of purpose. They closed them in Northampton, Great Barrington,
Springfield, Concord, Taunton, Worcester; finally they marched on
the Springfield Arsenal to arm themselves against reprisal.

There was a curious innocence about these rebels. Many were god-
fearing men, their consciences trained in Calvinist doctrine. At first
they expected to be applauded as patriots as had happened on their
foray as minutemen; that they were now called traitors bewildered
them. They were singularly guiltless of bloodletting. When they marched
on the arsenal and were commanded to halt, they did not raise what

rifles they had; they continued to march, probably expecting what had happened elsewhere, that the defenders would come over to their side, since their cause was just. When the defenders fired, killing three, they still did not fire back. They fled in grief and confusion; at a later rally a touching and Biblical cry was heard, "What must we do to be saved?"

Shays' Rebellion, as it was called, was easily suppressed by the militia, but the issues it presented were not so easily disposed of. Massachusetts could not bring itself to hang what rebels it captured. Northampton people assembled for an advertised hanging and so crowded the meetinghouse to hear the final admonition to the condemned that the latter couldn't get in and had to listen to their funeral sermon from an open window. Then they were marched to the gallows, and the congregation marched with them. At the foot of the scaffold the sheriff waited with a document, Governor Hancock's reprieve. Those who had been petitioning for mercy for the condemned, one of whom was very young, wept in relief. Others felt let down and some consciences were outraged. This method of tempering justice with mercy, however, had not originated in Northampton; George Washington had sometimes found such a demonstration expedient.

Of all the founders of the republic, only Thomas Jefferson, then in Paris, where a greater rebellion was about to take place, approved the efforts of the rebels. To him it seemed both natural and desirable that common men should take up the unfinished work of revolution. Samuel Adams did not share this sentiment, nor did Washington. The latter had no thirst for vengeance, but he saw as Hawley had, that the building of a united nation was still incomplete; reluctantly he applied himself to the task.

And the veterans? Opportunity awaited them in the West; they began to move out after it, leaving crabbed fields to revert to golden rod and teasel, their chimneys to crumble, until all that was left of many a homeplace was a cellar hole and lilac bushes growing wild. There was regret in New England as the movement became massive, and new work for the congregations. The westering pioneers, bred to godliness in meetinghouses now abandoned, must not be allowed to revert to paganism as their fields were reverting to weeds. The home folk resumed the practice, begun in Colonial times, of sending good men into the wild places to minister to the spiritual needs of the wanderers. Though the Home Missionary Society was not formally organized until 1826, it was in operation long before then.

XIII
HOUSE DIVIDED

Not all problems had been solved by the new federal Constitution. Delegates to the convention had been bothered with the difficulty of reconciling the continuing existence of slavery with the powerful statement in the Declaration of Independence on the inalienable rights of man. They did not succeed; the republic was launched without the removal of a growth that was to become malignant. One could not forget the spirit of the older document, whose phrases became blended in the popular mind with the Preamble to the Constitution. For a time southern slaveholders sensitive to the dichotomy resolved the dilemma by freeing their slaves, either in their lifetime or by their wills.

New England was spared just this dilemma. Whatever the defects of the Massachusetts Constitution, it abolished slavery. Agitation against the practice on moral grounds had begun as early as Samuel Sewall, and had been heard from some pulpits during the Stamp Act crisis. One of the martyrs of the deadly street riot known as the Boston Massacre, canonized anew on every subsequent fifth of March, had been the Negro Crispus Attucks. On high moral grounds and also for the sound economic reason that since rugged New England soil didn't favor large single-crop plantations requiring many hands, the institution was unprofitable, Massachusetts ended slavery, and its sister states in New England followed suit.

And now with the long war over at last, with the upheavals that followed it settled and discontented veterans either appeased or on their way to a new life in the Northwest Territory, many congregations built new meetinghouses. This was the period when the spires of what is thought of as the "typical" New England churches began to give a peculiar grace to the New England landscape. Since it was also the period when the surge to the West gained momentum, they also graced the forests of Ohio and Indiana, and presently the cornfields of Iowa. New Englanders making a first visit to the West would be startled to see how faithfully homesick pioneers, with or without the aid of the Home Missionary Society, had reproduced the effect of a New England village dominated by its steepled meetinghouse. The buildings were painted white, and though usually designed by no better architect than the local carpenter, had a classic simplicity and purity of outline. The "Lord's barns" had become little temples.

Interiors were also plain, but here there were innovations. Arrangements were made to keep the congregation warm through a long winter sermon. Stoves were installed, often over outraged protest. "I have attended church fifty years," said one New Hampshire worshiper. "I have fought the Revolution seven years; I have slept in a tent on frozen ground with nothing but a blanket to cover me; I have trod the snow path with bleeding feet nearly naked—and if [the minister] needs a fire, let him go to the place where they keep one the year round."

Musical instruments were coming in. Brattle Street Church did not indefinitely refuse an organ. More modest congregations sometimes let a country fiddler accompany the singers; since not everyone could master the new-style part singing, choirs were assembled of those who could.

What would have seemed stranger still to the founders, the division of church and state was symbolized in the fact that few town meetings now took place in the church. The old arrangement had grown up largely as a matter of convenience in frontier communities where people were racing the season to build shelters. Nor was the custom exclusive to New England; in early Savannah the same building housed both Anglican divine service and court, the Holy Table being turned in opposite directions for each purpose. In theocratic Massachusetts the custom had a special symbolism; the "city on the hill" was a church-state, the same people voting on congregational and town business.

The new separation was also partly a matter of convenience. Worshipers were sometimes wroth to find what havoc a stormy town meeting had wrought in their orderly house. Town meeting more often ran to high feeling and disorder than Sabbath meeting, except perhaps on those occasions when there was a really rousing revival in progress.

But the separation also had its symbolic side: the congregation and town meeting members were no longer identical. Besides replacing the religious qualification for the franchise with property qualifications, the "rates" for the support of the minister were no longer set in town meeting. The "Separatist" adherents of the New Style, the Baptists and Friends and all the rest were no longer taxed for a faith not their own.

Dismaying, positively ungodly as some of this seemed to followers of the old Way, worse was in preparation. The beautiful new meetinghouses were not always theirs to keep. Strange heresies were infecting some congregations; yet another separation was in the making. And when it was consummated it was often the heretics who were left in triumphant possession of the fine new meetinghouse and the faithful who were locked out of it. It happened in Boston again and again; it happened even in hallowed Plymouth.

The Locking Out of the Saints

In 1820 the Massachusetts Supreme Court made a decision and established a precedent that was to deliver a third of the state's congregations to the heretics. The crisis did not boil up suddenly in that year; it had been in the making since the turn of the century.

The specific decision applied to Dedham, to a congregation first gathered in 1638, the fourteenth in the Bay Colony. Characteristically the crisis had come over the choice of a new minister.

Since 1803 the pastor had been Joshua Bates, who had come fresh from Harvard, and had been recommended by the distinguished Fisher Ames as a man of liberal views. The recommendation perhaps appealed to the parish at large rather than to the communicants, the saints of the visible congregation. The latter were now admitted to full communion on a liberalized basis; since 1742 a public confession had no longer been required for membership.

Bates, however, was no liberal. He preached hellfire, predestination, and infant damnation with an emphasis that had been going out of fashion. The old guard nodded amen to such topics, but others, particularly the non-communicating members of the parish, who also attended and supported the church, were repelled. They became antagonized when the War of 1812 broke out and Bates preached not only the gospel but politics. Unlike most of Dedham he was a Federalist, one who advocated that Massachusetts secede from the Union rather than support the war. He was, moreover, intolerant of any other view.

Congregation and parish got through the war somehow, but it was a relief when in 1818 Bates asked for his dismission, and his flock could look for a successor more to its taste.

The distinction between parish and congregation had a new significance in Massachusetts. The latter was what it had always been, the saints who enjoyed full membership and the privilege of approaching the Lord's Table. The parish included those who attended meeting, paid rates, but had not been received into membership. The distinction was not entirely new, but there was now a difference; mindful of the battle cry that taxation without representation is tyranny, members of the parish now voted in the election of church officers.

It was the parish which found a candidate guaranteed to be liberal, Dr. Alvan Lamson, and which formed a committee to stump the town and insure his election. Every home, every shop was visited and revisited. Sometimes the candidate was hauled along with the committee, a procedure some saints found distasteful. They had nothing personal against Lamson, but it struck them that pastoral dignity forbade open electioneering.

In separate elections, the parish voted for Lamson in a landslide, 81 to 44, the congregation against him in a near tie, 17 to 15. The saints had harsh things to say of the electoral returns. They charged that the parish landslide had been maneuvered by inducing some Episcopalians, who had their own church, to cross party lines in support of the parish; that the closeness of their own vote had been due to the deafness of an oldster who mistook the side he was voting for and the blackmailing of another. The latter, so they claimed, had been threatened with public exposure of a hitherto private sin.

The faithful still had hope; surely no pastor of any delicacy of feeling would accept a pulpit offered under such circumstances. When Lamson did accept and the congregation was given the supreme insult of being asked to ordain him, its dissenting members seceded. Let the parish and such members as had voted for Lamson go find their own meetinghouse.

It was the parish, however, that got the meetinghouse, the church records, all the church furniture (with one exception), and all the property. The minority of the congregation that had voted for Lamson had sued for possession of these things on the grounds that not they but the dissenters had seceded. In the lower court a jury debated all night and in the morning plaintively asked the judge, "Which is the First Church?" The judge reprimanded them and sent them back to find out for themselves. They were in a quandary worthy of the intervention of Solomon. They examined a law of 1754 which vested church property in the deacons. But which deacons? Those recently elected by the parish or those of the seceding congregation? When one of the latter broke under the strain and was declared *non corpus mentis,* the jury found for the group that remained with the parish.

The dissenting majority of the congregation carried their case to the Massachusetts Supreme Court and held afterward that its decision was biased by the fact that the judge was a Unitarian. He denied their right to secede, held that "where a majority of the members of a Congregational Church separate from a majority of the parish, the members who remain, though a minority, constitute the church in such parish and retain the rights and property belonging thereto."

The bitterness of the blow lay not alone in the fact that the faithful were locked out of their own meetinghouse, but in that the decision denied the whole tradition of the Congregational Way. Always it had been accepted that the government of the parish belonged to the small, consecrated band of the sanctified, the elite. It was God's law; to rule otherwise was to sanctify the anti-Christ. God help the Commonwealth of Massachusetts now that the deed was done.

Dedham went through something like a civil war that divided families, destroyed old and loyal friendships. The winners were ungallant: for a long time the seceding congregation was denied access to its own church records. The dissenters were poor losers: one bit of church furniture the parish did not get was the silver communion service. Someone stole it. The new congregation, named the John Allin Church in honor of the pastor of 1638, couldn't use it either. It was hidden for a century and then placed in a neutral corner, the Dedham Historical Society.

As for the Reverend Alvan Lamson, after so stormy a beginning, which probably afflicted him little after the opposition left in a body, he prospered and performed his duties in peace for two-and-forty years.

The "Unitary" Conception of God

Dedham's plight was no novelty; it merely clarified the law on situations that had been arising for more than a decade. The Pilgrim Church of Plymouth had gone over to what was still called only "liberalism" as early as 1800. Had William Bradford returned to see how it fared with the First Church, begun so bravely in a stockade, he would have rubbed his eyes to see that The Church of the Pilgrims bore the strange device of Unitarian. The inheritors of the Way were housed nearby in what they called the Church of the Pilgrimage; being a minority, they had seceded without trying to possess the church property.

Bradford may have heard something of the sect called Unitarians before he left England. They had existed there then, and much earlier, not long after the times of Luther and Calvin, in Hungary and Poland. An inclination in this direction had been manifest in America during the Great Awakening. It was a peculiarity of the faith that such manifestations arose spontaneously and independently. The English had not been influenced by the Hungarians, or the Americans by the English; or at least not until later, when the Unitarians became a conscious denomination.

In America it had begun as yet another response to the revivals of Whitefield and Edwards, arising unheralded and unnoticed amid the far more conspicuous controversy of the Old and New Lights. Quite simply, there were ministers who began to feel that enough had been said about damnation. They had observed Whitefield; they had watched his congregations writhing in the mortal agony of regeneration; they had observed the backslidings in the emotional slump that followed. They had become convinced that this was not the way.

They began to preach Christ with a difference that lay more in emphasis than explicit doctrine. Hitherto much stress had been laid on the Christ who in the words of the Apostle's Creed, having undergone the mysteries of vicarious atonement "sitteth on the right hand of the father, whence He cometh to judge the quick and the dead." Such judgment was visited on ungrateful humanity who had not accepted the miracle of the atonement. It was time to say more of what Christ had done between birth and Resurrection, His role on earth as teacher, healer, comforter. Without recourse to such ponderous phrases as "Antitrinitarianism," which hardly existed in the ministerial vocabulary, their preaching tended to center less in mystic concepts of divinity than in a man working among men. He was the perfect man, the climax of creation and as such the Messiah; nevertheless man he was.

A tactful minister groping his way to a fresh concept of eternal truth seldom had trouble with his congregation. Sometimes a captious element did awaken, as happened in Leominster, and demand the dismissal of a preacher suspected of heterodoxy. More often the congregation moved with the times, enabled to do so by a latitude in the Way itself. It was an odd fact that even in the most rigid days of theocracy, Orthodoxy had been stressed only when challenged by an Anne Hutchinson or a Roger Williams. A new minister was indeed closely catechized, but the public confession of an applicant for Church membership had seldom contained a statement on creed. It was taken for granted. Presumably the candidate had imbibed it in childhood with his catechism; if he had heterodox inclinations as an adult, these were dealt with in the privacy of the minister's study. All that was required of him in public was his statement of his personal covenant with God.

An occasional minister was not reticent about his new beliefs. Such was Jonathan Mayhew, brilliant scion of the Mayhews who had been missionaries to the Indians of Martha's Vineyard. His published sermons attacking the Calvinist doctrine of the Trinity had disturbed Jonathan Edwards. They had not disturbed his congregation. Boston's West Church, already suspected of heterodoxy before it called him, had been unable to persuade the Boston Association of Ministers to ordain this pastor. He had to be ordained by more permissive pastors outside of Boston. This was in 1747; by the end of the century the

West Church was not exceptional. Whether they preached it openly or not, the Boston ministry had turned almost to a man to the "Unitary" conception of God.

Many things had happened to make this possible. Newton's *Principia,* long included in Harvard's reading program, had led to Deism, which may be crudely defined as presenting God as a divine clockmaker, who having set the works of the universe in motion, lets them run of themselves without supernatural intervention. So orthodox a believer as Cotton Mather, who read Newton as he read everything that came his way, had shown a certain receptiveness to this point of view.

Studies in John Locke, and the sermons inspired by Locke with which so many pastors prepared their people for revolution, continued the trend to a freer concept of creed. During the Revolution, obsessed by practical urgencies, few pastors preached on doctrine at all, and many of their parishioners, scattered on the far-flung Continental Line, were learning ways of life, ways of thought to which they had not been bred. The skepticism imported by some of the French had been made explicit by Thomas Paine. Earnest believers might consider such views as atheism; Thomas Jefferson was later denounced in New England on this ground. But many without becoming either Deist or atheist were unconsciously revising the basis of their belief.

Boston was on its way to becoming cosmopolitan. During the war others than John Adams must have visited Roman Catholic services, and while using stern Puritan phrases like "being taken in," yielded to the magical beauty of the Mass and the concept that godliness need not be restricted to a bleak, ungarnished meetinghouse. Before the century ended the bodies of the founding fathers must have caused a small earthquake when they turned over in the Copps and Granary Burying Grounds. Boston, of all places, now had a Catholic Church, established in the sacred meetinghouse of an "expired church" that good Congregationalists had founded.

The English Unitarians were now being heard from. A short-lived church was founded under that name in Portland, Maine. Joseph Priestley, leader in the English movement, visited America and founded the first permanent church in Philadelphia. His writings and those of other Englishmen of this persuasion were being read in Boston.

Yet in spite of the swing away from Trinitarian doctrine in eastern Massachusetts, even the most radical ministers did not call themselves Unitarian. The term still had questionable connotations for them; they did not accept it until it was forced upon them by the opposition. They preferred to call themselves liberal, rational, or catholic Christians, just as those who took issue with them called themselves evangelical. What need to call names at all? Under diplomatic leadership there was room for everybody, evangelical and liberal, to live comfortably together in the same congregation. That was how matters long stood. Occasionally as in Plymouth the calling of a new minister split a congregation, but that had always been so, not only since the time of the Old and New Lights but sometimes during theocracy.

Jedidiah Morse's Disastrous Crusade

It might have gone on thus forever, the emergent views resembling a change of climate rather than a new creed. There need not have been the outbreak of violent controversy and the calamity of the Unitarian Separation but for a crusader who arose in 1803 to say, "They shall not pass." However, the emergence of the crusader was probably as inevitable as the drift to liberalism.

He was Jedidiah Morse, father of the Samuel Morse who was to invent the telegraph and send as his first message, "What hath God wrought." He was a native of Connecticut, which as yet had been little exposed to the Unitarian trend, and trained at Yale, whose staff remained more securely Calvinist than Harvard. In 1789 he was called to the church at Charlestown, where good old John Wilson had begun his American ministry by preaching under an oak. He joined the Boston Association and only gradually became aware of doctrinal weakness among its members.

At first he was tactful. He remained on friendly terms with the Boston ministers and began his work not by overt attack but by improving the occasion when it fell his turn to deliver Boston's Thursday lecture, to preach on the divinity of Christ; he preached three successive lectures on the subject. Their reception was polite, but the

Kingdom of Heaven is not achieved by politeness. Presently his conscience caused him to withdraw from the Boston Association and found the Union Association among ministers who shared his principles. The withdrawal was also accomplished politely; he no longer exchanged pulpits with the Boston ministers, whose doctrine he at the moment called Arian, but relations remained friendly.

It was only in 1805 when Harvard appeared to be delivered to heresy that he made an open break. The occasion was the passing over of an orthodox candidate for the Hollis Professor of Divinity in favor of Henry Ware of Hingham, a confessed Arian. The Hollis chair was all-important to students preparing for the ministry; as yet Harvard had no divinity school and it was this professor who guided their studies.

Bitterly Morse denounced Ware's appointment as betraying the Calvinist faith of the founders of the "school of prophets" and the purpose of the Hollis chair. Resigning from Harvard's Board of Overseers, he devoted himself to restoring orthodoxy to Massachusetts. Thanks to him the Andover Theological Seminary was founded in 1808. Two years later Boston got a church guaranteed to defend the faith, the Park Street. Andover was raided for its first pastor, Professor Edward D. Griffin, one of whose early sermons was "The Use of Real Fire in Hell." His determination to restore a wholesome concept of damnation to a creed grown weakly permissive earned his church the title of "Brimstone Corner."

Meanwhile Morse issued a monthly call to arms in *The Panoplist*, which he published at his own expense and wrote almost singlehanded. And being from Connecticut where the "consociations" of ministers had almost presbyterian power to outlaw congregations of undesirable views, he tried to wield his Union Association into a body of similar authority. He was renewing the efforts of the Mathers to curb the questionable practices of Brattle Street, and the results he achieved were even more unfortunate. The congregations were not going to surrender their cherished autonomy to any ministerial association, however orthodox.

But he was fatally successful in stirring up the controversy which the preachers of the new liberalism had tried to avoid, until the latter began to accept the designation Unitarian thrust upon them by the enemies, as Wesley's followers had resigned themselves to being called Methodists. The orthodox took alarm, and the little civil war that split Dedham apart was duplicated all over eastern Massachusetts, southern New Hampshire, and even in the new state of Vermont.

Separation was sometimes accomplished amicably, the church property divided by agreement instead of by the law courts. Sometimes it was the Unitarian element that seceded without making such claims. Sometimes nearly the entire congregation went over to the new creed, leaving only a pathetic remnant of old men and women to function as a "praying company" rather than a congregation and presently to become an "expired church." In Boston, John Winthrop's proud city built upon a hill, only the Old South remained faithful, and for a time the Park Street, though more handsomely housed than any, had a hard time keeping its head above water.

When in 1840 the process was approximately complete, it was estimated that of 544 churches originally Congregational, 135 had gone over to the Unitarians, and these were usually the largest, best-endowed churches, most of which had carried with them their endowment, not only in treasure but in family and intellectual prestige. The pride of the old Way had been in its emphasis on education, in rigorous ministerial training. Now Harvard itself, in response to the activities at Andover Seminary, had a Divinity School to train ministers in heresy. Many of the best minds, the most intellectual ministers, had gone over to the Unitarians.

Of the eighty-one Congregational Churches which had seceded, forty-six had become "deprived churches," locked out of their meetinghouses, constrained to worship in the town hall, the local schoolhouse, sometimes in a front parlor until they could marshal their shattered energies to rebuild and refurnish.

Would Morse have begun his valiant campaign if he could have foreseen the result? He became unpopular in his own parish. In 1816 its liberal members went Unitarian, and the orthodox were so discontent that he resigned three years later. He died in 1826, having lived just long enough to see an end he had by no means desired, the founding in 1825 of the Unitarian Association.

A Denomination from the "Way"

The near disaster of the separation forced the orthodox for the first time to consider themselves as a denomination. While the secessionists organized themselves under a title they had at first indignantly denied, the faithful of the Calvinist old guard became the Congregational Churches. One would have supposed that the sect had existed since the Pilgrims came. Yet the term church was seldom used; the physical structure was the meetinghouse, the worshipers the congregation. They represented a Way rather than a sect. Presbyterians had mingled with them from the first; later some communicants became Baptists. Sometimes a minister moved from one group to another without causing discord. But the pressure of the separation forced the recognition of Congregationalism as a distinct denomination, still adhering to local autonomy, advised not ruled by its ministerial associations, but a denomination nonetheless.

It also happened that during this time in an agreement made just before the Unitarian controversy broke into the open, the Congregationalists adopted a measure which would have a more far-reaching effect on their future than anything the Unitarians could do. No contest was involved. The Congregationalists simply did not foresee the long-range results of the Plan of Union they formed with the Presbyterians in 1801.

The plan was a natural extension of the Home Missionary Society, first heard of in the late 1700's to bring the gospel to frontier settlements in western Massachusetts. It began as a system of branch churches too feeble to support a pastor, allied to the nearest stable congregation, whose pastor visited them when he could, and whither they repaired to receive communion.

When at the close of the French and Indian Wars and again after the Revolution, settlers pressed beyond the Berkshires into New York and Vermont, the Home Missionary Society was strengthened to insure that the new settlements received religious guidance. When the opening of the Northwest Territory brought about large-scale emigration, the Massachusetts General Assembly made a proposal to the General Association of Connecticut ministers which resulted in the Congregational-

Presbyterian Plan of Union. The sects would cooperate in sending missions into the new territory. When differences arose they were to be referred to the nearest presbytery for arbitration. And this arrange-ment, willingly consented to, was to make all the difference to the Congregationalists.

Why did they consent? There was one theory that the Presbyterian form of church government was better suited to the frontier. Those who held it couldn't have looked into their own history or considered the fact that the Way, originating in Plymouth, had spread to Massa-chusetts less because its leaders preferred it than because of its exact fit to frontier conditions. Perhaps the temper of the times made the Congregationalists diffident. The Unitarian controversy was already in-cipient; they may have reasoned that firm Presbyterian control was better adapted to preventing heresy than Congregational autonomy. Or perhaps they didn't anticipate at all. But the results were saddening. Presbyterians rather than Congregationalists took over much of upper New York State and Ohio. No less than two thousand churches of Congregational origin are estimated to have become Presbyterian.

But if this was saddening, it was not embittering. No doctrinal dispute was involved, for both sects were firmly Calvinist.

XIV

THE HAYSTACK AND OTHER MISSIONS

The stresses of the Unitarian Separation were like a moral winter to the faithful of the old Way, the sort of winter that men of the Stone Age knew, when summers became too brief to melt the snows, and the glaciers, ponderously inching southward, engulfed the forests.

New England was not, however, entering a glacial age. Feeble stock might be winter-killed, but on sturdy trees, buds were waiting their time, and in the frozen ground good seed waited for the sun to complete its turn and release them to an exotic and luxuriant growth such as New England had never seen. The Congregational Churches were about to enter an adventure as notable as the sailing of the *Mayflower*.

An association of ministers initiated this adventure: the General Association of Massachusetts Proper. The "proper" referred nominally to the fact that the body represented the state at large; more subtly it also implied that its membership was restricted to followers of the old Way. The group that met in Bradford on June 27, 1810, to consider a remarkable proposal included no Unitarian schismatic.

Four young men, all students at the new Andover Theological Seminary, were there to present a petition. Their action had its origin in what was to become famous as the "Haystack Meeting" in Williamstown four years earlier. At that time an undergraduate of Williams College, Samuel Mills, often met in the groves with a group of fellow students who called themselves the Brethren, to pray and discuss their religious experience. They were youths whose good sense matched their zeal; when a thundersquall caught them in the open they knew better than to take shelter under the trees. They burrowed into a haystack, and with the storm crashing about them there continued their devotions.

Like Cotton Mather they heard the voice of God in the thunder. Looking out from their snuggery at forked lightning splitting a sky as black as doom, they had a vision, or their leader did. In his childhood at Litchfield, Connecticut, long before he had found faith, Mills had been awed to overhear his pious mother tell a neighbor that she had consecrated this child as a missionary to the heathen.

During the storm he suddenly understood his destiny. If the spirit languished in New England it was because the faithful ignored the greatness of their mission. There were other fields for the harvest beyond the spent grounds of New England, beyond the Northwest Territory, the Pacific, and the Atlantic. Asians lived in darkness because they had never been shown the light; so did Africans, South Americans, Sandwich Islanders. It was for New England to go forth to proclaim the gospel to all the waiting world. With the spirit of God enkindled within, with the faith that moves mountains, missionaries could convert every heathen on the planet to Christianity in the space of a single generation.

Mills communicated this vision to the Brethren; when after taking his degree at Williams, he began his theological studies at Andover, he communicated it to the friends he made there.

Now he and three companions stood before the ministers to ask for the means of realizing their vision. The spokesman was Adoniram Judson, Jr., a recent graduate of Brown University; the others were Samuel Newell, recently out of Harvard, and Samuel Nott, Jr., who had his degree from Union College. They presented for prayerful consideration "the duty and importance of personally attempting a mission to the heathen." Modestly they sought guidance, "whether they ought to renounce the object . . . as either visionary or impracticable." If practicable it was, could they "expect patronage and support from a mission society in this country or must [they] commit themselves to the direction of European society; and what preparatory means . . . take previous to actual engagement."

Some members of the association snatched at the term "impracticable." Convert the heathen of the wide world indeed while at home so many bred to the faith were swinging to heathenism! One man, while honoring the dedication of the youths, pronounced them "infatuated."

Bringing the Gospel to Asia

But the majority found the appeal deeply moving, especially as presented by Judson, of whom it would be said, "If his faith is proportioned to his voice, he will drive the devil from all India." Samuel Worcester, pastor of the Tabernacle Church in Salem, who had helped get them this hearing, was for them. So were others, notably the indomitable layman, Jeremiah Evarts. The latter spoke of "the deep sense of the sublime position and devout consecration of this missionary band. They were unpretending, modest, of a tender and childlike spirit, well understanding their aim, consecrated, a felt power." His recommendation: "*Try* it! If the project fail, it would have . . . an honorable burial."

On June 29 a mission society was formed and given a long name: The American Board of Commissioners for Foreign Missions. Nine members of the General Association of Massachusetts Proper were chosen to it, and the Association of Connecticut invited to join. The body held its first meeting in Connecticut in September, and assigned the executive power to a Prudential Committee. Then it issued an appeal for public support and adjourned its deliberations for a year.

To the ardent young men the delay was unthinkable. Mills, who needed time to complete his studies at Andover, could wait; Judson could not. He visited the London Missionary Society and came back with a promise that while London could not undertake joint action with the American Board, it would accept Judson and his friends as its own missionaries. It was the prospect of losing such consecrated men at the start that moved the Board to action in 1811. It commissioned three of the original applicants (Mills was to concentrate on raising funds on the home front), added a fourth, and assigned two others to prepare for the service. The first field would be Asia.

In February 1812, when word came that passage to India was available from Philadelphia on the *Caravan,* Judson, Newell, Gordon Hall, and Luther Rice were solemnly ordained at the Salem Tabernacle. Judson and Newell reached Calcutta June 17, 1812; the others followed on the *Harmony.*

It was a courageous act of faith on the part of the Board. Money had not yet been received in quantity in response to the appeal. The treasury had barely enough to pay passage and a year's support in the field. For a time it looked as if Judson, who had married the day before his ordination, would have to leave his bride behind.

In the meantime war with England broke out, and in Calcutta Judson and Newell were ordered to get back on the *Caravan* and go home. They did not. Newell got permission to go to the Isle de France off Madagascar; the others managed to elude the authorities. Hall and Nott made it to Bombay, Judson and Rice to Burma.

The next thing that the Board heard was that its Burma contingent had turned Baptist. It was not as in the heydey of theocracy when "Anabaptists" were equated with the anti-Christ. The Board, though prevailingly Congregational, had not included the term in its title the better to cooperate with other sects, especially the Presbyterians. But that its most eloquent and gifted missionary should turn was almost as severe a blow as other bad news that began to come, the death of Mrs. Newell with her infant at sea, and of Hall by cholera.

But having put its hand to the plow the Board did not turn back. As Mills had anticipated, the boldness of the project stirred fresh spirit in languid congregations. Collection plates circulated for this cause overflowed; wills were rewritten to include bequests to the Board. This was well, for the expectation that each mission would become self-supporting proved fallacious. Soon the Board, which at first could hardly raise the fare to India for a handful of missionaries, was supporting hundreds, in India, Ceylon, South Africa, the Sandwich Islands, Turkey, the American frontiers; and had opened a school in Cornwall, Connecticut, where talented protégés of missions in the field were brought to receive more advanced training than was possible at the mission stations.

The difficulties remained mainfold. In India, where the missionaries made it a first duty of the new convert to renounce the caste system, they found themselves entrusting the conduct of their schools to the Brahmin caste. Until they could master Hindustani, they had no choice. Cholera and malaria carried off some of their best workers. Mills died on a visit to Cape Palmas in the "white man's graveyard" of Guinea where he had gone to assess the prospects of setting up a mission in

West Africa. Nearer at home, in Georgia, two missionaries went to prison.

But such circumstances only deepened the missionary spirit; a great cause thrives on the example of its martyrs. The human cost was less than that of founding Plymouth and Massachusetts Bay. The spirit of the Founding Fathers lived again in the "rooms" of the Prudential Committee on Boston's Beacon Hill.

America's Own Indians

Even after the War of 1812 the English governor of Ceylon was obstructive. There were, he said, enough English missionaries to take care of the island; let the Americans go home to work among their own heathen, the still-unconverted Amerinds. Given the difficulty of getting news from home, the missionaries were unable to point out that the Board had begun that task in 1817 and was prepared to continue it on a massive scale.

Work among the Indians had, as a matter of fact, begun in earliest colonial times, from Roger Williams among the Narragansetts, Mayhew on Martha's Vineyard, to John Eliot and his Indian village at Natick, governed by Mosaic law. Eliot had applied his scholarship to mastering the language of his charges and for their benefit had performed the tremendous feat of translating the whole Bible into "American."

Harvard had welcomed such Indians as could be induced to attend; David Brainerd and Jonathan Edwards had worked among the Stockbridge Indians. Dartmouth College had been founded in Connecticut expressly for the red men, though it did not flourish until it removed to Hanover, New Hampshire, and admitted whites.

If the achievement of these first workers in the vineyards had been small, the intent was pious. In 1817 the American Board opened the first of its Indian missions; soon it had scores, among the Choctaws, Chickasaws, and the Cherokees. With the latter it achieved mightily, participating with them in a genuine renaissance and joining them in a moral contest that was to rouse the United States as did no other episode on the far side of the Civil War.

The Cherokees were the most advanced of the "Five Civilized Nations," but neither their civilization nor their acquaintance with Christian doctrine derived primarily from the American Board. By the time Cyrus Kingsbury set up his mission in Tennessee, their once extensive hunting grounds had shrunk to lands spread across the borders of Georgia, Tennessee, North Carolina, and Alabama, and they had turned from hunting to agriculture. After the Louisiana Purchase they had become the crossroads of western migration and had consented to the construction of a federal highway through their land, from Georgia to Nashville. At the Treaty of Hopewell in 1785 they had taken to heart George Washington's advice that they become farmers. They had small choice; the shrinking of their lands had made a hunting economy no longer feasible. They profited from the proximity of white communities to learn the best methods of tilling the soil and breeding livestock. Prosperous farmers among them made use of the federal highway to drive their cattle and hogs and cart their grain to market. Many had comfortable, well-provided homes.

Though the bulk of them still followed their ancient religious practice, they had early acquaintance with Christianity. In the 1760's a Jesuit, Christian Priber, had come from the French settlements to the west to live among them, master their language, and guide them in strengthening their government from a loose federation of tribes to something approaching nationhood.

The Cherokees: Teaching, not Preaching

Seven years before the American Board reached them, they had accepted missionaries from the Moravians, and later they admitted Baptists and Methodists. The Cherokees imposed conditions: what they wanted was not preaching but teaching. They wanted their young taught writing and ciphering to aid them in trading with the whites. They would listen docilely enough to sermons, but only if instruction was made available to their children. When the Moravians were laggard in setting up a school, they got a peremptory warning: teach or get out. The school was duly supplied and chiefs of distinction such as The Ridge sent their children to it.

In 1817 when Kingsbury reached the neighborhood of the future Chattanooga and set up on Mission Ridge the station that he named for David Brainerd, he came to a nation long committed to peace, whose leaders set great store on book learning for their children, and had no aversion to Christian doctrine. Parents were pleased with the classes he set up on the "Lancastrian plan," whereby more advanced scholars helped the teachers coach the younger, and made no objection to Kingsbury's requirement that the students help support the mission by spending part of their time at work in the fields or dairy. Now and then a parent startled the missionaries by bringing a slave to school with the proposal that he take over his child's chores. Living in the South, exposed to southern ways, affluent Cherokees often owned slaves. It was a more permissive form of slavery than prevailed in Georgia, and many slave children attended school with their young Cherokee masters.

When Kingsbury left to work among the Choctaws, the Cherokees were genuinely sorry to see him go. However, he had left trained workers to carry on, not only at Brainerd, but at many points in the nation.

Mission life did not always run smoothly. Such Indians as could afford it still practiced polygamy, and the Christian concept of marriage did not yet prevail. Moody Hall saw a fine opportunity to enforce its sanctity and publicly demonstrate the hellfire that awaited those who disregarded it when he caught a young girl in his charge at the Carmel mission with a Cherokee lad. He assembled his students and as much of the community as he could gather to watch him burn the cabin and bedstead and listen to a sermon on sin and its consequences in hell.

It didn't go over. His congregation thought the destruction of a good cabin and bed a shocking waste, and didn't grasp the point about sin. Nothing unnatural had taken place. Were the white men of so exotic a composition that conception was achieved on an entirely different plane?

Moody was already unpopular because when parents dropped in at mealtime to visit their children, he pointedly did not invite them to the table. One day a whooping brave invaded the mission, brandishing a knife and shouting threats. Moody ran one way, his wife another, dropping her baby into the arms of a Cherokee girl as she fled. This cowardice had its effect on the parishioners. Had the missionaries, they asked, so little trust in their God? Moody asked the Board for federal protection, and when he did not get it, he resigned.

In time Christian marriage became popular among the Cherokees, if only because the ceremony had style. At one national council the chiefs considered formally renouncing polygamy. They refrained because it would have made too many complications in the lives of too many of them. The missionaries recommended that they renounce all wives but the one with whom they had lived longest. But one missionary so well understood Cherokee ways that he demanded of the Prudential Committee where justice lay in the not uncommon situation when a man took two orphaned sisters in one ceremony, not from concupiscence, but from the benevolent motive of providing both with masculine protection.

Scandal arose when several Cherokee youths were sent to complete their education in the school in Cornwall, and two of the most promising, The Ridge's son John and his cousin Elias Boudinot, married white girls that they met in town. Cornwall was convulsed to the point of near riot, and the Prudential Committee so disturbed that it closed the school.

The Cherokees were disturbed for a different reason. Why were the missionaries, who set such store on Christian marriage, outraged when it took place? Cherokees and whites had intermarried before this time, and there was no objection in the nation except when the chiefs had reason to suspect that a white man wanted an Indian girl only for the purpose of getting his hands on good Cherokee land. Both marriages were happy in spite of the uproar, though Harriet Boudinot died after giving birth to her fifth child—and was promptly replaced by a young mission teacher from New England, Delight Sergeant. This marriage produced no scandal, though Delight's superior officer did remark to the Board that he didn't admire her taste.

"Butrick, Dear Man"

One missionary, vowed to celibacy (temporarily, as it turned out), applied himself so sympathetically to studying Cherokee ways that the Board sometimes wondered who was proselyting whom. He was Daniel Butrick, "Butrick, dear man," as his colleagues called him when they reported his idiosyncracies to the Board. He came to the nation young and with boundless zeal. When there was a house-raising at his own Creek Path, he didn't direct from a safe distance—he climbed to the rooftree and fell off.

He loved riding out with his Indian friends, swimming his horse across the rivers, mounting dizzy mountain trails. More than most he understood the Indians, who affectionately indulged him for all that he too had odd notions about sin, and sometimes had half his congregation under suspension at once for one cause or another. Other missionaries were asked by derisive young braves how it was, if God were as good as reported, that He hadn't fenced off that fatal tree in Eden. Butrick drew more sincere queries. The Ridge, no believer, though he committed his children to the Christians, earnestly asked him what sin was, how one could know.

Butrick smoked a peace pipe and ate hickory hominy with an upland chief. Once when he came upon a cabin where a rowdy dance was in full swing and whisky kegs in evidence, the little man wanted to do what he knew the Apostles would have done, charge right in and break it up. Gently, tactfully, his Cherokee companions drew him away.

He was the first to attempt to master the language, so that in his sermons he need not depend on the sometimes questionable translations of the "linkister." He threw himself into the task headlong, and deemed Cherokee the most gracious and eloquent of human tongues. More remarkably, at a time when Christian missionaries characteristically believed that they being possessed of the one truth had nothing to learn from the heathen, Butrick made a strenuous effort to understand what religion the Cherokees already had. He was guided by a hypothesis not original with him that the Indians were a lost tribe of Israel.

He identified the Green Corn Festival with the Jewish Feast of the Tabernacles. The rite of the New Fire in spring, when the cabins were cleaned and the hearth extinguished to be relit from the sacred fire magically kindled by the medicine man, had something in common with Passover and Easter. The cleansing rite of "Going to the River" was a kind of baptism.

Butrick was no Baptist and he forbade his people (not always with success) attendance at the Corn Dances because of the drinking, but often he forgot his Judeo-Christian preconceptions while he let an Indian point out the stars, telling their names and their origins or listened to an old chief discourse on the wonderful Thunder Boys.

He grew older and more conservative. The conservatism was connected with his abrupt disavowal of celibacy for a somewhat absurd reason, at least as reported to the American Board. One evening he stopped at the Carmel Mission to find the young teacher Elizabeth Proctor alone with her students. "Dear souls, said I, how can I leave them immediately alone in this wild desert?" He spent the night there, sleeping with the boys in their cabin.

During the night his horse ran away. He could not leave without it, but he could not with propriety spend a second night in a mission managed by one unchaperoned female. No neighbor had room for him; the only way to avoid compromising young Elizabeth was to marry her. The girl made no objection; in fact she agreed with alacrity.

So Butrick abandoned celibacy, and though he continued to study Indian speech and folkways, it was with a difference; he no longer identified himself with the Cherokees. Not long since, his colleagues had found it unwise to leave Butrick in charge of a post while they were afield because they found their stores of provision greatly depleted on their return. Butrick subscribed wholeheartedly to the Cherokee custom of freehanded hospitality, denounced the frugal mission custom of drawing apart at mealtime while parents who had come to see their children waited hungry. After marriage Butrick was somehow no longer so openhanded. And when the Cherokee Nation entered its period of trial, his conduct was more common sensible than heroic.

XV

THE TRAIL OF TEARS

Late in 1825 Brainerd was taken over by a freshly ordained and very aggressive young missionary who was to play a decisive role in Cherokee affairs, in both the days of their glory and their misery. He was Samuel A. Worcester, nephew of the Salem pastor who had helped found the American Board.

One of his first tasks was to provide a Testament for the Cherokees in their own language. The American Board was already attempting to supply their far-flung missions with Bibles translated into the local vernacular, and had recently engaged the philologist William Pickering to devise a system of transliteration suitable for all Amerind languages. Working independently, Butrick had invented one of his own, had gotten a Knoxville printer to publish what he called a Cherokee speller, and was now translating the New Testament.

The Cherokee Renaissance

Worcester brushed aside the efforts of "Butrick, dear man," and with some difficulty persuaded the American Board to ignore those of the eminent Dr. Pickering. He had reached the nation just in time to share its wonderful little renaissance. With no aid from white men, a Cherokee had invented an alphabet. At the last national council the chiefs had earmarked fifteen hundred dollars of the federal annuity for the purpose of setting up a printing press to publish a newspaper in their own language.

The alphabet was the work of an unlettered Cherokee named Sequoia. Though his father was reputedly the white man George Guess, whose name he also bore, he had never learned to speak English, much less to write it. At about the turn of the century he and a friend had been impressed to observe that characters written on paper could instruct a white man about the thoughts of a friend in the distance.

"White man's magic," said Sequoia's companion. Nothing of the sort, said Sequoia; it was a code, and red men could construct one as well as whites. His friends laughed, but for twenty years Sequoia applied himself to proving his point.

First he made little pictures, one for each word in Cherokee. They were charming pictures, for Sequoia had skill in draftsmanship, but the words were too many. He himself could not long remember which word a drawing was designed to represent. He visited the Moravian school at Spring Place to get further insight into how the white man's system worked. A missionary gave him a speller, and studying it, he realized that it was done not with pictures but symbols, each representing a sound. How many sounds were there in Cherokee? For years Sequoia worked to identify them. His task was still incomplete in 1817 when he joined a group of Cherokees who accepted a federal invitation to move into what was to become the Arkansas Territory. It was in the West that he finished his syllabary, a rough phonetic system. Just before Worcester came he had made a visit to the Cherokee Nation East to demonstrate his invention.

The eastern Cherokees had not forgotten how they had mocked him for neglecting his farm to mutter in his cabin over arcane abracadabra. They still mocked. But the demonstration impressed those who thought it over. Sequoia had some chiefs dictate to him, and then called his six-year-old daughter from a distance to read what he had set down. The chiefs heard their own words in the treble of the child.

They still doubted; it was a trick. But one had afterthoughts. Big Rattling Gourd sought out Sequoia privately and said, "Teach me." And soon the whole nation was saying, "Teach me." For the invention worked. To know white man's writing one had first to learn his language, and the whole process could take years. Parents sometimes withdrew their children from the mission schools in exasperation that three whole months of book learning had not trained them to keep accounts. With Sequoia's method an intelligent learner, willing to make a supreme effort of concentration, could become literate in a day. Even the less gifted could manage it in a week.

A passion for letters swept over the nation. Children scratched characters in the dirt to instruct their parents. Young men who could get hold of a bit of paper journeyed to the other side of the mountain to compose a letter to a sweetheart and entrust it to a friend for delivery. Medicine men, conjurers, conservative by nature and the last to respond to the missionaries, craved instruction. The efficacy of their incantations depended on rote repetition without a syllable lost and memories were fallible. Earnestly, with many consultations, they undertook to commit their lore to Sequoia's writing.

Into this situation came Worcester. Even old hands in the mission field who had been given to remark that Cherokee progress had been much overrated, now notified the Board that mission schools would soon become obsolete; all that was needed was a sufficient quantity of white paper and let the Cherokees teach themselves. Worcester forwarded a copy of the syllabary with the request that it be cast into type and shipped to the nation with a printing press.

The Prudential Committee had been excited by the reports, but the syllabary dismayed them. Some characters resembled ordinary English letters; others were so elaborate, so complicated that they doubted any Cherokee's ability to master them. Moreover there were eighty-six of them, sixty more than the English alphabet. Cherokee not being one of the languages familiar to learned Bostonians, they were slow to grasp that this was no alphabet but a kind of shorthand system. They could not in conscience encourage the Cherokee Nation to lavish so much of its annuity on a toy that was bound to be a passing fad. They approved the Cherokee press, but told Worcester to induce the Cherokees to adopt Pickering's alphabet.

Worcester did no such thing. It was Cherokee money and the Cherokees must have their way. "Their enthusiasm is kindled," he wrote. "They are circulating hymns and writing letters every day. At National Council they have listened to a proposal to substitute an alphabet like Mr. Pickering's and have rejected it. . . . Tell them now of printing in another character and you throw water upon the fire which you are wishing to kindle. . . . A crisis in the nation is passing by, and when at such a crisis such an enthusiasm is kindled, it must be cherished, not repressed, if you would save the nation."

Reluctantly the Board gave in. The type was cast, a press purchased, shipped to Savannah, and then up the roads by oxcart to the Cherokee capital of New Echota. Worcester looked about him for printers, a printer's apprentice, and a Cherokee editor.

The printers he found in Tennessee. One did not last long; he was surly and refused to work on anything but the English section of the paper. The other, John F. Wheeler, was a decent sort; he mastered the exotic characters, gave sound training to the Cherokee apprentice, lived companionably with his neighbors, and in the end underwent nearly as much hardship in behalf of the Cherokees as Worcester.

Finding an editor was more difficult. He must not only have an accurate command of English, but if possible he should know Greek, for Worcester, not yet fluent in Cherokee, needed a collaborator for his proposed translation of the New Testament. At the Cornwall School, David Brown had distinguished himself in Greek and had aided in Butrick's translation. But Brown, who now spoke English by preference, no longer had an idiomatic command of Cherokee; Butrick had to have his text corrected. Worcester settled on Elias Boudinot, whose marriage with Harriet Gold had caused the closing of the Cornwall School.

There were still difficulties. Boudinot objected to an inequity in the proposed salary: $500 for a printer; $250 for the editor. Worcester's post was at Brainerd, and Boudinot would not leave New Echota. The Board in its turn objected to Boudinot; they had heard that he had recently attended a Cherokee ball play, a rousing, warlike sport which the missionaries tried to suppress partly because of its violence, partly because it led to gambling.

Worcester overrode all objections. He assured the Board that Boudinot's devout young wife would keep him in hand. He reduced the printers' salaries to $400 and added part of the difference to the editor's. He met Boudinot's objection to Brainerd by removing his own family to New Echota.

The latter arrangement caused new misgivings in Boston. Some members of the Prudential Committee had visited the nation and questioned its capital as a proper site for a mission. Only during national council was it populous; visitors had been impressed to see crowds walking away from council at dusk, carrying flickering pine knots in their hands, creating the illusion of a little city. But it was a transitory metropolis. Out of season it was only a hamlet, and worst of all it was in territory claimed by Georgia. Worcester was to pay a high personal price for settling there.

On February 21, 1828, the first *Cherokee Phoenix* rolled off the presses, and for more than six years it did so weekly. In the mountains those who knew the syllabary fitted needless spectacles to clear eyes (a peddler had recently been by with a packful of them) and solemnly read and reread. Those who lacked such learning craved it, and asked meantime that the paper be read to them, and looked for a mission-trained child to construe the English columns. The Cherokee section was for a time filled with serial publication of the new Cherokee constitution; the English also covered local events and tidings from places like St. Petersburg, Turkey, and Paris, France. Boudinot lifted the latter as filler from his exchanges, but never at the expense of news directly affecting the Cherokees. Visitors were amazed at the quantity of exact information commanded by people living in the remotest reaches of the nation. The mountain folk of the Aquohee District, where the Valley Towns were, became especially effective in the uses they made of what they read in their *Phoenix*.

The paper went much farther afield. Pickering's friend Baron von Humboldt sent from Germany to New Echota for a subscription. Mission societies in New England read the English columns, and their ministers quoted from them in meeting. The English section, which relieved the printers of laboriously setting all four pages in a character they imperfectly understood, was designed to inform white friends of Cherokee affairs. They too read the constitution and exclaimed over its excellence, especially as the chiefs had, unlike the Americans, adopted an establishment, a national religion. Their constitution proclaimed them a Christian nation.

Far away in the Cherokee Nation West, the aging Sequoia rode his pony regularly to the nearest post office to get his *Phoenix*. He pored over it with solemn satisfaction; he had not lived in vain.

The Looming Crisis

The crisis of which Worcester had warned the Board was soon painfully apparent. It originated in Georgia, whose officials were bringing heavy pressure to bear on the federal government to evacuate Cherokees from the land they considered rightfully theirs.

In 1802 Georgia had relinquished its claim on the territories on which Alabama and Mississippi were to be founded in return for a promise that Indian titles would be extinguished in the western part of the state. None of the Indians involved, the Creeks and Chickasaws as well as the Cherokees, had been consulted in making this agreement. The former were eventually induced to remove west, but the Cherokees held fast to the Treaty of Hopewell and the white men's promise that the cessions they had made then would be the last ever asked of them. They had followed Washington's advice that they learn agriculture, had fulfilled their treaty obligations faithfully, and when Georgia politicians made petulant noises about the delay in pressing their state's claims, the Cherokee shrugged them off.

In 1817 the group that included Sequoia had accepted an invitation to remove; from time to time some families, bothered by their proximity to the intrusive Georgians, followed suit. But they were a small minority. The great majority of the Cherokees loved the hills and fertile lands on which the Great Spirit had placed them, and had no intention of leaving.

The years of 1828–29 marked their triumph and the beginning of disaster. Their constitution had been ratified and put into orderly effect; the wonderful printing press had reached New Echota and began publication in Sequoia's wonderful characters. Great things were projected at the capital: a Cherokee museum, a national academy. The future promised glory.

The glory faded when they looked to Georgia. Ominous things had happened in these hopeful years. Gold had been discovered at Dahlonega within the nation, and no effort by the lighthorse guards who policed the nation could keep disorderly Georgians out. The discovery, no Klondike, but substantial, had reinforced Georgian demand for full control of what it regarded as its own. Hitherto they had been restrained by President John Quincy Adams, who had refused to force the Cherokees against their will. But in 1828 he lost the election to Andrew Jackson, and both Georgia and the Cherokees knew that Jackson would not brook any interference with American Manifest Destiny. After the election the legislature extended Georgia law into all parts of the Cherokee Nation that lay within state limits; in 1830 they put them into effect; a year later they ordered the missionaries to get out.

The latter had called attention to themselves by formal resolutions adopted in New Echota December 29, 1830. The gathering had been a kind of ecumenical council attended not only by nine missionaries of the American Board, but two Moravians and one Baptist. Butrick presided, rather surprisingly since he would shortly decide that the Apostles would not approve political action. However, a chief point of the resolutions was a denial that the missions had ever exerted political influence; the Cherokees' refusal to remove was their own; given their progress they had the soundest reasons for refusing, and the missionaries sympathized. Georgia's threat was a moral issue on which they could legitimately take a stand.

In taking such a step, representatives of the American Board needed no express authority from Boston; in the field they enjoyed much the same autonomy that did the Congregational Churches at large. The Prudential Committee, holding the purse strings and passing on the qualifications of its missionaries, could indeed exert influence, but its policy was to trust to the judgment of its representatives in a given situation. Only those on the spot could know what an emergency required.

The Missionary Herald

The adventures of the missionaries, not alone here but in India, China, Greece, and Turkey, were eagerly followed by readers of that excellent monthly, *The Missionary Herald,* founded in 1820. Every contributor to the missions, whether an individual or the hundreds of auxiliary mission societies, received a copy. Most societies were connected with Congregational Churches, but not all. Young ladies from the Second Presbyterian Church in Charleston, South Carolina, sent not only $30 of their own in 1831 but added $20 from "a widow lady" and $3.87 from "two colored members of Dr. Palmer's Church" (Methodist). Contributions were listed in the *Herald,* the societies being designated as "gent," "la," "gent and la," and occasionally "fem juv." A Young Ladies Sewing Circle in Boston raised $20 for Ceylon; a Worcester lady contributed a ring to be sold for the cause. A New Hampshire pastor in 1831 raised his annual contribution for $12 to $15 as a "thank offering to the Lord for the health of my family and the hopeful conversion of a daughter thirteen years of age within the past year."

There were inducements. A contribution of $50 or more gave the donor honorary membership on the Board; he could attend its meetings, though not vote. Societies often pooled their resources to get this privilege for their pastor. Donors who supported a child at any mission school could name him. The Charleston young ladies called their protégé Wheeler Gilbert; the lad apparently did not appreciate the distinction and incurred a discouraging report: "very unsteady at school; his talents appear to be rather below mediocrity, his habits rather indolent."

One lad answered to the name of *Boston Recorder* at school; at home he probably reverted to plain Rising Fawn or Rattling Gourd. But some clung to their school names, notably Elias Boudinot, who not only retained by preference the name of the Philadelphia patriot and philanthropist, but named one son William Penn. The Penn he had in mind was not the founder of Pennsylvania, but Jeremiah Evarts, who used this pseudonym for the two dozen articles in which he publicized the Cherokees' case against Georgia in the *National Intelligencer*.

The popularity of membership in the mission societies was not entirely due to evangelical zeal. The Board was the National Geographical Society of its day. Though wealthy Americans made the grand tour of Europe, no one got to the Far East, South Africa, or the Sandwich Islands except an occasional sailor, trader, or missionary. Of the three the latter were by far the most articulate, and readers pored over their reports in the *Herald*. The American Board broke new ground; Borneo and Patagonia were unknown until agents were sent to prospect for suitable sites for missions. Patagonia had to wait, but the exploration was reported in the *Herald*, and Miss Sophia Sawyer had her Cherokee charges praying regularly for the souls of the neglected Patagonians.

For a few years after 1831 the Cherokees came close to monopolizing the space in the *Herald*. Two missionaries had landed in Georgia jail for refusing to leave their posts, and the American Board was taking their case to the U. S. Supreme Court.

Missionaries in Jail

It wasn't the first time the Supreme Court had heard of the Cherokees. When Georgia extended its laws, forbidding the Indians to rule or police their own territory, the Cherokees had taken action. A few decades earlier they would have dealt with the situation with the tomahawk, and there were some who yearned to do so now. But their chiefs, committed to non-violence, allotted some of the precious annuity funds on which their fiscal economy was based to hire a first-class lawyer to plead their case before the Court.

The Court was sympathetic, but the suit was disallowed on a technicality: the Cherokees could not qualify as a "foreign nation." At best they could only claim "municipal status." But when this blow fell a new case was in preparation, that of Worcester *vs.* Georgia, and thanks to the American Board, Worcester was going to vindicate the rights of the Cherokee Nation.

Less than a month after the New Echota resolutions, Isaac Proctor and his brother-in-law Daniel Butrick, both stationed in territory claimed by Georgia, united on an urgent appeal to the Prudential Committee. The Georgians were coming. What were they to do? Remain and go to jail, or get out as Georgia ordered?

It was an emergency in which they craved no reminder of local autonomy; they wanted orders. Butrick did not conceal his anxiety to get out of reach of the Georgians. Since presiding over the December meeting he had been searching the Acts of the Apostles for guidance, and now had every relevant text by heart. He could not find that in a political situation the Apostles had ever taken a stand. The Georgia situation had become political. Would not the Board approve his following the example of the Moravians who planned to cross the Tennessee or North Carolina borders when the Georgia Guard was known to be on its way?

In March the Guard did come, and Butrick was in Carolina. Whether by God's grace or his own good management he had chosen this time to visit the Valley Towns. Proctor was arrested, and Worcester and some others, but not he.

All the prisoners were soon home again. To the annoyance of Governor Gilmer a Georgia judge had held that the missionaries were federal officers and not subject to the new law; each served at his station as postmaster. For two months, during which His Excellency industriously pulled wires in Washington to get the missionaries dismissed from these posts, there was no more trouble. In May the Georgians were back.

The first arrests had taken place with a decorum that surprised the missionaries, who had braced themselves for the ordeal of the early

Christian martyrs. The officers had been gentlemanly, deprecatory, had even allowed Worcester an extra night to remain with his sick wife. On the second invasion they were ungentle. Elizur Butler was marched off in chains, one end of which was fastened to the neck of a horse. Or he started thus; it happened that his captor fell off his horse and required first aid for a broken collarbone from his captive, who was a physician. Since the Guardsman then found it too painful to remount his horse, it was Butler who rode.

In Georgia the missionaries found that contrary to report the state was by no means seething with a passion for conquest. On the contrary they found real sympathy for the Cherokees and their missionaries. The seething appeared to be centered in the legislature and state officialdom. But it was these who had the say at their trials; Worcester and Butler were found guilty of trespass and sentenced to four years of hard labor in the state penitentiary at Millidgeville.

The labor was not very hard. Butler was happy to find medical books in the prison library, and took the opportunity to catch up on his reading. In working hours he labored at the cobbler's bench and found that he enjoyed it. Worcester applied himself less effectively to cabinetmaking. Perhaps he was too much the intellectual to excel at manual training, or perhaps he was too often interrupted by visitors. Distinguished Georgians came to the prison, the governor, ministers, the president of the University at Athens; they brought little comforts to the prisoners, expressed admiration for their principles though usually deploring their practice. It was Worcester whom they sought most often. He was manifestly the leader, and the case that the Board was bringing to the Supreme Court bore his name.

While Butler, who had no such connections as Worcester and lacked even a college education, applied himself in apparent content to his reading and his shoemaking, his fellow prisoner went through a subtle corrosion of spirit as the months lengthened to years.

The Women Carried On

In New Echota Anne Worcester and Miss Sophia Sawyer ran the mission school. The Georgia law had chivalrously exempted women. Mrs. Worcester, recovered from her illness, was afire with pride in her husband. Her only fear was that the influence of his Georgian visitors might confuse his vision of the rightness of his stand. She and Lucy Butler knew what charm Georgians could exert when it suited their purposes; they had visited their husbands, and the governor had gone out of his way to befriend them. They were not beguiled by his mannerly persuasions, but what of their husbands? They would be proof against any brutality, but compassion was an insidious persuader. Anne wrote her misgivings to the Board.

Miss Sawyer had an encounter with the Georgia Guard. It was a judgment on the Guard that when it tried to molest a woman it was Miss Sophia that it ran into. She had been the most difficult of the teachers under Worcester's direction, outspoken, given to fits of temper. He had finally dismissed her from Brainerd, and that she remained in the nation at all was due to the affection that the Cherokees felt for her, and the sympathy of the wives of John Ridge and Elias Boudinot. They had taken her in and prevailed on the Board to maintain a nominal connection lest the sensitive woman think herself the subject of charity.

She was a gifted teacher. Her charges not only learned their three R's but celestial geography; they progressed from their readers to *Parlin's Magazine,* the *Youth's Companion,* and apparently *The Missionary Herald,* for they were taught to look beyond their own troubles to those of people in Patagonia and Greece. She encouraged physical fitness; on a warm day she sat on the riverbank while her girls splashed happily in the water. When an older girl showed symptoms of interest in forbidden fruit, Miss Sophia read her what the Bible said about the lewd woman of Proverbs. It was more effective instruction than Moody's burning of an unhallowed bed; the girl's mother sought her out and asked to see that interesting passage for herself.

Miss Sophia too had suffered an affront from an uproariously drunken father. She did not quail. Nor did she when she found members of the Georgia Guard knocking at her classroom door. She told them to wait: before receiving them she must consult God in prayer, and it was not seemly for a woman to pray before a man.

"Yes ma'am," said the Georgia Guard, and waited.

When admitted, its spokesman complimented her on her good work, but pointed to two Negro boys, Sam and Peter. Did she not know that Georgia law forbade the teaching of Negroes? She did, replied Miss Sophia, but what had that to do with her school? She taught not in Georgia but in the Cherokee Nation, and the Cherokees were too civilized to pass such laws.

"No ma'am," politely replied the Guard, this here was Georgia. "That," said Miss Sophia grandly, "is for the Supreme Court to decide. And until it declares in your favor, I will not yield to the laws of Georgia."

The Supreme Court was rather over the head of the Georgia Guard. Its representative could only say "Yes ma'am" and withdraw for further instructions.

Instruction came at once. The Supreme Court spoke and for the Cherokees: "The Cherokee Nation then is a distinct community . . . in which the laws of Georgia can have no force and which the citizens of Georgia have no right to enter but with the assent of the Cherokees. . . . The act of the state of Georgia . . . is consequently null and void . . . repugnant to the constitution, laws, and treaties of the United States."

Nevertheless the instructions to the Georgia Guard did not change. Neither President Jackson nor the Georgia governor had any intention of enforcing so eccentric, so un-American a judgment. It was on this occasion that the former is said to have remarked, "John Marshall made his decision; let him enforce it." Jackson had nothing against the Cherokees; some of his best friends were Cherokees. But they were in the way; they must listen to common sense and get out. This was the last territorial concession that would ever be asked of them; the western lands would be confirmed to them in perpetuity. When the Cherokees, who had heard all this before, inquired how he proposed to protect them at such a distance when he could not in territory so much closer to Washington, they were ignored.

The Impotent Supreme Court Decision

A great wave of thanksgiving went through the nation when the Supreme Court decision was published in the *Phoenix*. In the penitentiary, Worcester and Butler hardly rejoiced at all. They got the news late, and it coincided with the information that the decision would not be implemented.

Worcester had been undergoing the corrosion of spirit that his wife had feared. His visitors had been persuasive, particularly Dr. Alonzo Church, like Worcester a Vermonter by birth and now president of the University. Dr. Church expressed admiration for the courage and integrity of the prisoners but asked if they had considered the ultimate consequences of their stand. A decision against Georgia could be enforced only at the point of the bayonet. The state would join South Carolina on the nullification issue and there would be civil war. Was the Cherokee cause so important that Worcester would risk such a calamity?

Worcester was deeply disturbed. What troubled him was that the most eloquent of his visitors were not fire-eaters but men who seemed sincerely anxious to preserve the Union. He was also receiving misleading information about the Cherokees. For this, the lawyer, Elisha W. Chester, who had defended the missionaries in the Georgia court, was responsible. He had become the confidential agent of Jackson, and was telling the Cherokees that Worcester and Butler were suing for pardon. It was Chester who arranged a visit from the Cherokee whom Worcester best knew and trusted, Elias Boudinot.

The latter had been hit hard by the impotence of the decision. Despondently he and John Ridge and John's father were yielding to the persuasion of Jackson's agent that removal was inevitable. In August he brought himself to announce his conviction in the *Phoenix:* "I love my country . . . and for that reason I should think it my duty to tell . . . the whole truth. . . . I cannot tell [my countrymen] we shall be reinstated in our rights when I have no such hope."

He spoke for a slim minority and his statement cost him the editorship of the *Phoenix.* But Worcester was in no position to assess Cherokee opinion at large. On December 7 he wrote a long letter to the Board, which Butler also signed, urgently asking for guidance. Should the missionaries surrender and ask for pardon or risk civil war by serving their term? On Christmas Day the Prudential Committee gloomily considered the dilemma.

The possibility of war had already been faced by that indomitable crusader, Jeremiah Evarts. "Better that half the states of the Union

were annihilated and the rest left powerful in holiness, than that the
whole nation should be stained by this guilt. We would rather have a
civil war, were there no other alternative, than avoid it by taking shelter
in crime." These fighting words were imputed to Evarts by the present
governor of Georgia, Wilson Lumpkin. Under the present circumstances would he still speak so? The Prudential Committee had no
way of finding out, for Evarts was dead. Their own attempt to force
Jackson's hand had only caused the President to malign the whole
mission cause: "Here as in most other countries they are by their injudicious zeal (to give it no harsher name) too apt to make themselves obnoxious to those among whom they are located."

A decision was reached: the missionaries could honorably seek pardon; the Cherokees must be told that there was no longer hope for
them but in removal.

"Salvation" in Removal

Returned a free man to the nation, Worcester found intermittent re-
assurance that the ignominy of appealing to "the magnanimity" of
Georgia, as he and Butler had been forced to do, was justified. During
his two years of absence the once prosperous, happy nation had undergone a demoralizing change. Restrained by Georgia law, the lighthouse
guard could no longer enforce order. Grog shops were being set up
everywhere; even Sophia Sawyer couldn't always keep her children out
of them. Their incautious elders were being made drunk, and in that
state made to sign papers surrendering their property. There was no
redress for them, for Georgia had extended its "black code" to the
Cherokees; their word could not be received in court against that of a
white man.

National Council had been harried from New Echota to Alabama,
and then when under Georgian pressure Alabama forbade it, to Tennessee, where there was sympathy for the Cherokees and great indignation with Georgia. The chiefs now operated without funds, for
Jackson had arranged that the annuity no longer be paid to the nation,
but niggled out to each individual. Georgians were everywhere. Cherokee
lands had been surveyed and then distributed by lottery. Even the

Moravians at Spring Place had been invaded by a "fortunate drawer" who not only took over but demanded back rent.

Worcester knew his surrender had been right. Salvation lay only in removal west, where there would be no more intruding white men, no more grog shops. His work was done here; he moved west to discover that it did have intruders and grog shops, and what was worse, an explicit expression of what had been tacit in the east, the suspicion that he who had suffered so much for the Cherokees had connived with the Georgians. For years Worcester could not rid himself of the painful query: Had he done right to sue for pardon? "He who endures to the end shall be saved." But had he?

It was given to Butler to endure to the end, at least to the end of the Cherokee Nation. When he left prison Cherokee friends did not avoid his eyes as they did Worcester's though he too had sued for pardon. That was not really the point. Worcester suffered as Butler did not from guilt by association: with his double-dealing Georgia lawyer, the kind visitors who lost no time in broadcasting any weakening they detected in his spirit, above all his intimate friendship with Boudinot. The latter's defection had taken place shortly after a visit to prison; when Boudinot later committed what the Cherokees judged as treachery, Worcester was believed to have inspired the act. The Christmas Day decision of members of the Prudential Committee had not helped him; they were within their rights to advise the missionaries to seek pardon; when they urged the Cherokees to remove they were guilty of overt political interference.

These suspicions did not extend to Butler. Worcester, though four years younger, was his superior officer, and Butler was bound to follow his lead. Congregational insistence on an educated ministry also applied to the missionaries, who were to be grounded in theology and the ancient languages. Given the need, the American Board couldn't always get such men; in the Cherokee Nation only Worcester and the somewhat unstable Butrick met these qualifications. Butler naturally deferred to his more highly trained colleague. The Board had once ordered him to give up his medical practice and concentrate on teaching and preaching, either because it did not appreciate the importance of the medical missionary or thought his training inadequate. He was nonetheless a good doctor, and shrewd observer of Cherokee *materia medica* and treatment.

Initially Butler like Butrick had questioned the wisdom of resisting the Georgians, whereas Worcester had no doubts at all. In prison Butler had made the better adjustment. "Whilst in confinement," he had written, "I have had many happy hours, some of the happiest of my life." And there, while it was the eminent Worcester who got the attention of distinguished visitors and listened to their distressing comments, it was Butler who got letters from the Cherokees. "I do not feel sorry that you are willing to go to prison," wrote Little Turtle, "for you have done no wrong, and I do not think you will be unhappy."

He was welcomed when he came home to his Haweis Mission. Soon both he and Worcester at New Echota were ordered out. Worcester promptly obeyed, and began his preparations to move west. Butler resisted, and when that proved futile, crossed the Tennessee line to build a new mission at Red Clay, now the site of National Council. The Cherokees had no intention of surrendering, and by God's will he cast his lot with the Cherokees.

This intransigence was due to more than native stubbornness. They still had grounds for hope, for the Americans had been aroused in their behalf as they were not to be aroused again until the eve of the Civil War.

Such sentiments were not unanimous. Some Americans, including good Congregational ministers, put Manifest Destiny above fidelity to a contract and excused cruelty to the Indians on the grounds that the latter were incapable of true human feeling; they must have been judging from the stoicism Indian braves demonstrated under torture. "We are not insensible to our sufferings!" protested the Cherokees in one memorial. "We feel them!"

One of Jackson's first messages to Congress had concerned the Removal Bill, applying not only to the Cherokees but the Five Civilized Nations. It had been opposed by such congressional leaders as Henry Clay, Theodore Frelinghuysen, and Edward Everett. The latter, presently to share the platform at Gettysburg with Abraham Lincoln, had said, "We ourselves when the interest and passion of the day are past shall look back on it, I fear, with a self-reproach and a regret as bitter as unavailing."

When the Removal Bill passed in the spring of 1830, it could not be implemented without a legitimate treaty. Jackson's agent, J. F. Schermerhorn, a former minister of dubious reputation, finally succeeded in 1835 in making an illegitimate one with the Cherokees, the Treaty of New Echota, signed only by the Ridges and Boudinot, some of their friends, and a handful of stray Cherokees who were tempted by Schermerhorn's offer of blankets. Immediately Chief John Ross circulated a memorial of protest, which was signed by nearly the entire nation and presented to the government by Jackson's own emissary, Major William M. Davis, who added a personal protest: "Sir, that paper called a treaty is no treaty at all. . . . I solemnly declare to you that upon its reference to the Cherokee people it would be instantly rejected . . . by nineteen-twentieths of them. . . . This treaty cannot be carried into effect except by the strong arm of force."

It was one of the crosses of Jackson that nearly every agent dispatched to bring the Cherokees to their senses at once became their advocate.

The treaty still had to be ratified by the Senate. Again the Cherokees had friends in high places—Henry Clay, Daniel Webster, Henry Allen Wise of Virginia—and the bill passed by only one vote. It was urgently protested by citizens in Alabama, Georgia, the whole North, and by readers of *The Missionary Herald* and of the "William Penn" articles, who recognized that the country was faced by a moral issue whose outcome would affect the integrity of the young republic. Indians who in such a crisis had taken not to the warpath but to the Supreme Court, who thanks to the courage of the missionaries had been vindicated there, were no savages. If any race could claim superiority, on what basis other than the willingness to honor the sanctity of a covenant? It was the Cherokees who preserved that sanctity; it was the Americans, whose very beginnings had been in a covenant with God, who had become the violators. If this treaty were executed, not the Indians but the whites were the savages.

Executed it was in the summer of 1838, not by Jackson, but most reluctantly by his successor, Van Buren, and even more reluctantly by Army officers who once on the spot turned pro-Cherokee. Nevertheless they set up camps, and aided by the Georgia militia, rounded up the Cherokees.

Butler and Butrick, who had also remained in the East, watched them come. There were babies, some born on the road to the camps; there were people so old and intricately wrinkled that they were like figures out of their own folklore; there were the ailing who had to be carried on litters, the blind who had to be led. And once in the camps they began to die. "Carried off as by a flood," reported Butler. And Butrick said that the government had chosen "a most expensive and painful way of putting these poor people to death."

The Cherokees must have once undergone their own "Indian sickness" when they were first exposed to the white man's diseases, but that had been long ago. The missionaries, themselves often subject to "agues," had known them as a generally healthy folk. But now crowded in the heat of summer into encampments with inadequate sanitation, fed unaccustomed food, they fell prey to dysentery, measles, and sheer heartbreak. Butler had been preaching to them, choosing his texts from Lamentations, had opened his stores to feed them at Red Clay; now let the American Board say what it liked, he picked up his doctor's bag and ministered to them. The best he could do for them was too little; he estimated that two thousand died in the camps alone; by the time he had completed with them the "trail of tears" to the West, he estimated their losses at more than four thousand.

Butler did not at that time remain in the West. It was Butrick who reported the assassination there of the Ridges and Boudinot for negotiating the fraudulent Treaty of New Echota, and he who startled the Board by defending the act. It was not, he explained, assassination but execution; under a Cherokee law to which they had assented, their conduct was punishable by death.

Butler had returned to Red Clay to close up the mission which he had left in the charge of his Lucy. He was saddened to observe that some Georgians, lately so hot to possess Cherokee lands, were already tired of their bargain and were abandoning the fields so lovingly tilled by the Cherokees to move farther west.

He also heard something that he could not remain to investigate. Even now the Cherokees had not left their hills; there were fugitives who had eluded the soldiers, perhaps a thousand of them, their numbers augmented from time to time by small parties returning from the West. They concentrated on the North Carolina side, somewhere in the neighborhood of the Valley Towns, beloved of Butrick. When Butler heard of them their state was precarious, but eventually they found an honest white man who bought land for them in his name, which when North Carolina at last consented to Indian titles, became their own. The Cherokee Nation East had been extinguished, but not the Cherokees; they drew together in a modest community among the loveliest of the Great Smokies, and there to this day their descendants abide.

But they are no longer the responsibility of the American Board of Commissioners for Foreign Missions.

XVI

THE ABOLITIONISTS

On Sunday afternoon, August 25, 1839, householders near Montauk Point, Long Island, were startled by an exotic visitation. Knocking at their doors came men who were very black and very naked; a few wore loincloths, others a blanket over their shoulders, some nothing at all. One of them carried a fistful of gold in Spanish doubloons which he desired to exchange for food and water.

They communicated by signs. However, one, by the name of Banna, had picked up a bit of English on the West African coast, and he improved the occasion to ask for rum. For his doubloons he got a bottle of gin.

By Monday everyone was making for the shore to see the castaways, forty-one men and manboys and three young girls. Their provenance was a schooner anchored offshore, their leader a young African named Cinque, who questioned the sightseers through Banna. Did the people in this country hold slaves? Were they Spaniards? When the answer to both questions was no, the castaways raised such a clamor of joy that some whites ran to fetch their muskets.

Wordlessly Cinque reassured them. His companions possessed two guns and a knife. These he presented to the whites, who laid aside their own weapons and made what conversation they could with Banna's scant vocabulary.

That afternoon a cruising coastal survey brig, the *Washington,* caught sight of the schooner and sent a jollyboat to inquire. Its officer knew mutiny when he saw it. The Africans on deck were armed with cane knives; these he confiscated at the point of his pistol, and going below he found as he expected two white men, Ruiz and Montez, whom he released. The Africans he removed to the *Washington.* Cinque sprang overboard, but he was recaptured, and taken with the rest to New London. When the judiciary got the story from the Spaniards, the Africans were charged with murder and piracy and put in New Haven jail.

The Spaniards reported that the slaves had been landed in Havana during the spring from a Portuguese slaver, and then put on the schooner *Amistad* for transshipment to another Cuban port. Since the journey was short, they had not been chained. On the second night out they got hold of machetes and cane knives, killed the captain and the cook, wounded Montez, and made him and Ruiz and a mulatto cabin boy their prisoners. Some of the crew had escaped in a ship's boat.

The jeering of the cook had set off the mutiny. He had somehow managed to inform them that the white men were planning to eat them. West Africans, who knew white men only as strange creatures living aboard ships with no visible land of their own, commonly believed that the slave trade was conducted for cannibalistic purposes. Since they were doomed anyway, they rose in rebellion, and since the cook with his huge pots and pans was obviously the chief cannibal, they killed him.

Mutinies were common on slavers while they lurked off the African coast and the mutineers had a chance to swim for it or let the ship drift ashore. A mutiny in America was a rare and desperate expedient. West Africans knew only enough navigation to propel their canoes through the surf, and any African who had endured the "middle passage" knew that the distance from home was beyond reckoning. The *Amistad* rebels knew only that it lay three moons to the east. They had to rely upon their prisoners to direct the voyage, Ruiz, whom they had taken unharmed, and Montez, whose wounds were not fatal.

Cinque set them by turns at the helm and laid the course due east. By daylight, when the Africans could see the sun, the steersmen perforce followed orders; but no African aboard seemed to know the position of the stars, at least not in this latitude. At night they regularly turned the ship to the north. They had been following this erratic course two months when they made their landfall on the north shore of Long Island.

Defense of the Amistad Mutineers

Their trial in New Haven in September became an international incident. Spain demanded surrender of the Africans as Spanish property, and Secretary of State John Forsythe, a Georgian, approved the claim;

President Van Buren also concurred. But the fate of the Africans lay with Judge Thompson of New Haven, who ruled that the slaves had committed no crime under American law. An appeal to the district court brought a ruling that the prisoners were freeborn, had been kidnaped, and should be put in the custody of Van Buren until they could be returned to Africa. The case went to the Supreme Court, which in February 1841 pronounced the Africans free and ordered them released from custody.

That the cause of the mutineers was contested so far, that they were defended before the Supreme Court by no less than ex-President John Quincy Adams, that they finally did get back to Africa, was due to the friends they had made among American Abolitionists. Their plight called a new society into being, interdenominational but largely Congregational in composition, the American Missionary Society. The good offices of the American Board of Foreign Missions had first been invoked, but the Board, many of whose Indian missions were in the slaveholding states, was loath to get involved in another *cause célèbre*, this one involving the explosive Abolitionist controversy. A new society had to be organized in behalf of the Africans.

The Amistad Committee had been formed to defend them. It included two Connecticut ministers, a professor of the Yale Divinity School, and a devout member of Henry Ward Beecher's church in Brooklyn, New York, the silk merchant Lewis Tappan. The professor had made a linguistic study that identified the Africans as belonging to the Mendi group in Sierra Leone. Lewis Tappan's brother Arthur provided most of the wherewithal for returning them to their homeland in 1842 and setting up the Kaw Mendi Mission to protect them. By 1846 when the Amistad Committee joined several other groups to form the American Missionary Society, the missionary at Kaw Mendi reported that his trade school was training thirty-nine young men and women in the manual arts. The boys were learning to become carpenters, sawyers, blacksmiths, the girls cooks and seamstresses.

The future activities of the new society would sometimes overlap those of the Mission Board: missions among the Indians in the United States and Canada; in the Hawaiian Islands; among the Eskimos. One benefaction with the latter was the importation of a herd of reindeer from Siberia and training the Eskimos to care for them.

But their most important work lay in their efforts to improve the lot of the Negroes. One of their parent societies had been the American Anti-Slavery Society, which, while deploring the extremism of Abolitionists like William Lloyd Garrison, sought emancipation as earnestly as he, and also destruction of the caste system that made the life of even the free Negro so difficult.

Just before the Civil War it set up an interracial school in Berea, Kentucky, to educate not only former slaves but underprivileged mountain whites. The war interrupted this project, which was successfully renewed afterward. Unlike some Abolitionists, the Society did not assume that its task was complete when Lincoln signed the Emancipation Proclamation, but redoubled efforts to educate the freedmen. Its missionaries followed the Union Army, improvising classes for the freedmen. When the war was over scores of primary and grade schools were founded in the South, and at least a dozen colleges. Hampton Institute, Fisk, and Talladega all owed their inception to the tireless fund-raising of the American Missionary Society.

No Unanimity

At the time of the *Amistad* incident, Congregationalists were by no means unanimously committed to abolition. Indeed, with many New Englanders as with most Southerners, it had become a dirty word. Some northern communities imposed a more rigid caste system on the free Negro then did the South. Connecticut adopted something like a black code by passing a law (later declared unconstitutional) forbidding the education of Negroes brought in from outside the state. The law had its origin in a proposal to set up a Negro trade school in New Haven, which the city vehemently resisted, and Miss Prudence Crandall's seminary for colored girls in Canterbury. The town had been proud of her well-conducted seminary until she admitted a colored girl. When the town violently objected, she disbanded her school and set up another expressly for young colored women. This time the town rose in arms and drove her out.

Within the memory of the elderly, ministers had thrown caution to the winds in nerving their flocks for the impending conflict with Great Britain. As of this time few enheartened their congregations for the "irrepressible conflict" with the South. Some who dared preach aboli-

tion paid a penalty; the former Congregational minister, William El-
lery Channing, often called the founder of American Unitarianism, was
ostracized by his own congregation when he refused to be silent on the
subject in his fashionable Brattle Street Church.

Somehow the notion of extending the inalienable rights of the Declaration to the Negro aroused the ugly worst in many of the Harvard-bred
elite. They denounced the extremism of Garrison, who attacked even
the Constitution because of its historic compromise with the slaveholding states. Garrison himself, however intemperate his language, preached
non-violence; when violence came it was from the upper-class Bostonians, who mobbed him.

Those renegade southern Quakers, Angelina and Sarah Grimké, who
had abandoned their heritage in South Carolina to bear witness against
slavery, got harsh treatment in Massachusetts. Small boys were encouraged to tear down placards announcing their meetings and to pelt them
with green apples. Church doors were locked against them; the Massachusetts General Association of Congregational Ministers passed a resolution forbidding their members to admit the sisters to their meetinghouses. As expressed in their resolution, their objection was not to the
Grimkés' doctrine but to their sex. A woman should not be heard in
public; "the power of a woman is in her dependence." When Garrison
got the New England Anti-Slavery Society to permit women to sit
among the delegates, eight Congregational ministers promptly resigned.

The real objection was to anyone's stirring up discussion on a topic
so emotionally loaded as slavery. There was fear, fear of the local explosions that followed such discussions, fear of the cataclysmic explosion
that would result if the South were pushed into civil war, the same
fear that had impelled the American Board to yield to Georgia in the
hour of victory. Ironically there was also self-interest. Massachusetts,
which had led the way in emancipation, now owed much of its prosperity to slave labor. The Industrial Revolution was gaining momentum,
and the thriving textile mills in Lowell and Lawrence were dependent
upon cotton planted, cultivated, and picked by slaves.

Ministers who closed their meetinghouses to the Abolitionists did not
formulate, let alone preach so cold-blooded a rationale; but there had
always been a trace of such thinking in the Puritan composition, in the

high regard for property as one of the visible signs of grace bestowed by God on the elect.

Thus as of this time few ministers advocated emancipation, and those who did sometimes went through perplexing mutations. Lyman Beecher thundered against slavery so long as he was a country parson in Litchfield, Connecticut. When he accepted a call to Boston to hold the fort against the Unitarians, he found temperance a more congenial topic; and when he went to Cincinnati to head the Lane Seminary he ran into real trouble. His students were hot for abolition; when Beecher tried to restrain them from stirring up the town by holding public debates, when the trustees forbade any discussion at all, the result was disastrous for Lane. Most of the students withdrew and went to Oberlin, founded under Congregational auspices with an interracial student body.

But if Lyman Beecher equivocated and compromised, it was otherwise with most of his seven sons, all of whom became ministers, and his daughter Harriet. Edward worked closely with the Abolitionist martyr Lovejoy, and in his fashionable Plymouth Church in Brooklyn, Henry Ward dramatized the infamy of slavery by bringing slave women to the pulpit and auctioning them off to freedom. It was presently given Harriet to sway most of the North to a moral indictment of slavery.

Yet there remained ministers who to the last questioned the virtues of emancipation. Such was Hartford's Horace Bushnell, a man so liberal in other respects that but for the loyalty of his congregation he would have been cast into outer darkness with the Unitarians. On the eve of the Civil War he told a group in Clifton Springs, New York that emancipation would solve nothing and must be left to God. Then he suggested how God would resolve the problem: "The superior lives the other down and quite lives it away." Left to themselves the indolent Africans, a prey to crime and vice, "will become extinct like the Indians." In effect he condemned not only the freedmen, but by implication the valor of the Cherokees.

One group of Congregationalists held slaves and could produce Biblical texts proving the righteousness of their doing so. This was the "Dorchester congregation," which had migrated to South Carolina at about the time of the witchcraft. (John Wise had once considered joining them.) Fifty years later the same circumstances that caused pious

Moravians to move out of Georgia caused the Dorchester congregation to move in. Georgia, originally founded with a ban on slavery, had removed that annoying restriction. Its lands were broad and fertile, and the congregation moved in a body to the place they called Midway, taking with them a multitude of bondservants, all African in origin. And there they flourished until the time that one General Sherman came their way in the course of his march to the sea.

The Arms Known as "Beecher's Bibles"

But well before the guns began their dialogue at Fort Sumter, there came a change in New England. Abolition was no longer a dirty word. When mobs roved the Boston streets they were no longer out for the blood of an Abolitionist, but bent on rescuing a fugitive slave from his captors. Congregationalists and Unitarian clergymen were ending their silence. No less than three thousand of them put their names to a petition demanding that Congress end slavery.

Had the South been content with the status quo there might not have been this change. But the South was applying the concept of Manifest Destiny to extend slavery from coast to coast. It had long since taken Alabama, Mississippi, Louisiana; in the 1840's it took Texas. Now it demanded an end to the Missouri Compromise, objected to the admission of California as a free state, maneuvered the passage of the Kansas-Nebraska Act with the provision that the status of these territories be decided by the settlers, and passed the Fugitive Slave Act to counteract the work of the "underground railroads" whereby fugitive slaves were passed from one station to the next on their way to freedom.

The situation in "bleeding Kansas" aroused the North. When Missourians invaded Kansas to rig the elections, merchants like John Lowell and Amos A. Lawrence ignored their dependence on southern cotton and financed the Massachusetts Emigrant Aid Company, which transported settlers to claim the territory as free soil. When the contest became bloody, they provided the emigrants with Sharp rifles. Henry Ward Beecher raised some of the wherewith from his congregation, and the arms became known as "Beecher's Bibles." This was because he saw to it that every rifle sent to Kansas was accompanied by a Bible.

Leadership was furnished by John Brown, a Connecticut man whose Calvinist conscience was obsessed with a blazing hatred of slavery. With his sons he went to Kansas and struck terror into the heart of the Missourians with his bloody raid on Ossawattamie. The bloodletting did not dismay his gently bred New England backers; some of them began to plot the conspiracy that would result in the raid on Harper's Ferry.

Uncle Tom's Cabin

There was another cause for the change of heart. In 1850 a housewife of many cares, from a hypochondriac husband named Calvin Stowe to a brood of children ranging from the teens to a babe in arms, pushed her housework aside long enough to set down a picture of slavery as she saw it. She wrote in the heat of her girlhood indignation at the fate of an aunt who had married a West Indian planter to find herself surrounded by his mulatto slave children. She wrote of a plantation she had visited in Kentucky while her husband taught at the short-lived Lane Seminary. She added the experience of a minister who conducted a "railroad station" on the Ohio shore; he had once received a young woman who crossed the river on the ice moments before it broke up in the spring floods. She wrote what she had learned of conditions in the Red River plantations in the Deep South.

She worked at top speed, rereading her copy only when her husband and children demanded to hear the latest installment. She wrote like one possessed; when *Uncle Tom's Cabin* brought her world fame she preserved her Puritan conscience from the charge of vanity by saying that not she but God was the author.

Her book created a new moral climate in America. Until then slavery was usually attacked or defended on abstract principle. Harriet Beecher Stowe, child of the stern preacher Lyman Beecher, bred in the Calvinist sense of sin, evoked for America the living, bleeding reality of slavery. Her book was not great literature (though so supreme a novelist as Tolstoy would rank it thus) but it was a great document. It was to perform the function of Milton's dragon teeth, which being sown sprang up armed men. No one in his right mind wanted open conflict between the North and South. But by the time the guns of Sumter spoke, men and women who had wept over the fate of Eliza, Tom, and Little Eva were nerved to accept war as their moral duty. What ministers had done to prepare their congregations to fight the Revolution, their granddaughter had done to prepare them for bloody civil war.

"Sweet Land of Liberty"

On New Year's Day 1863 people from the neighborhood of Beaufort, South Carolina, thronged into Camp Saxton, headquarters of the Union forces. A ceremony was scheduled: the presentation of colors to a newly organized Negro regiment, the reading of Lincoln's Emancipation Proclamation.

The latter was read first, and by a South Carolinian, Dr. W. H. Brisbane, who had not waited on Mr. Lincoln to free his own slaves. Then the colors were presented to Colonel Thomas W. Higginson, recently pastor of the Free Church of Worcester, Massachusetts, and one of the conspirators who had backed John Brown.

Solemnly, spontaneously, the Negroes began to sing, and their choice of song moved the colonel nearly to tears. Yankee invaders of the South had been discovering the spirituals and finding them "quaint," but this was no spiritual. "My country 'tis of thee," they sang, "sweet land of liberty."

It was an incident, reported Higginson, "so simple, so touching, so utterly unexpected and startling that I can hardly believe it on recalling, though it gave the keynote of the whole day. . . . It made all other words cheap; it seemed the choked voice of a race at last unloosed."

It would have startled Lincoln. His tentative plans for emancipation were very Southern. The one form of abolition that the South had accepted in the decades before the Civil War had been repatriation to Africa under the auspices of the American Colonization Society. Lincoln had hoped to continue the work. If the little state of Liberia, founded by the Society, was too small to receive masses of freedmen, he would look for land in Central America. But it was not to be. "*My* country," sang the freedmen at Camp Saxton. "My country," said the freemen at large, who indeed had never known another.

Already the American Missionary Society was hard at work preparing the freedmen for citizenship in the country they could at last claim as their own.

Teachers Following the Armies

The work had started hardly a year after the war began, at Fortress Monroe in Virginia, among the "contrabands," as General Butler called the ex-slaves. This mission had been entrusted to the Reverend L. C. Lockwood, who promptly requisitioned fifteen hundred primers with pictures to be sent for use in the Sunday School he had opened in the home of former President Tyler. A free woman of color, Mrs. Mary Peake, also opened a day school, which in the first week jumped from an enrollment of twenty to fifty.

There was drama at Monroe and nearby Hampton. One March day in 1862 classes were suspended while pupils and teachers watched from the shore the battle of the *Monitor* and the *Merrimac*. Hampton was burned by its own citizens in a scorched earth policy; freedmen were building shelters in the ruins, and soon attending classes in the courthouse. It had been gutted by fire, but its walls stood and repairs were possible.

By the end of the war, the day school which had started so modestly numbered six hundred pupils and had moved to a building erected by the Freedman's Bureau. A year later General Samuel Chapman Armstrong, son of a missionary in the Sandwich Islands, arrived to superintend the bureau's work in ten counties, and recommended to the American Missionary Society the purchase of acreage on the Hampton River for a permanent school. So began Hampton Institute, headed by General Armstrong and staffed by missionaries from the North.

The work begun at Hampton did not end there. In the course of the mission work known as "following the armies," eighty-three teachers had been sent to schools set up in Tidewater, Virginia and coastal South Carolina by 1864. When the war ended, a massive educational campaign was launched. Berea made its second and successful start, and another Kentucky school was founded at Williamsburg, which though serving primarily the mountain whites did not refuse a Negro applicant. Fisk was established in Tennessee, Atlanta University in Georgia, Talladega in Alabama, Tougaloo in Mississippi. Though the schools were not denominational, all had Christian and Congregational emphasis. Williamsburg had never had a church until the American Missionary Society came to it.

Wherever the schools were set up, their principals were importuned for teachers for back country communities. The head of Talladega had an answer: "Pick out the best specimen of a young man you have for a teacher, and bring to church with you next Sunday all the corn and bacon you can spare for his living. I will take him into my school and make a teacher of him." And so the "best specimens of young men" came, bearing provisions on their backs, sleeping on the floor of cabins in Talladega, frying their bacon and roasting their corn by the open fire, learning their alphabet, aiding in instruction as soon as they mastered the Third Reader, using their summer holidays to go home and set up "bush schools."

It was an imposing record. In 1865, when the National Association of Congregational Ministers, whose resolutions were to be as far-reaching as the old Cambridge Platform, first met in Boston, it recognized the achievement by voting a third of its budget to carry on the work.

XVII

REUNION, 1865

They were assembled in Boston, "the Jerusalem of our tribes, whither they should go up for the high festivals of their progress." They heard these words in an address by the Reverend Andrew L. Stone, D.D. of Boston in the Old South Meetinghouse, the only one of the original Boston churches that had remained faithful to Congregational orthodoxy during the Unitarian secession. Later they would adjourn to the Mount Vernon Church, where there were better facilities for the committees to deliberate in seclusion.

It was Wednesday, June 14, 1865, and other speakers would remind them that this was the first national council since the Synod of 1648 which drew up the Cambridge Platform. Dr. Stone also mentioned that of 1637, "which gave its crushing deliverances concerning the heresies of Mistress Anne Hutchinson." (After 228 years was he really so hot after poor Anne? But she had not "sealed" his ancestor.)

The sessions continued through Saturday, June 24, with an intermission on June 22 for an excursion to the holy of holies at Plymouth. There was a briefer interruption to visit Charlestown's Bunker Hill on June 17, when a delegate from Ohio was startled by "the firing of guns and crackers and the ringing of bells," and being told that this was the seventeenth of June "in my simplicity I said, 'What is the seventeenth of June?'" And hearing the explanation remarked, "Then it is like our seventh of April." Since Boston knew nothing of the seventh of April, President Rufus Andrew of Marietta College explained that it was on that day in 1788 that a band of Revolutionary veterans founded a colony on the banks of the Muskingum, "the Plymouth of the West," Marietta, first capital of the Northwest Territory.

There were 516 delegates to the National Council of 1865, plus sixteen from foreign countries. The voting delegates represented twenty-four states and one territory, Colorado, coming from Congregational Churches scattered coast to coast. Oregon sent one, California three;

the Confederate and border states were represented by one delegate from Tennessee, three from Missouri, one from Delaware, two from Maryland. New Englanders were in preponderance, led by ninety-eight from Massachusetts. Rhode Island, largely Baptist, sent only two. New Hampshire, whose State Association had replied to the invitation that it "failed to appreciate the reason for the call of such a convention," nevertheless sent fifty-eight.

But the Middle West, particularly Illinois (thirty-nine delegates), with its newly founded and aggressive Chicago Theological Seminary, was not far behind. But for the Seminary, which had sponsored a convention of Congregational Associations of the Northwest in April 1864, there might have been no national council. It was this group that had summoned Congregationalists "to inquire what is their duty in this vast and solemn crisis such as comes only once in ages."

It was a magnificent challenge. In the excitement of assembling in Boston so many delegates that many of them had to be housed out of town, parochial New England for the first time realized how little parochial its faith had become. "Tell Mr. S. that he cannot make New England in the West," President Julian M. Sturtevant, of Illinois College, quoted a reproving friend. It had been supposed half a century back when the plan of Union had been made with the Presbyterians that Congregationalism would not survive west of the Hudson. Yet here was proof that it had not only survived but flourished west of the Ohio, the Mississippi, on the Pacific Coast.

The western churches were New England transplanted. To most delegates, no matter how distant their parishes, this was a homecoming. Nearly 90 per cent had been born either in New England or New York State; all but a tiny minority of the rest had parents of New England stock. Some were foreign-born, mostly German and Welsh, and there was one very rare Georgia Congregationalist, now of Illinois, whose mother had been born in Savannah, and whose father in England.

That so much was known of the delegates was due to the Credentials Committee. Tirelessly, thanklessly, it worked to induce representatives to complete the registration forms, which some found confusing. Do I, asked one, "report myself as pastor of my church and representing one-fourth part of seventeen other churches, and my fellow delegates . . . report that they represent one-fourth part of seventeen churches? Or what does it mean?" Doggedly Credentials persevered, ultimately achieving a notable and revealing statistical statement.

Seven Canadian delegates presented a difficulty; six were from the Congregational Union of Canada, and one represented a dozen churches in the Congregational Union of Nova Scotia and New Brunswick. Were they to be seated with the voters, or relegated to honorary membership with the Welsh and English guests and the lone Frenchman? At first they were given full membership on the grounds that the "committee expected the United States to include Canada at no distant point [Laughter]." Possibly the Canadians didn't join the laughter; later their membership was made honorary. That didn't silence them; all foreign delegates were given their say.

"It's Time Somebody Was Hung!"

War and assassination were still a bleeding reality. Difficult to remember when they duly composed a message to the President of the United States that it went not to the Emancipator but to a man named Johnson. "John Brown's Body" was sung on request by George Eliashib Adams of Brunswick, Maine, who had vocal gifts. A report on the State of the Union evoked harsh commentary. It "would suit me better if it spoke out a little more plainly about hanging somebody. . . . It does seem to me it is time somebody was hung." These sentiments came from no Reverend, but an Honorable, Samuel C. Pomeroy of Atkinson, Kansas, born in Southampton and kin of the river god Pomeroys of Edwards' day. But if violence of language could be excused in a layman, the deacons and ministers applauded.

A minister had much to say of restoring civil rights to the rebels. He was Alonzo Quint, formerly pastor of Boston's Jamaica Plain Church, now of New Bedford. "I am not prepared now to welcome back those people who have fought against us to full fellowship. . . . These men have been fighting through the war against us. They were brave men—for I have seen something of their work—but they are uncommonly stupid and ignorant. They do not know anything near as much as the blacks there. I say that until they repent they are unfit to come back and be trusted with a vote. . . . It goes terribly against my grain ever to see one of these scoundrels under the old flag again."

England's part in the war evoked nearly as much emotion. All foreign delegates, including one from Boston, England, had presented greetings; the Welsh invoked a traditional blessing in their own language; the young Frenchman, who mourned the death of Lincoln as if he were a near relative, presented a series of letters from French evangelical societies. Reply was made in one statement, read by the Congregational historian, Dr. Leonard Bacon. Its terms were measured, but in addressing the English it did not conceal regret that of all English classes, not the Congregationalists but the cotton mill workers had openly sympathized with the Union cause.

"Our brethren who bring to us . . . the congratulations of the English Congregational Union must not be permitted to return under any impression that we have not felt deeply and sorrowfully through these four years of national agony the actual position of the English Congregationalists . . . that dominant influences in the Congregational Union were against us, or that honored brethren who went from us to them for the purpose of explaining our position and asking for their sympathy and their prayers were refused a hearing."

Instantly Quint was on his feet to underscore the rebuke in terms not at all measured. "England is now, I suppose, converted and on our side; for England is like Providence 'always on the side of the strongest battalions,' always ready to follow the powerful and crush the weak [a few hisses] robbing in India, plundering in Ireland, and in connection with our affairs, worse with us."

He turned on the hissers: "When you have earned the right to feel as strongly as I do, and earned it in the same way, by a three years' devotion of your life in the service of your country, then you may hiss if you please. . . . When . . . I saw friends from Wisconsin, Indiana, and New York dead side by side, I knew that they fell by British bullets from British muskets, loaded with British powder and backed up by British sympathy."

A New Yorker, Dr. Joseph P. Thompson, hastily rose to temper his colleague's fiery attack. He too ratified the rebuke, but he could see reasons for the silence of the English Congregationalists. "Have we not as a nation been in such complicity with the system of slavery as to blind our brethren across the sea?"

The breath of the British had been taken away by the violence of

Quint's attack. After Thompson's remarks, Dr. Robert Vaughan, one of the founders of the Congregational Union of England and Wales, nerved himself to reply. Yes, he was a sinner. He had deplored the attempt to conquer the South as impossible except at extravagant cost. Yet he had never known an English Congregationalist opposed to the North. Only now did he appreciate that the society of the South was so corrupt that only conquest was possible. "I think if you could have drifted the southern states a thousand leagues into the Atlantic to take their pest house with them and left them there, it would have been a good thing. . . . Why have I said this? Not that I might win favor from those who have cast their sneers on me. . . . I should like to live in your hearts with the character of an honest man."

Henry Ward Beecher, recently returned from England, and one of those who composed the American statement, was loudly called for. He expressed surprise that the French, "speaking another language, could see daylight through all our difficulties and appreciate our position so well, while those from whom we formed our customs, our polity, and most of our ideas of government, and spoke our language stumbled and could not see. . . . I would rather have any Englishman back me in a difficulty than any other man on the face of the globe. And now, Sirs, I hope there is peace among us."

There was. The Englishman Dr. Alexander Raleigh cracked a small joke and pronounced an affectionate invocation: "May God bless you and make you a blessing; and in the memory of the suffering you have passed through and in the prospect of the work waiting for you to do, may He make you patient and loving as He has made you strong and fearless and free."

The luncheon recess was half an hour overdue. A motion that the afternoon session begin half an hour late was sternly voted down. There was too much work ahead.

Temperance and Evangelization of the West

The remarkably detailed transcript of the Council's deliberations was due to the services of two "phonographic reporters." The invention referred to was not that of young Thomas Edison but the shorthand system of Sir Isaac Pitman. The reporters had an expertise that a tape recorder could hardly have bettered. They had assistance in committee secretaries and in the fact that formal addresses, sermons, and resolutions were presented in manuscript; but even these they followed closely to insert the sound effects: laughter, applause, renewed applause, a few hisses. And they retained the lively discussion that followed formal presentation.

"Rev. Mr. Jenney, of Illinois. 'I move to amend that passage which speaks of the use of "all other honorable means" by erasing the word "honorable"—as if there were any other than honorable means that we could use!'

"Rev. Dr. Dutton, of Connecticut. 'There are other means, and Congregationalists sometimes use them.'

"Rev. Mr. Jenney, of Illinois. 'If that be so, let us not publish it to the world.' "

His motion was lost.

Or the asides during the discussion of British perfidy during the Civil War. "John Bull boasts down in the belly and we in the mouth. He feels as large as anybody." This from Dr. Edward Morris Kirk of Boston, for the reporters, who must have had a politician's memory for faces, caught not only the speech but the identity of the speaker. Only in a throng were they sometimes forced to record: "A Member. 'You ought to be ashamed!' " (From the context this remark can be certified as jocose.)

The agenda for the Council had been drawn up at the final preliminary meeting in New York's Broadway Tabernacle in November 1864. The topics were sevenfold: Evangelization of the West and South; Parochial Evangelization; Education for the Ministry; Ministerial Support; Statement of Church Polity; Declaration of Christian Faith; Systematizing Benevolent Contributions. The direction of the agenda, plus a multitude of miscellaneous items not easily classified, was assigned to thirty-two committees, of which the most strenuously active was the Business Committee, whose work subsumed almost everything else.

Temperance was one subtopic, and a subtopic under temperance was an attempt to restrict the use of tobacco, at least by men of the cloth. Such topics had not been considered by the synod that had evolved the Cambridge Platform. Drunkenness was then abhorred, but it did not follow that a minister found it beneath his dignity sometimes to drain a dram at a respectable public house, or to "drink tobacco," as the indulgence was then called.

The committees toiled in the conference rooms in the basement of the Mount Vernon Church. "I have just come up from a week in the cellar," genially remarked one member, emerging to make an address "on the floor."

No discussions were livelier than those on Evangelization of the West and South. Speakers were limited at first to twelve minutes, then to eight, but when a delegate from the Far West spoke, the fascination of his listeners impelled the moderator to extend the time. How interrupt the Reverend George Henry Atkinson of Portland, Oregon, who had been there since 1847 as successor to the martyred Marcus Whitman, whose dramatic appeal to Congress had saved the Oregon Territory from the Canadians?

He described his struggle to maintain his little church after the cry rose, "There is gold in California," and the men went for it, "traveling seven hundred miles where never a wagon had gone before," leaving him with a congregation of little more than women and children. "He that maketh haste to be rich shall not be innocent!" thundered the pastor to the departing brethren. When they wouldn't stop, he was forced to re-examine his premises. "Sir, I have learned this lesson, that God had a mighty magnet in the Sierra Nevada and Blue Mountain regions, and I have learned that our people have just as much right to go mining as your Cape Cod fishermen to go fishing. . . .

"Now what is the meaning of this immense mining magnet? It means that God intends to draw population there. He has made a California, a Nevada, and an Oregon there; he is making an Idaho and two other states. . . . They are earnest men, these miners; they are men in an unsettled condition . . . but if you will only give them a standpoint around which they can cluster, give them any kind of organized institution which commends itself to their common sense and Christian conviction, they will gather around it with characteristic energy and great zeal. . . .

"We want men to say, 'Here is a church, and here are men who will help you, and I will start the matter and preach the gospel to you and establish a common school and a Sunday School and get matters well organized.' . . . I came here for nothing else but to say to you . . . that we must have help, and to ask this Congregational Church to feel with us that we must have help and have it now."

Kinsley Twining of San Francisco made a similar plea. California "is away off toward the setting sun, and there is no connection between you and it. When the churches of the West fall back from the outposts, they fall back upon an older country, upon stronger churches . . . upon colleges, and at last they come back to Plymouth Rock. . . . But when Californians fall back from their cities, when they move away from San Francisco, they fall back upon the wild Indians and the wilderness. . . . Send us MEN."

The needs of the freedmen were described by the delegates from Delaware and Tennessee. Thomas E. Bliss, whose Memphis represented the true South, described the chaos in the conquered Confederacy, the slaveholders who said, "You can't raise cotton enough with free labor to make nightcaps for the old women." People who felt "the curse of Cain upon them" were moving West "like a great tidal wave." The freedmen were "in a most interesting condition," and evil reports circulating against them must not be believed. "There are already two thousand scholars in the colored schools of Memphis. We have already a high school established among the colored people. . . . Every single church in Memphis was swept overboard by the tide of treason. . . . Now we must build there the institutions of New England, and among them our own liberty-breathing and liberty-loving Congregationalists."

J. M. Sturtevant of Missouri spoke of similar problems and opportunities. His church received people "just as we marry people. We marry people that love one another and are not already married to somebody else; and we receive people into the church that love God and Christ . . . and are not already connected with any other church. Somebody has accused me of building a church out of Methodists. . . . I put no Methodists into the church but what I found lying around loose; and every Christian man that I find lying around loose I propose to build into a church of Christ." He knew of fifty communities craving a Congregational minister; the opportunity wouldn't last indefinitely.

More Preachers Needed

A problem in finding preachers was presented by Jesse Guernsey of Iowa. He told of "a good brother in Massachusetts" who volunteered his services. "But what sort of a parish do you suppose he asked for? He wanted first a village of some two or three thousand inhabitants; and we have plenty of them where the gospel is needed. He wanted an academy; he wanted a meetinghouse; he wanted as good society as he should leave behind him in New England. These are all very pleasant things, and no man is to blame for asking for them, but he might as well have asked me to locate him in Paradise as to make such a proposition in relation to my field." He recommended the use of lay preachers to supply the need; those found satisfactory could be ordained later.

The sum of $750,000 was allotted to carry on the work of evangelizing the South and West, roughly a third of it to enable the American Missionary Society to continue its remarkable work among the freedmen. The suggestion was made that northern businessmen might be induced to underwrite specific undertakings of the latter for the glory of getting their names on the schools, and the remark was prophetic. Someone urged that the general fund be raised to a round million.

The latter was a minority of approximately one. In general the most devoted shrank in dismay of the magnitude of the generosity they were expected to evoke from their parishes. The sum was not on hand; it must be collected, and those ministers who were hard put to it to collect their own salaries were appalled at the prospect. They had already taken one collection to provide traveling expenses for the most distant delegates. The total expenses of these came to $7818, and the collection had netted only $3972. The Finance Committee was calling upon the wealthier churches to make up the deficit; it refused to reduce the fund for evangelism; a special committee was appointed to distribute the sum along members of the Council according to ability to pay.

Adequate support of the ministry brought forth a long report. Ministers should not undergo the humiliation of begging for their lawful due. Their salaries should enable them to live without anxiety for the future of their children; they should be able to buy books. What was considered a fair salary the committee didn't specify. To judge from another context, $1500 was considered respectable; no delegate receiving so much was privileged to put in an expense account. There was a reference to a graduate of the Chicago Theological Seminary who in his eagerness to serve the pioneers was content with $400.

Ministers also had perquisites. In many New England towns firewood was still supplied in the tradition of "the minister's woodspell." Henry Ward Beecher's Brooklyn congregation (loyal even when scandal later came to him) added to a salary of $3000, later much increased, a coach and four. The report certified such gifts as honorable, but "if they put to him as a present what they owe to him as a debt, it is not honorable to either of the parties."

A resolution adopted by the Committee on Collegiate and Ministerial Education might well have outraged the college-bred founders of the Bay Colony, who before they had finished building their homes, undertook to reproduce England's Cambridge University in Cambridge, Massachusetts. Given the pressing need, they recommended that "earnest-minded and vigorous young men whose hearts are in the Lord's work" be admitted to theological schools without "a previous collegiate training, in order that with as little delay as possible they may engage in preaching the gospel to the many thousands who wait for it in our land." The Chicago Theological Seminary had already adopted this practice.

Had standards of education so sadly declined since the 1600's? Obviously they had changed. The discourse of the delegates, ranging from prepared statements to chance remarks, evinced lively intelligence, sound reasoning, and a fund of information about the problems they faced. But Cotton Mather would have listened in vain for a learned reference to Josephus or Herodotus, or for more than a crumb of Latin and Greek. He might have considered the current crop of ministers a race of barbarians, especially if he caught the scholarly Dr. Leonard Bacon saying "it don't." Aside from the laymen among them, the congressman from Kansas, and a number of deacons, probably the majority knew their classics, but they didn't parade their learning. They still revered it, they wanted the best education possible for the ministry, but the needs created by the extraordinary expansion to the West and the emergency in the South couldn't wait on paradigms; they were willing to compromise.

Adoption of the resolution on Church polity was preceded by a long statement by Dr. Bacon, who opposed complete independence of churches. As pastor of the First Church of New Haven, he belonged to the Connecticut "consociation." Its power had been waning conspicuously; within a decade it was to disappear. But without using the term, Bacon advocated it as a means of counteracting irresponsible independence.

He cited instances of its evils: congregations where a faction had won a majority by calling in the women and children to vote. One had "voted out just about a moiety of the members of the church without trial. . . . Then they said, 'We are independent and don't want any counsel about this.' Now I say, if a church says it is independent and won't have any counsel, then it don't belong to us—we have nothing to do with it; and wherever that church is, whether it be in Boston, in New York, in Chicago or San Francisco, it don't belong to what we call our denomination."

The resolution finally adopted contained nothing to disturb the framers of the Cambridge Platform. Each church was responsible to Christ, not exterior authority; but each was also "bound to observe the duties of mutual respect and charity . . . in the communion of churches with one another, and every church which refused to give an account of its proceedings when kindly and orderly desired to do so by neighboring churches, violates the law of Christ." The ministry itself had no power of government and did not constitute a hierarchy.

A Revolutionary Omission

But the most far-reaching resolution was the Declaration of Faith, which contained a revolutionary omission.

On Thursday, June 22, a special train left Boston for Plymouth at nine-thirty. Two hours later the delegates stood on Burial Hill to begin a festal day by listening to the proposed Declaration.

They had been looking forward to the excursion for days. A New York minister had opposed it, thinking it "better to carry out Plymouth Rock principles upon which all could unite than visit the Rock itself, where no two men could stand at the same time." But delegates from the Plains, the Rockies, and the Pacific would not be defrauded of their chance to visit "the holiest spot of all the earth." Above the graves of the spiritual ancestors of all and the personal ancestors of many, they listened to a draft of the Declaration. It had been ardently debated in committee, and even on the train Alonzo Quint had revised one moot paragraph.

The outspoken veteran prefaced reading the document with a statement of unwonted diffidence: "The idea was entertained that it might possibly meet the view of all present. If it did, well; if it did not, it could be quietly dropped."

"Standing on the spot where the Pilgrims set foot upon these shores," he read, "we . . . do now reiterate our adherence to the faith and order of the Apostles and primitive churches as held by our fathers, and as substantially embodied in the confession and platform which our synods of 1648 and 1680 set forth and reaffirmed. We declare that the experiences of nearly two and a half centuries which have elapsed . . . have only deepened our confidence in the faith and policy of these fathers. . . .

"It was the faith of our fathers that gave us this free land in which we dwell. It is by this faith only that we can transmit it to our children, a free and happy because a Christian commonwealth. . . . We confess our faith in God the Father, the Son, and the Holy Ghost. . . ."

Dr. Bacon remarked on the fitness of the place for ratifying the Declaration in its essence if not *ipsissima verba*. "I felt that on this consecrated spot . . . we should become, all of us, more deeply and fervently conscious of our relation to the past and of our relations to the boundless continent and to the boundless future . . . and that there was a fitness in our here uniting in giving our testimony to the faith and to the order which our Pilgrim Fathers brought with them."

It wasn't to be easy. George Allen of Worcester cried out at once: "In the name of our fathers I protest from this consecrated hill against that declaration! It is sectarian!" A Boston deacon retorted: "I hope the declaration will be adopted."

The souls of those whose dust lay underfoot must have stirred at the prospects of a full-throated congregational dispute such as they had known in the old stockade meetinghouse. But Dr. Bacon's suggestion that the Declaration be ratified in substance, leaving details to be perfected in committee, was adopted with only two dissenting voices.

After a prayer and the Doxology, the delegates trooped down the hill to inspect the Forefather's Rock, then to Pilgrim Hall to see Peregrine White's wicker cradle, his mother's one surviving satin slipper, and bits of Miles Standish's armor. They enjoyed a collation; they listened to a series of addresses. They avoided public reference to a scandal: the original Pilgrim Church had gone Unitarian.

It was because of that scandal and from a determination that it not recur that a significant deletion had been made in the Declaration: a reference to the Congregational faith "commonly known among us as Calvinism" had been struck out.

The omission had been hotly debated almost up to train time. Dr. Joshua Leavitt of New York City had spoken of the difficulty of winning Methodists if Calvinism were insisted on. "I have known . . . able men and better preachers than the average among us who have been deterred from accepting invitations to become the pastors of our churches simply by the dread of the scrutiny and screwing to which they might be subjected by an examining council to see whether they were Calvinists or not."

"I consider it a great blessing that I was not born in the Lutheran denomination," this from Dr. William W. Patton of Chicago, "to bear all my life long a man's name in connection with my religion. I consider it a happy thing that the Congregationalists, although we hold to the substance of his doctrine, do not bear the name of Calvin."

"Why not call ourselves Edwardeans as well as Calvinist?" inquired Dr. Samuel Dutton of New Haven. "We propose to take the Bible as our rule of faith instead of Calvin. It is customary with other sects to put horn and hooves upon Calvinism; and if we adopt the name, they put horn and hooves upon us."

Dr. Zedekiah Barstow of New Hampshire made a passionate protest. For all his respect of the council, "I should alter my opinion of it at once and totally if it should desert the name of Calvinist. . . . I should be utterly and perfectly ashamed to have this amendment pass. I should be ashamed to see it published in the newspapers."

Yet pass it did; the reference to Calvin was not restored when the committee resumed its work after the Plymouth outing. It was not that the majority had forsaken Calvin. The contrary was probably true, but if the Council had taught its members anything, it had taught the most parochial New Englanders that America was no tight little rockbound pasturage, but a wide world where people lived and worked out their destinies in a manner impossible to anticipate. Almost as sacred as Calvinism was the conviction that a minister must be college-bred; yet they agreed that during the current emergencies exceptions must be made. If they imposed a doctrine too rigid, who knew what secessions might take place in the unfettered West, as the Unitarian Separation had already taken place in the East? They would not take such a chance.

A bit of unfinished business concerning the Separation arose at one point. The Massachusetts Convention of Congregational Ministers had a fund for the aid of "widows of poor ministers" collected before it took place. Their scribe requested the Council to clarify its status by adopting the name Trinitarian Congregational in order to distinguish its membership from "Unitarian and other Congregational churches in this commonwealth."

The proposal was gravely considered and denied. "This denomination has always had the distinctive name of Congregational Churches." Many founded by the Unitarians were said "to be Independent not Congregational. . . . If we prefix this name to distinguish us from Unitarians and Universalists, we must take some other prefixes to distinguish us from Baptists and Free Will Baptists. We see no need of either. . . . We are happy to know that so many of these churches still retain the old polity. And whenever their convictions of duty will allow them to stand on the old platform of faith of their and our fathers, gladly will feel that we are one again."

XVIII

THE HARTFORD PROPHET

The National Council of 1865 became a watershed in the Congregational Way; it brought about a widening of the horizons, geographical and spiritual.

The geographical horizons had been expanding for half a century, thanks to the intense interest most Congregationalists took in the worldwide activities of the Board of Foreign Missions. Even earlier the Home Missions had called attention to "westering." Most New Englanders were aware of gaps in their communities as old-timers abandoned their farms to try their luck in the Northwest Territory, the prairies beyond the Mississippi, the mountains, the Oregon country.

All this had been going on for decades, but it was one thing to acknowledge a fact and another to feel its impact. No one who attended the Council, listened to the reports of those who did, or even read about it in the papers, could think of the Way as circumscribed by his own village and the fellowship of neighboring towns.

The white horns of the Rockies glittered beyond the Berkshire pastures. New Pilgrims found their Rock on a western shore washed by waters that rippled in from the Orient. Nor were Congregationalists now a prosaic breed of small farmers and tradesmen. Gold miners also followed the Way, and so did ex-slaves trying to find their footing in freedom. The new evangelism was as exciting as anything achieved by the American Board among Asians and Africans, and it was more intimate. What was involved was not a pack of heathen of strange ways that had to be rectified, but one's own flesh and blood.

Was this true of the freedmen among whom the American Missionary Society was setting up not only schools but churches? Perhaps less so, especially as this movement had its difficulties. Could the freedmen have been introduced to the Congregational Way when they were fresh from the tribal councils of Africa, it would have been simpler. A palaver of African village elders had much in common with New

England town meeting. But interposed between their native villages and emancipation had been centuries when impulses to individual initiative, to freedom of choice, had been ruthlessly suppressed. To such a people the self-government which was the essence of the Way was as difficult as walking upright to a man long crouched in chains. It could be learned, but it took time. The Methodists, who had founded many churches among the Negroes during slavery, made out better. It was a situation favorable to bishops.

In another and more important sense the horizons were widened by dropping any reference to Calvinism from the Declaration of Faith. It was not a matter of proscribing the old doctrines of total depravity, infant damnation, and predestination. Many congregations, possibly the majority in the East, still held to the high heroic faith of their fathers. There were as there still are "brimstone corners."

Yet even these would gradually be influenced by concepts recently deemed heretical. And the loyal parishioners of the likes of Horace Bushnell of Hartford would not have to spend the better part of a decade preventing neighboring Congregational associations from casting him into outer darkness with the Unitarians.

A Latter-Day Cotton Mather

Bushnell had some points in common with Cotton Mather, last of the theocrats. Both had a poetic vein. Mather was haunted by angelic visions that served his vanity. Bushnell, who had no vanity, saw theological concepts not as mathematical axioms demonstrable by logical proof, but as poetic symbols to be felt, experienced, appreciated rather than demonstrated. Christ, he once said, was God's supreme metaphor; it was the sort of remark that got him into trouble with the literal-minded orthodox.

Both were caught between adherence to outmoded tradition and insight into the future. Mather went in both for witchcraft and medical inoculation, and was as much abused for one conviction as the other. Bushnell, while deploring slavery, was something of a racist in his belief that Negroes and Indians were inferior breeds who were doomed to be "lived down" by the superior whites. He was hardly advocating genocide; it was just the way he supposed God would arrange it. Meanwhile he was personally benevolent; he extravagantly sentimentalized a Negro who came to inquire when he was ill. He deplored the agitators for women's rights almost as much as he deplored the abolitionists. Heaven forbid that female purity be sullied by politics. "Do save one half of society free from the broiling and bruises of demagogy. . . . God made woman to be a help for man, not to be a wrestler with him." His letters to his daughters were full of sweetness and counsel to high moral uplift.

At the same time he brought to childhood an understanding never inherent in Calvinism. His doctrine of "Christian nurture," initially shocking to the orthodox, became incorporated into the Congregational Way.

Both men had influence in their time. Mather would have been heard often in the Council of 1865 had he been born in the proper century. So would Bushnell, but for the fact that invalidism had recently forced him to retire from active ministry. Both were sought as president of infant colleges, Bushnell for one in California, where his congregation had sent him to restore his health. Both declined for similar reasons; Mather was too loyal to Boston, Bushnell to his devoted congregation in Hartford.

They had very different childhoods. Mather, son and grandson of the most distinguished of Puritan ministers, imbibed Calvinism with his mother's milk. Bushnell had a near-miss from similar influence. He was born in Litchfield in the heydey of Lyman Beecher, and might have grown up with the Beecher boys, all destined for the ministry. But his family moved to New Preston before the Beecher influence could take hold, and his family was not Calvinist.

This was especially true of his doughty little grandmother, who after struggling in youth to accept predestination heard a Methodist preacher and immediately accepted his creed. It was given her to raise up a Methodist bishop. In Vermont, to which she and her husband removed, she induced a promising youth to read sermons at little Sabbath gatherings in her home and presently bade him prepare for the ministry. The youth, unsure at the moment that he was even a Christian, was aghast, but he obeyed, and rose through the Methodist hierarchy to a bishopric. Bushnell seldom saw this grandmother, but he loved and revered her, and his memories of her influenced his own choice of vocation, though he didn't move in the direction of bishops.

His father was not at all a Calvinist. Perforce he attended Congregational meeting, there being no other in New Preston, but after a sermon he exploded at the dinner table in his impatience at the "tough predestinationalism or the rather over-depravity" of the minister. Young Horace looked from his father to his mother at the other end of the table, trying to catch the man's eye and shake her head in a gesture which meant, "Not in front of the children." She was less Calvinist than any, having been bred an Episcopalian. But she was deeply pious and would not expose her children to defiance of religious authority.

Briefly her eldest son did defy it. One Sunday he and some playmates played hooky from meeting to climb a mountain. Divine retribution was immediate and dreadful; the boys were caught in a tremendous thunderstorm, and huddling under a rock, gave thought to their sins. It was a manifestation of God's Providence that deeply impressed New Preston people, who discussed it for years.

Mather, brought up in his father's booklined study, learned Latin almost at his mother's knee and entered Harvard at a tender and defenseless age. Bushnell was nearly twenty when he entered Yale. He could have gone earlier; his family, especially his mother, who in her prayers had dedicated him to the ministry, wanted him to enter it from high school; it was the boy who objected.

He was a hulking, strenuous youth, too fond of country life to commit himself early to scholarship. He loved fishing, swimming, boating, riding; he enjoyed farm work, especially in such vigorous details as felling a tree or laying the stones for a dam. His father had not only a farm but a little mill to which the village brought wool to be carded, and homespun to be finished. From his early teens the boy spent his school holidays helping in the mill; he had a lively interest in mechanics, liked to tinker with machinery and invent improvements. Yale would have had more appeal if it had had a technological department.

Then suddenly he craved learning. He applied himself to repairing some defects in his country schooling, and in the fall of 1823 entered

Yale, a serious, determined student, who laid down strict conditions on his roommate: study, not sociability. In 1827 he took his degree and set out in every direction except the ministry.

He tried his hand at teaching school in Norwich, and fretted. He put in a year in New York as editor of the *Journal of Commerce*, performed ably, but neither was this what he wanted. He returned to Yale in 1829 to tutor and to study law. Two years later he was about to leave to enter a law office in Ohio, when his mother's prayers were answered.

Lightning Strikes the Church

Yale had been caught in the fervor of a revival. The excitement swept the college, with the exception of Bushnell and the youths he tutored. At no time of life would he relish revivals; at this period, beset by doubts, he cut an awkward figure when it was his turn to lead prayer in chapel. What troubled him now was not only his inability to resolve his doubts, but the fact that he had apparently infected his charges with them. They were devoted to him; they would not follow their classmates into a movement from which their beloved tutor remained aloof. Was this well done?

It was under the pressure of his responsibility to them that he achieved his personal conversion. Instead of demanding "scientific" proof for creed, he evolved the concept of poetic experience that would later make his faith so questionable to many. It was as a mature man with highly developed critical faculties that he gave up his plans for law practice to enter the Yale theological courses. Late in the summer of 1833, already ordained to preach in Hartford, he realized his mother's prayers by preaching his maiden sermon in the little meeting-house in New Preston.

It was an electric occasion in all senses of the word. A storm was gathering as the congregation assembled; during prayer the skies opened with sheets of rain and the clatter of hail. When Bushnell rose to preach he could hardly see to read his sermon. Mather in a similar predicament had sensibly cast aside his manuscript to discourse on the God of thunder. Bushnell had small faith in the virtues of improvisation; he was and would remain a preacher who read word for word what he had carefully composed in his study. Nor did he deliver it from memory, this because his memory was undependable. There were to be occasions in Hartford when a small daughter would have to be urgently signaled during preliminaries to run home and fetch his forgotten manuscript. Now under darkness so deep that he had to bring the pages close to his eyes, he doggedly read, while the faithful tried not to jump as each flash and crash came nearer.

Then there came such a crash, accompanied by a light so blinding, that even the pastor looked up. The house had received a direct hit, folks in the gallery had been flung to the floor; there was smoke, and the screaming congregation was threatening to stampede. Only the firm, self-possessed voice of the young preacher stopped them, and even he did not resume his sermon at once. One man had been struck unconscious and had to be revived. A check had to be made for fire. Only when it was clear that none had been killed or seriously hurt did the pastor methodically resume his reading.

He did offer some extemporaneous remarks. Mather would have called attention to the devil's fondness for striking meetinghouses, and would have found cause for complacency that the devil so obviously feared him. Bushnell limited himself to an expression of the comfort of being in God's hands. He had at the moment quite forgotten the day in his boyhood when a similar storm had punished his truancy from Sabbath meeting; old-timers in New Preston had not, but they did not intrude their reflections on so dignified and composed a young man of the cloth.

A Lifetime of Controversy

He had been called by Hartford's North Church (later the Park) for a six-week trial. He occupied the pulpit for life, or that part of his life that his health permitted. He began at $1200, rose to $1500, then to $2000, and when his grieved parishioners accepted his resignation they made up a purse of $10,000. In the meantime he enjoyed uncommon perquisites; his flock sent him to Europe, the Midwest, Cuba, California in the hope of restoring his once rugged health, which went into an irreversible decline when his spiritual life began.

He was, in short, greatly loved, yet in some ways his performance was less than adequate. Congregations usually preferred the minister who preached from notes or memory to one who persisted in reading from manuscript. Bushnell misread sometimes; a small boy long recalled his dismay when having safely ticked the pastor's "sixthly" off his fingers, what came next was "secondly."

The obligation of visiting every family in his parish once a year bothered him; he learned to do it in one lump, devoting the fine days of early autumn to the purpose and taking his wife with him to relieve his awkwardness. This reluctance applied only to formal duty calls; he was not awkward when he encountered distress. When a call uncovered a homely need, the reserved man, whose colleagues did not venture to address as Horace, was delighted to supply it. Once finding a blind man shivering in a cold house because no one had come to set up his stove, the pastor happily reverted to handyman and got the fire going.

He troubled his parish on the score of orthodoxy, especially at first, when the congregation was divided into followers of the Old Style and New Style. The two factions listened intently to see whose side he was on, and were confused at his failure to take a recognizable stand on either. An elderly deacon was moved to remonstrate. Deferentially, apologizing for the temerity of differing with so reverend a figure, he called his pastor's attention to his failure to emphasize doctrinal points like original sin and regeneration. "I would have a child of mine told that he was all the time sinning and rebelling, and that he must yield himself to God as a living sacrifice and nothing short of that will avail."

In time Bushnell would reply in detail to that sort of reasoning in his most famous book, *Christian Nurture,* which would cause some ministers, especially in Massachusetts, to accuse him of heterodoxy if not outright heresy. By the time it appeared, however, most of his parish and indeed many Connecticut ministers who would later join the clamor against him, would accept it.

The book that nearly cost him his pulpit was *God in Christ,* and the series of pieces he composed immediately after publishing it on the semantics of religious expression, in which he set forth his conviction that theological points were not scientifically verifiable, but akin to poetry in that they revealed the absolute and the divine through imaginative figures of speech.

The appearance of *God in Christ* stirred up in New England, from

Bangor, Maine, to outermost Connecticut, the same furor that had once forced "liberal" pastors to acknowledge themselves Unitarian. Bushnell knew the Unitarians, and their doctrine was not his. Yet he might have been forced into their ranks but for the stubborn loyalty and eventually the legal finesse of his congregation, where even the deacons now understood him.

The issue was brought before the Hartford Central Association in 1848, and Bushnell was cleared of the charge of heresy, though not by unanimous vote. But another association, the Fairfield West, was determined to bring the pastor before the Connecticut Consociation, which still had judicial powers, for formal trial. When Fairfield West refused to let the matter drop, Hartford North withdrew from the consociation to avoid the buildup of perhaps eventually overwhelming pressures. Bushnell, who in spite of ill health had borne himself through the controversy with grace and good will, was troubled no more. Some Connecticut pulpits were now closed to him, but that was not calamitous.

Christian Nurture vs. Day of Doom

It was to avert just this sort of unprofitable wrangling that the National Council had deleted the reference to Calvinism from its Declaration of Faith. Bushnell's fame was, however, not to rest on the fine academic points of *God in Christ* but on his *Christian Nurture*.

New England Calvinists had never given realistic attention to the psychological needs of small children. It was not entirely their fault; they shared the view of their times that children were only undersized adults, to be so dressed and so treated. They did acknowledge that the miniature adults were of unripe intelligence, hence the construction of catechisms to be memorized as soon as the children could speak, and the fact that few children were admitted to church membership before their teens.

Otherwise there was no concession to childhood, except as individual parents tempered the wind to the shorn lamb. From a tender age, in their catechism, in the sermons they sat through, children were faced with the high heroic reality of a doctrine which, as Harriet Beecher

Stowe reported, "regarded human existence itself as a ghastly risk, and in the case of the vast majority of human beings an inconceivable misfortune."

They knew that thanks to Adam they had been born in mortal sin; they knew that the baby brother who died before he could be rushed to the baptismal font was damned for all eternity. They knew that before the foundations of the earth had been laid, every human soul had been predestined to hell or heaven, with election never sure, though that didn't excuse the individual sinner from striving for salvation.

As food for the imagination of the sensitive, all this would seem to have more devastating impact than latter-day television shows specializing in monsters and gangster brutality. Add to this the fact that few children were unacquainted with the meaning of that ominous epigraph on the tombstones, "As I am so shall you be." Mothers died in childbirth; siblings and playmates were carried off with "summer complaints," smallpox, or farm accidents. When little Phoebe Bartlet tearfully besought her unregenerate sisters to repent she was not at all necessarily impelled by holier-than-thou smugness.

Nor was there much playtime in their lives. Some parents encouraged it, especially with their boys who in the country enjoyed hunting and fishing with their fathers. Cotton Mather was not always explaining damnation to his children; he told them Bible stories, probably very delightfully. Nevertheless the spirit that brooded over a Calvinist childhood was grim. How did the children take it?

Many by a simple act of evasion. On the testimony again of Mrs. Stowe, who in late maturity escaped into the Episcopal Church, many cultivated a gift for not hearing a word that emanated from the pulpit. On the testimony of the tithing men of colonial days, some desecrated the holy hour with surreptitious amusements. If their attention were not somehow arrested along the way (that came to be the purpose of the revivals) they would grow up in the indifference that made the Half Way Covenant necessary, and later produced Deism and the Unitarian heresy.

Not all children were gifted in evasion, especially if like the Beecher children they had to take notes on the sermon to be expounded later in family council. Some of these responded in different ways. Some, knowing that their parents as members of the visible church were among the elect, would assume that their own election would follow as a matter of course. Damnation was certain, but it was designed for someone else; they themselves would presently enjoy the celestial pleasure described by the Malden pastor, Michael Wigglesworth, in his *Day of Doom,* of leaning over the parapets of heaven to watch the unredeemed writhe in hell. It would be like watching a hanging, an edifying spectacle of which good Puritans did not deprive their young, with the added attraction that the writhing would never jerk to a stop but go on forever.

To sensitive natures, however, no such complacency was possible. Election was unsure and there was one sin accounted unpardonable. Who could be sure he had not committed it? The elder Joseph Hawley, who finally sought relief from mental agony in suicide, must have been such a child.

More rarely an awakening intelligence rebelled against "teaching which seemed to accuse the great Father of all of the most fearful cruelties and injustice." Only a remarkably tough intellect, aided by outward circumstance, could evolve such a view against the prevailing climate of opinion, but one of Lyman Beecher's daughters did, Harriet's elder sister Catharine. What precipitated her rebellion was the sudden death of her betrothed, and the prevailing view that since he was still unconverted he had gone to certain damnation. Catharine never returned to the faith of her childhood.

The Salem witchcraft had illustrated the differing effects of such a creed on the young. Samuel Parris's eight-year-old Betty was the defenseless child who could not shake off her conviction of unpardonable sin, and went through suffering so pitiful that her parents removed her from the other afflicted maidens and sent her away to recover.

Her eleven-year-old cousin Abigail was the tougher sort who took damnation as a judgment designed for others, particularly those people she didn't like, Martha Cory, for instance. It was she who exposed this unbeliever by spotting her spirit in the shape of a little yellow bird sitting on the beams, while Martha's corporeal presence sat solidly in its assigned pew. Abigail achieved what many a child of her ilk must have dreamed about; she took over Sunday meeting, hooting down her reverend uncle with complete impunity.

A slightly older child, Ann Putnam, was of a different kind. She was the daughter of tragedy, sharing her mother's grief at the death of many babies, in loyalty to her mother dedicating herself to uncovering the witchcraft that had caused these deaths. In her manifest if crazed sincerity she held the trust of the magistrates, and so in the end did far more harm than the hellion Abigail. She was the only girl on record who eventually recognized and acknowledged her delusion in a public act of contrition; more remarkable than her repentance was that those whom she had most wronged forgave her.

The concept of childhood of the 1690's still prevailed among the orthodox when Bushnell came to Hartford. It was what the deacon had in mind in his worried remonstrance to the new pastor when he said he would have his children always thinking on their sins. It might be expected that Bushnell, whose household had twice been visited by death, his first daughter and his only son, needed no reminding. But it was apparent that his mind worked on a different plane, and the publication of *Christian Nurture* proved it.

That he advocated such nurture was unlikely to arouse a deacon. When had the orthodox recommended anything else? But in his assumptions, in his program for childhood, there was a revolutionary difference. Why, he asked in effect, should not heaven instead of hell lie about the child in its infancy? What need to postpone redemption to adolescence, then to be achieved only after agonized wrestling with conviction of sin? What need of "revivals" to precipitate such a crisis? "The child," he wrote, "is to grow up a Christian and never know himself as otherwise."

If he didn't wholly dismiss such concepts as total depravity and predestination, he placed his emphasis elsewhere. He decried conversion in the form of an emotional explosion. Bushnell had never liked revivals. He found them self-defeating in that once beyond the high water mark of communal excitement, the convert was apt to backslide, much as the afflicted girls of Salem Village had sullenly settled down when people stopped paying attention to them. He admitted that there were situations where a revival might serve a necessary purpose, but he considered the very necessity dishonorable. Truly Christian people needed no artificial incentives.

It was said that Sarah Pierpont, who became Mrs. Jonathan Edwards, had once been denied church membership because she could not date the time she first knew Christ. Bushnell would make Sarah his model; it was thus that the vital experience should come, not with crying out and breast-beating, but as naturally and quietly as the unfolding of a bud. For all his doubting at Yale (and he now believed that doubts were not to be feared but to be faced and boldly examined) this was how knowledge of the eternal had come to him, in childhood, through the example and tender understanding of his mother, who had never preached at her children, but guided them by her innate piety into the light.

Childhood was also playtime. He did not advocate that the young be always thinking of death and damnation. Discipline, serious instruction should not be neglected, but neither should sport. Bushnell's parishioners were already aware that the little girls at the parsonage played games and shared jokes with their father. There was even something close to dancing on the high festival of Thanksgiving, when after turkey and pumpkin pie he led his household through the paces of a riotous grand march.

There was one game that even this sportive pastor did not approve. It was an affliction to his daughters that he had no patience with their dolls. From his exasperation when he found them at such play one might suppose that he had regressed to 1692 when many an innocent doll was deemed a poppet used by witches to torment the enemy. With him it was indeed something of the sort. He considered dolls a caricature of humanity, and since man had been created in God's image, caricature was blasphemous. On the same ground he objected to the hand organ man's poor little monkey, and wouldn't have the creature in his neighborhood.

It was the Massachusetts clergy that protested *Christian Nurture*. Some chapters had been delivered as lectures at Harvard; when the Unitarians approved his doctrine, it was a black mark against him, and the Congregational Sunday School suppressed the book. But not forever. Bushnell's ideas suited the new climate of opinion already beginning to pervade Congregationalism; soon they became an accepted part of the Way.

The Rugged Invalid

Where do Bushnell's writings stand in literature? Some of his sermons are memorable, like his charming reminiscence, *The Age of Homespun,* delivered at an anniversary in Litchfield. Not only *Christian Nurture,* but sermons like "How to Be a Christian in Trade" and "The Pattern of Society" anticipated the widening scope of Congregational social interests. He could stick to a subject better than could the discursive Cotton Mather, but beside the tough-minded, the almost scientific objectivity of Edwards he seems a little soft, sometimes in the vein of misty Victorian sentimentality. Yet he could also hit hard; an occasional sermon reveals a vein of the old Calvinist iron. Such was "Reverses Needed," delivered to his Hartford congregation the Sunday after the first Bull Run.

Officially it was no longer his congregation, for his health had forced him to retire in 1859. But he was happy to supply the pulpit in need, and never was he more needed than in July 1861, when his flock was sick with anxiety for the fate of sons and brothers, and shaken with the revelation that putting the rebels in their place was not to be the work of a summer's day, with congressmen and their ladies picnicking on the sidelines.

The battle had taken place the Sunday before; he spoke of the sons of Hartford in their "terrible worship in the day-long sacrifice of blood. . . . The flash feeling is over, the nonsense bubble of proud expectation is burst, but the fire of duty burns only the more intensely."

To him the crisis was a moral judgment upon a country founded in the brotherhood of worship only to deviate tragically under the Jeffersonian infidels who wrote the Declaration and the Constitution. In the former, Jefferson had "put in by courtesy the recognition of a Creator, flung in with his self-evident truths." The troubles with the South had grown out of "trying to make a government without moral ideas, to concentrate a loyal feeling around institutions that . . . are merely human compacts." It was this godless conception that had encouraged the demand for states' rights. Adversity was necessary to restore moral conviction. "Peace will do for angels, but war is God's ordinance for sinners, and they want the schooling of it."

He prayed for a new Washington. "If I were a prophet I would almost dare whisper his name. . . . Our old Washington, what would we not take for him now." The name he didn't quite dare whisper was that of Lincoln, for whom he had hope. For slavery, "that great and frowning misery," he no longer had a glib solution.

In spite of his tubercular tendency, or rather because of it, since

most of his journeys were taken for his health, Bushnell was a great
traveler. He had made one trip to Europe, where lacking the Mather
gift for languages, he fretted over his difficulties in communication and
wrote letters to his daughters urging them to study German and French.
He visited the cathedrals, was touched by their worshipers, and repelled
by their priests, all of whom struck him as "bloated." He embodied
his observations in an open letter of admonition to the Pope, which
found a place on the *Index Expurgatorius.*

Most of his travel was in his own country, ranging from visits to
the White Mountains and Adirondacks, fishing expeditions with fellow
ministers on Long Island, to the Far West. He enjoyed indulgences on
such holidays: "Come let us sin a little," he would say, pressing a
cigar on a colleague. Luckily none from the Fairfield West was present,
or he would never have lived down such levity.

He had his first glimpse of the Northwest Territory when he visited
Ohio in 1842 to deliver a commencement address. The landscape dismayed him: "Only think of a country that has no horizons . . . no
sweeping outline, no distant blue." But its people charmed. He could
preach what was in his heart without stirring up a deacon. "I am
convinced . . . that my peculiarities of thinking and style . . . would
go down much better at the West than the East, and partly because
they are offended by nothing new, glued to no habits of thinking and
not thinking, but ready to catch with eagerness at everything which
seems to be true. In a word, they are all alive in this region."

It was this spirit that probably drew him west when he needed a
change of climate. Once he was inspired to head for Minnesota in
November, risking his life by getting caught in a prairie blizzard in
dismal and unsanitary conditions. Eventually he got to California,
rounding the Horn both ways. No trip arrested his disease, but the
rugged constitution of his youth was still with him and made him a
most rugged invalid. Overtaken by a hemorrhage on a mountain climb
in the Adirondacks, nursed by companions who thought to lose him
then and there, he insisted on completing the climb once he had recovered.

In all his travels his heart remained in Connecticut, and both before
and after retirement he performed notable civic services for his beloved
Hartford.

It was a lovely little city, bounded on the east by the broad Connecticut, spreading west into residential streets planted so thickly with shade trees that the shy woodthrush nested and sang there. What it lacked was a park, and this Bushnell was determined to supply. There was talk of one on the outskirts; what he wanted was one in its center. For the purpose he selected a grim area bounded by the tracks of the New Haven Railroad and an unappetizing waste of dilapidated tenements, pig sties, and garbage and refuse dumps.

To conceive that such a place could be transformed into a park required vision, and this he had. In his country boyhood he had taken a keen interest in the lay of the land, and had never lost it. He kept an eye on railroad extensions, remarking sometimes to his family that a pass through the hills had been faultily chosen. Now hot on a project for which the term "urban renewal" had yet to be coined, he made an enormous map of the area he coveted for Hartford, placed it on the walls of the conference room of the City Council, and made his plea. The Council, inclined to smile at first, examined the walks and drives he had designed, listened to his lyrical exposition of the merits of a sweep of hillside looking into beauty instead of squalor, and was against its will impressed. "Why, it will cost ten thousand dollars," said one man plaintively.

He got his way. He had already facilitated it by dabbling in politics. First he got a friend to introduce a bill to the legislature amending the city charter so that the city could possess itself of land when needed; then he used his influence to see that when the amendment passed in 1853 and was submitted to popular vote, that it was so ratified. Buying the land titles cost five or six times the estimate of the despondent councilor, but Bushnell got his park, and in 1876 it was given his name.

"How Does Death Look?"

In spite of his ill health he lived more than the allotted three score years and ten, and in his last years, when he was well enough to get about, he watched the laying of the stones of the new state capitol. In itself this was not his project, though the state had long outgrown the one near the river where Hooker's meetinghouse had once stood, but its situation on the high land of his park was. Other sites were advocated, and to get his way, Bushnell again mustered his now very feeble energies to appear before the Council. The capitol crowned the hilltop in his park, though Trinity College had to be moved to make room for it.

Bushnell almost died in 1875. His wife Mary hung over him, and being of Puritan stock, a descendant of New Haven's founder John Davenport, she asked him the sort of questions Puritans liked to ask on such occasions. How did death look to him? "Very much like going into another room," he said. However, it was a year later before he entered that room.

Hartford was to give him another memorial long after, when it built the Horace Bushnell Memorial Hall. No one would have thought to dedicate such a structure to Cotton Mather, one designed for concerts, and not of sacred music only, to say nothing of ballets, operas, and dramas. But Bushnell was fond of music, particularly Beethoven's. On a gala night people with Abigail Williams' gift may glimpse him there, certainly not in the shape of a little yellow bird, but in the frail dignity of his ailing old age. In intermission he may sit in the comfortable chairs of the lounge, not to "sin a little" with a cigar, since he eschewed such indulgence in his parish, but to savor the fragrance emanating from those who did, the good tobacco, shade-grown along the banks of the Connecticut.

XIX

THE WIDENING WORLD

Bushnell had been enchanted with the freedom of spirit he had found in Ohio, but it is rash to generalize one observation to apply to the whole Midwest. Newcomers were capable of bringing in their prejudices along with their pots and pans, and the dead hands of the past could close on newly gathered congregations and become manifest in captious deacons.

Yet it was true that freshly broken soil often nourished liberalism as well as wheat and corn. Could New Englanders on New England soil have produced the likes of Oberlin, which New Englanders founded in Ohio, dedicated to education without regard to race, color, or sex? That the college was coeducational from the start was a more radical departure from tradition than its refusal to draw a color line. Red men at least had been admitted to Harvard long ago; but it took Harvard three centuries to consider women educable in the higher branches of the arts.

In Illinois one minister would have opened the Congregational meeting to Anne Hutchinson, let her "prophesy" before mixed assemblies. He went home from a discussion in the Illinois General Association on the Pauline stricture against women's so speaking to give thoughtful attention to Paul's exact words. Paul had indeed enjoined silence upon women; he had also prescribed other practices no longer in use: that in Sabbath meeting each member greet every other member with a kiss, that after devotions they all wash each other's feet.

If Paul was to be taken so literally at this date (1876), this man asked, why not also perform these other duties? He was the Reverend Flavel Bascom, New England-born, educated at Yale, a founder of Congregationalism in Illinois, though under the Plan of Union he had at first resigned himself to taking Presbyterian pastorates. When he spoke, he knew that many congregations, without making a point of it, were letting women vote in church affairs.

Though the Plan of Union with the Presbyterians was not officially ended until the Albany Convention of 1852, Illinois Congregationalists had renounced it in 1837. Congregational pastors sent into the new territory by the Home Missionary Society accepted government by Presbyterian synods, but more and more congregations had not. One had emigrated in a body, the Princeton Church, which had a formal ingathering of eighteen members before it left Northampton in 1831 for the Erie Canal and an adventurous progress west. Princeton Church had no intention of becoming Presbyterian. Others presently demanded the privilege of following the old Way, sometimes meeting with opposition from pastors, who though ordained as Congregationalists believed it their duty to serve here as Presbyterians.

There were several reasons for such demands. Those accustomed to self-government in their home churches objected to being curbed by a presbytery. There was division among the Presbyterians themselves, who had their own Old Style and New Style adherents. In 1833 the dissension provoked a heresy trial of three professors at Illinois College in Jacksonville. Those accused of unsound teaching were all good Yale men—Edward Beecher, Julian M. Sturtevant, and William Kirby. They were acquitted and their accuser charged with slander (he too was acquitted and by the same synod), but the incident was "humiliating and disgusting in the extreme" and left its mark. Congregations in Quincy and Jacksonville seceded from the presbytery.

Agitation against slavery accelerated the secession. Most of the settlers from New England were intensely abolitionist, as the Presbyterians were not. Many of the latter came from Kentucky and Missouri, where their church was strong; they were accordingly under an embarrassment which Congregationalists did not share. The latter had no slave-holding brethren to influence them; the anomalous "Dorchester Congregation," now in Georgia, was so far removed from their orbit that few had ever heard of it. They were also free of the circumstances that caused some New Englanders to look askance at abolition; in a new territory where capitalism had not yet taken hold, they were under no necessity of placating owners of textile mills depending on southern cotton. Free to follow their convictions, they did so with zeal, broke away from the Presbyterians, and threw themselves into politics. By 1843 they were strong enough to organize a General Association at Princeton and adopt a stern resolution: "No one shall be admitted to membership who does not regard southern slaveholding as a sin clearly condemned in the Bible." They became active in the organization of the Republican party and the election of Lincoln. They remained active when the slaves became free, and applied their social conscience to many fields.

Midwest Accent on Action

The influence that Congregationalists exerted in Illinois was not based on priority of numbers. They remained a minority sect. Settlers who had no New England antecedents inclined toward the Baptists or the itinerant ministers of the well-organized Methodist circuits. Congregationalists, who tried to set up academies in the New England style in order to give their children a grounding in Latin and Greek, were too intellectual for most pioneers.

That Illinois played a leading part in calling the Council of 1865 was remarkable. It had less than two hundred regular pastorates, aside from small congregations which irregularly received the attention of a visiting minister. Of the two hundred, only half were self-supporting; most of the rest were maintained by eastern benevolence through the Home Missionary Society. In the smaller communities ministers had to make ends meet on salaries ranging downward from $750, and they were lucky if they were paid in full. Few had parsonages, and their "perquisites" often came in the humiliating form denounced by the Council: "donation parties" held at the ministers' homes. With the kindliest of intentions, parishioners descended on the parsonage bringing gifts: bric-a-brac, cast-off furniture and clothing, provisions, and more rarely cash. Such "surprises" demonstrated how much more blessed it is to give than receive; accepting some of the items with grace required heroism of the minister's family. Cash and provision were welcome, but the party itself sometimes consumed most of the latter.

The Chicago Theological Seminary had barely made it through the Civil War, what with their young men going into the service. Three faculty members, scantily paid, managed to carry on until a timely benefaction got it through the crisis. When after the war good times came and Chicago mushroomed, the seminary confidently looked to a future when it would surpass New England's Andover, and began to patronize Boston, "a dear little place . . . on the Bay." They were not yet, however, in a position to dispense with New England; for a long time the majority of Illinois ministers as were college-bred had their degrees from Yale, Dartmouth, and Amherst.

What was true was that Illinois continued to lead the way in those services eventually given formal recognition in the Social Action Committee.

Those who had been hot for emancipation did not make the mistake of supposing that the issue had been settled when the ink dried on Lincoln's signature on the proclamation. The work of the American Missionary Society among the freedmen was as warmly supported in Illinois as the work of the more venerable American Board. After the war no meeting of a ministerial association was complete without a recital from the Fisk singers from the promising Negro college in Tennessee. And the Congregationalists kept a sharp eye on the civil rights of the freedmen.

In 1874 the Illinois Central Railroad drew a sharp reproof from the General Association for its discourtesy to the Reverend Barnabas Root, a Negro graduate of the Chicago Theological Seminary, who was about to go to Africa as a missionary. On his way to the meeting with white colleagues he had been refused service in a railroad dining room "with rudeness and profanity" and ordered to eat at the table provided for Pullman porters. The Association made this outrage the first order of business and exacted an apology from the Illinois Central.

Other minority groups served by the American Missionary Society had the sympathy of the Illinois Congregationalists: the Chinese in California where legislation deprived them of citizenship, the American Indians. The projected campaign in which Custer was to make his famous last stand was denounced at the outset by the editor of *The Advance*, founded in Chicago in 1867.

But the end of the Civil War thrust them into close contact with minority groups with which they were less sympathetic. The influx of Germans in Chicago was feared on the grounds that they brought socialism with them. The Irish were denounced as whisky-drinking, superstitious, ignorant, and "Romanish." A beginning was made to evangelize the German socialists in an informal plan of union with the

Lutherans, eventually with notable effect on the Scandinavian immigrants. Also notable was that presently Congregational leaders adopted measures they would once have considered socialistic.

Puritans, Railroads, and Strikes

The railroads were closely watched. No community could progress beyond subsistence farming until a railroad came near enough to carry its produce to market. But the coming of the railroad brought new problems. Somehow, whenever it reached a town hitherto noted for its sobriety, a saloon sprang up close to the depot. Railroads were also notorious Sabbath-breakers. Surrounded by settlers indifferent to such desecration, including Germans who would as soon dance on the Sabbath as any other day, ministers put up a manful fight to bring the railroads in line with ancient Puritan tradition. Learning "with grief and alarm" that the Rock Island was operating on Sunday, the Fox River Congregational Union in 1853 made a vehement protest: "We shall not feel safe in entrusting our persons or property to men who disregard the Sabbath." The Chicago, Burlington & Quincy was later praised for giving "those employed twenty-four hours of rest, running no Sabbath Day trains."

Simultaneously, irrelevantly, the associations had another running quarrel with the railroads on their reluctance to reduce fares for ministers and missionaries. Again the Chicago, Burlington & Quincy was commended for compliance; so presently was the Rock Island, although far from heeding the protest against Sabbath-breaking it had doubled its Sunday traffic. But no minister, even on a deadhead pass, would then dream of riding one of its Sunday cars.

Rapid railroad expansion and the consequent industrialization of the Chicago area precipitated the Congregationalists into situations that their Puritan ancestors would have ill understood, the strife between capital and labor. To be sure, in the first settlement of Massachusetts Bay, when difficulties of supply forced masters to release the servants they had brought with them from their indentures and let them shift for themselves, the magistrates had been wroth at the high pay the latter demanded for their services. Instinctively recognizing the law of demand and supply, ungrateful servants were asking more for their services than they could have hoped for in England. The notion of joining unions, however, had not occurred to them; presently the magistrates had some success in setting wage scales.

Illinois soon had unions, and Congregationalists hardly knew what to make of them. Ministers reverted to the sound Puritan practice of preaching to laborers their duty of remaining content with the lot to which God had called them. Some were outraged when unions demanded an eight-hour day. Ministers also preached to the capitalists: let them apply the Golden Rule and conflict between capital and labor would not arise.

Not all capitalists bestirred themselves to do so. Railroads set up discriminatory rates which afflicted not only laborers but the general public; their magnates showed a disinclination to hear grievances. Even so, strikes were not in accord with the Golden Rule, and when in 1886 the railroad workers struck, their act was denounced as "consummate folly." The leader who inspired the strike, Terence V. Powderly, was, however, even to the orthodox, a more sympathetic figure than the notorious railroad magnate, Jay Gould.

There was hardly a pulpit that failed to produce a sermon on the Haymarket Riots that followed the strike, hardly a preacher who failed to denounce the anarchists who were alleged to inspire them. The suppression of a German-language newspaper was approved, and Governor John Peter Altgeld was condemned for pardoning such anarchists as had not been hanged at the time.

Yet ministers and laymen were awakening to a new concept of the relations between capital and labor. They were ambivalently involved in the Pullman strike, of special importance because there was a Congregational Church in the "model town" set up by George M. Pullman for his workers. The trouble had come when Pullman simultaneously reduced wages and raised rents. That the workers struck did not meet with approval, but neither did Pullman's refusal to discuss grievances. When the American Railway Union struck in sympathy, *The Advance* called its leader, Eugene Debs, "drunk with a sudden sense of power" and praised President Cleveland for sending federal troops to break the strike.

Debs, very young then, went to jail on a contempt charge, and he who had not been one before, there became a socialist. Ministers also underwent a change of heart. Pullman's refusal to arbitrate went against the grain; some ministers disapproved the federal injunction against striking. The Chicago Theological Seminary set up a new chair to "teach social appreciation and application of religion" and called Graham Taylor to fill it. He allied himself with Jane Addams and set up a famous settlement house, the Chicago Commons.

Chess, Checkers, and Other Sins

Interest in social action was by this time not peculiar to Illinois. In New York Lyman Abbott, who followed Henry Ward Beecher as pastor of Brooklyn's Plymouth Church, and as editor of the *Christian Union* (which under his direction became the *Outlook*), took a consistent interest, and as the friend of Theodore Roosevelt approved the latter's efforts to control capitalistic excess through "trust busting." Much earlier Bushnell had preached sometimes on the application of Christianity to socio-economic problems, and his disciple, Washington Gladden, renounced the theory that a pastor should concern himself only with the spiritual life of his flock. Or more accurately, he expanded the scope of things spiritual to include all aspects of the Industrial Revolution and the politics that went with it. Bushnell had not hesitated to appear before city councils on projects close to his heart. Gladden went him one better; during his Ohio pastorate he served a term on the Columbus City Council.

Gladden read Bushnell's *God in Christ* when he was about to accept a pastorate in North Adams, Massachusetts, and what others deemed heresy was gospel to him. He had never found time to attend a theological seminary, though he had begun some studies in the subject at Williams College under Mark Hopkins. After his graduation in 1859 he had tried his hand at teaching, and then, not relishing the nervous strain of educating eighty ill-assorted pupils in one classroom, applied for a license to preach. By 1860 he was in Brooklyn, "City of Churches," in charge of a flock recently seceded from the Methodists. Soon after the outbreak of the Civil War he went to a less contentious parish in Morrisania, just north of the Harlem River. Here he found leisure to resume his readings in theology.

Since his study was undirected, there was no authority to warn him from what was then anathema to the orthodox, the German "Higher Criticism." To those who believed that the Bible must be taken literally on the grounds that if so much as one passage were challenged the validity of the whole were destroyed, these textural and philological studies were blasphemy. Gladden found them liberating to mind and soul. The concept of God was no longer static, established immutably before Eden, but a dynamic force, constantly revealed anew in a dynamic world.

Reading Bushnell's controversial *God in Christ* in this context was a further illumination. Gladden had not been able to explore the Calvinist doctrine of a God Who from the beginning of the world had predestined so many of the unborn to inescapable and eternal damnation without experiencing incredulity and shock. It was a concept he presently denounced as "immoral theology." How could humanity worship a God less humane than men? In Bushnell he found a God whose compassion and loving kindness precluded such jealous wrath. When North Adams called him as its pastor, it was Bushnell he asked to ordain him there.

The older man demurred, and not because ill health had forced him into retirement. He was worried that a young minister at the start of his career would incur guilt by association if he received the blessing of one still considered a heretic by many of the orthodox. Gladden did not propose to cower before his own deacons; he told Bushnell that he would accept ordination from none other, and Bushnell came. The voice in which he preached the ordination sermon was so faint that if it contained heresy few heard it. What the congregation could hear was impressive, and Gladden, who never disguised his own views, never had trouble even with the strictest Calvinists.

Bushnell also examined the North Adams topography with practiced eye and pointed out to Gladden the proper site for a park. But Gladden never found time for that enterprise. His field was what was to be designated as "social action." Never forgetting that his grandfather had been a humble cobbler, he was intensely interested in the lot of the workingman. North Adams was an industrial town of shoe factories. When the laborers demanded better pay, the management imposed a lockout and imported Chinese coolies from California to replace them. Gladden's concern for this situation, his sympathy with the workers, and his anxiety that the Chinese receive fair treatment gave him no leisure to lay out a park.

It was not that he disapproved of recreation. At about the same time he was opposing with more amusement than indignation the refusal of the local YMCA to set aside a room where checkers and backgammon could be played, on the grounds that Christian young men should be above such frivolities. Gladden was a minority among the local ministers in his insistence that godliness need not preclude a bit of fun. Eventually the Y got its recreation room. It got it after the minister most violently opposed to such sinfulness left his wife to elope with a girl in his congregation. After that exhibition, chess and checkers looked less sinful.

Preaching Social Doctrine

Gladden's social philosophy, which he continued to evolve in Springfield, 1875–82, and in Columbus, Ohio, thereafter until his death in 1918, grew out of his acute awareness of the events of the day. His *Recollections,* a neglected autobiographical classic, is superb personal history of the vital period from just before the Civil War through Reconstruction, and the first contests between capital and labor.

Intensely alive to the issues of the Civil War (he served briefly in an Army hospital), he saw the terrifying draft riots in New York, shared the solemn thankfulness with which the North received the surrender at Appomattox, a mood untouched with thought of recrimination until Lincoln's assassination loosed the victor's fury upon the South. Unhappily he watched the vindictive course of Reconstruction, and the moral collapse in politics, from New York's Tweed Ring to the seamier details of Grant's administration. He found comfort in the honesty of President Hayes, and mourned at another assassination, that of his fellow alumnus at Williams, James Garfield. This President did not die as quickly as Lincoln; he lingered for more than two months, and Gladden protested assemblages of the devout who made it a tenet of faith that if they believed and prayed, God would save Garfield. "That is not prayer which assumes to dictate to the infinite Wisdom what He shall do in any given case," said Gladden. "There is no true prayer which is not summed up in the prayer, 'Thy will be done.'" Garfield died, and so did the faith of some of the suppliants.

The lockout in the North Adams shoe factories had set Gladden to thinking about labor problems. His ministry in Springfield gave him further food for thought. The Panic of 1873 had been followed by industrial depression and unemployment. The unemployed were thronging to City Hall in search of relief, and in 1875 one of them urged Gladden to address such an assembly. The crowd was turbulent, and afterward Gladden was dissatisfied with his remarks: don't expect too much of the city; accept work at any pay rather than go begging. Only later did it occur to him that the city had a responsibility in giving relief.

Some of the unemployed accepted his invitation to attend his church the following Sunday to hear what he had to say to their former employers. There they heard him exhort his parishioners to take advantage of low wages to build, remodel, and repair. It was a makeshift solution, but it did produce some results, and the man who had induced the minister to help him fight City Hall was so impressed that though an Irish Catholic he joined the church.

Gladden began a series of sermons which he published under the title *Working Men and Their Employers*. It was a subject until then largely avoided by ministers as secular and hence none of their business; parishioners and colleagues who had not protested his theology did protest his meddling in such affairs. They viewed such preaching as at best superfluous; the "saved" would naturally practice Christianity in their relations with employer or employee and there was the end of it.

Gladden, his observation sharpened by recent experience, knew better. He knew that devout church members could commit acts of injustice and cruelty without any sense of the evil of their conduct. Nearly all assumed that the Christian rule of life did not apply to business, that the law of supply and demand "was the only law, which in the world of exchanges, they were bound to respect." Some specifically maintained that "economic forces are beyond the reach of moral laws." These people took exception to his discussing such subjects on the grounds that "the minister was not competent to deal with them. Concerning economic questions and business questions he was not apt to have any adequate knowledge, and therefore he had better let them alone."

To this Gladden firmly replied that it was time ministers acquired competence in matters of such moment. Very well to say that their business was to save souls; how could souls be saved when self-interest was made the whole rule of life? "Is not the selfishness which is expected to rule in this department of life the exact antithesis of Christianity? . . . I fear that some . . . may have grave accusations to bring against us one of these days, for having failed to tell them the truth about their conduct."

His reasoning curiously echoed that of Jonathan Edwards when parents protested that their children were too young and tender to be told of hell and damnation. Gladden after all had a very Calvinist conscience; he believed in damnation, had seen it in the Civil War, Reconstruction, political corruption; now he was seeing it in current business practice, and no more than Edwards would he pass it in polite silence.

By 1882 when he went to Columbus he was concerned with the workers' right to organize and to strike. Two years later coal miners struck in the Hocking Valley against employers who were conspicuous members of his congregation. The manager of the mine, a member of the church's board of trustees, fought the miners' union not only on their demand for higher wages but on their right to organize. "We'll kill that union if it costs half a million dollars," he told the pastor, and so he did. The miners surrendered after signing a promise never to organize again. Three months later they had a new union, and Gladden did not condemn them. "They felt no more bound by [their promise] than they would have been by a promise made to a highwayman at the point of a pistol."

Another strike was averted by arbitration between union and management, and the manager confessed to Gladden his change of heart. "It is far better to have an organized and disciplined force to deal with than to deal with a mob."

Gladden's Columbus congregation was a microcosm of the Industrial Revolution, containing both capital and labor. He accomplished the remarkable feat of exposing the faults of both sides and commanding the respect of both. As time went on he perceived that inequities were not confined to management; labor could be as blind to the rights of the capitalist as the latter to the needs of the workingman.

His social philosophy, "applied Christianity," as he called it, was his interpretation of the Golden Rule: thou shalt love their neighbor as thyself. Not more than thyself, he pointed out; decent self-interest was as important as altruism. What was necessary was that each apply the rule in recognizing the needs of the other, while justly calling attention to his own. The *laissez-faire* policy so long followed in the industrial world led only to ruthless competition and the creation in industrial relations of a state of war which the nations of the earth had finally renounced. (Such was Gladden's impression in 1909 when he published his *Recollections.*)

His sermons and writings received a hearing far beyond Columbus. The Ohio State Association of Congregationalists ratified his conviction that the ministry's duty of saving souls had a wide application when they made him chairman of a committee to investigate industrial conditions in Ohio. A sermon in Cleveland on the subject "Is it Peace or War?" made such an impression that he was called to Boston's Tremont Temple to repeat it. He did so first to a group representing management, and then at their request, to a group of workingmen. He won applause from both, not only when he defended their rights but when he exposed their misdeeds. By the time of the Des Moines Council of 1904, which he served as moderator, he had long lived down the opposition with which many Congregationalists had received his social doctrine. He had supporters like Dr. Graham Taylor, who had been working on parallel lines in Chicago, and Theodore Munger of New Haven. The program adopted at the Council prepared the way for the formation in 1934 of the Social Action Committee.

Doctrine and "Tainted Money"

Along the way Gladden had two disputes with the American Board of Foreign Missions, one on theological grounds, one in the field of social ethics. He was perhaps predisposed to challenge the Board, by now grown so ramified in its power that it could almost be classified as big business. His own affiliation was with the American Missionary Society, and for the reason that had called the latter into being, the Board's diffidence about offending slave-holding Southerners. The contest, however, arose when slavery was long a thing of the past.

The first had to do with a committee chosen by the National Council of 1880 to attack the perennial problem of drawing up a creed which Congregationalists at large would accept. What came of this was a liberal document which two members of the committee refused to sign, one being the secretary of the American Board. Their reason: "The creed failed to declare that all persons dying impenitent were forever lost, that there was no possibility of repentance beyond the grave." The issue was what came to be called "the second probation." The secretary of the American Board said that no missionary would be commissioned who entertained such loose thinking, for "there would be no adequate motive to work for the salvation of the heathen if such a thing could be believed."

It took twelve years to convert the American Board from what Gladden called its "medieval conception." It was finally done less by the efforts of Gladden than by missionaries in the field, especially those in India and China who reported that intelligent Chinese and Hindus refused to accept any part of a doctrine that held that all "heathen" who died without hearing and receiving the word of Christ were damned for all eternity. To these there was no attraction in a Christian heaven if from it they must watch their honored ancestors writhe in torment, and if this was the will of the Christian God, they would not follow Him. In 1892 the missionaries were released from the obligation of preaching such doctrine.

In 1905 Gladden again attacked the Board, this time for accepting "tainted money," $100,000 of it. The gift had come from the Standard Oil Company, then under fire for many reasons. When Gladden heard of the gift he expressed himself on the subject in the *Congregationalist*. No church, he argued, could accept benefaction from such a source without entering into a "dishonorable alliance." Members of the Board demurred. Money was money, in itself blameless, however obtained. They were no more under obligation to reject an unsolicited gift than was the church steward to inquire into the provenance of every coin in the collection plate and reject those whose donors he did not approve.

The Standard Oil Company entered the dispute, less than pleased at the kind of publicity its generosity had incurred. The gift, it seemed, had not been unsolicited; indeed it had taken two years of solicitation on the part of the Board to induce John D. Rockefeller, himself a Baptist, to part with the money. No one asked for its return, but the company did want to set the record straight. Gladden and others demanded that the money be returned. It was not; the Board had taken the precaution of expending it before the gift was announced.

Gladden's protest seemed somewhat at variance with the practice of the American Missionary Society, of which he was then vice president. Long ago it had considered inviting northern millionaires to become philanthropists by contributing to Negro schools and colleges, and they had success. The likes of Hampton Institute could not have flourished as it did without the generous endowment furnished by capitalists, one of whom was Rockefeller. The Society must have worked more discreetly than the American Board; Gladden was not roused to protest.

XX

ZEAL FOR EDUCATION

Boston had become the Athens of America, some said the Hub of the Universe. But it was little Plymouth that remained a holy place, not only to Congregationalists but to America at large.

Its story was more touching than Boston's. One saw its settlers guided across the seas as mysteriously as a flight of migrating birds, buffeted by wind and circumstance, half extinguished during their first year, and yet lifting their hearts in thanks for their first inadequate harvest to give America its first holiday that Calvinists would accept. Not that Thanksgiving was original with the Pilgrims; Puritans observed it as a movable feast whenever occasion arose. But a recurrent harvest festival, roughly corresponding with the Jewish Feast of Tabernacles, became a tradition in Plymouth and was adopted elsewhere until during the Civil War it was nationally recognized.

For children still denied Christmas trees, Christmas stockings, and all such pleasures by strict constructionist parents who pointed out that there was no Biblical authority for the date of Christ's birth, Thanksgiving was indispensable. The day was sacred; it was also jolly. After sermon and prayer came the feast, the stuffed turkey, the cranberry sauce, the pumpkin and mince pies. And since though sacred it was not the Sabbath, in genial households there were games.

Preparing for the feast everyone thought of the Pilgrims. While the children hung about the kitchen to chop nuts and raisins and watch mother stuff the turkey, they heard again the old story, how the *Mayflower* came, how the Pilgrims starved and yet gave thanks for what they had left, inviting Indian guests, who brought venison. Children listened to the story not only in New England, but in Ohio, Iowa, California, and thanks to the missionaries, even Hawaii.

Plymouth and its Rock (so much weathered, so much hacked by souvenir hunters that it was difficult to visualize its ever having served as a pier) took precedence over anything that had happened at the founding of the more important Bay Colony.

So in memory Plymouth outclassed the great neighbor without which it might not have survived. Plymouth had given American Congregationalists their first church, their first holy day. But no one called Plymouth the Athens of America. One of the most distinctive contributions of the Congregationalists to American life, their insistence on education, derived from the driving power and foresight of the founders of the Bay.

The Pilgrims were not indifferent to education. They had left Holland that their children might grow as Englishmen instead of Dutch, and in 1624 had talked of setting up a common school. But it couldn't be done, not then, while they had to struggle so hard for the leanest subsistence, not until they could find a "fit person" with leisure to conduct one. Such parents as knew their own letters taught them to their children. Bradford gave instruction to his sons, his stepsons by his second marriage, and his nephews. Dr. Fuller's wife Bridget, who reached the colony on the *Ann* in 1623, opened a dame school. But not at once; either because her first home was too tiny to admit scholars or she was too busy with childbearing, it was 1634 before she got around to it.

Not until 1671 did Plymouth open a public school. Long before then its neighbor across the Bay had a college, half a dozen grammar schools, and since the mid-century the beginning of a public school system. A college was beyond the dreams of a village that had not so much as one university graduate, Brewster having left Cambridge without taking his degree. Massachusetts at the time of its settlement had more university graduates in proportion to its population than England, and these gave thought to the future of their children. Harvard was founded before Boston was made presentable; Boston Grammar School, Roxbury, and others were set up to prepare students for Harvard. Dame schools sprang up wherever there were dames with sufficient learning to instruct the young in the first rudiments. Before the turn of the century most of the more prosperous towns had heeded General Court's order to provide schools and schoolmasters.

The system had its crudities, especially below the grammar school level. Country school terms coincided with the seasons when boys could best be spared from their farm chores; the pay of the schoolmasters from town assessment was meager. It was often supplemented by the practice of boarding them around for free; parents took turns at making the schoolmaster their guest for two-week intervals. There were some illustrious schoolmasters; no less than President John Adams in his youth put in a few terms in the neighborhood of Worcester.

The Ivy League

Nearly all the colleges of the "Ivy League" were begun in colonial times and under Congregational auspices. Even Presbyterian Princeton, founded in 1746 as the College of New Jersey, was not really an exception, nor was Jonathan Edwards' reluctance to accept its presidency due to denominational scruples. Many New Jersey Presbyterians were descendants of John Davenport's New Haven congregation, who had moved south in protest after New Haven was absorbed into the rest of Connecticut, whose religious practice was more liberal than they would accept. Much as Yale had been founded as a defense against the growing liberalism of Harvard, Princeton was founded in response to similar tendencies at Yale.

For the better part of a century Yale drew its students from both Connecticut and western Massachusetts. To a resident in Northampton or Springfield it was far easier to get down the Connecticut to New Haven than overland to Cambridge; young Joseph Hawley was a Yale graduate.

Then western Massachusetts set up a college among the lovely Berkshire hills surrounding Williamstown by raising the Williamstown Free School to collegiate rank in 1785. This conversion of academy into college set a precedent. It would be said that if you gave an ambitious principal the direction of an academy he would forthwith try to make a college of it.

The Massachusetts section of the Connecticut Valley got another institution in 1821 when Amherst College was founded to meet the need "for a college not quite so far west as Williams and not quite so far towards Plato as Cambridge." Its auspices were orthodox, and President Edwin Griffin regularly asked his students to pray for the people of Boston, then conspicuously succumbing to Unitarianism. Long before, in 1794, Maine had begun the difficult task of founding a college to save its talented youth the long trip to Cambridge; the result was Bowdoin. Six

years later Vermont, "the new state," achieved Middlebury. And ever
since 1769 New Hampshire had had Dartmouth; its origin went back
to 1754 when it was founded in Lebanon, Connecticut, as yet another
mission to the Indians. It achieved collegiate status after its removal to
Hanover.

All these colleges derived from Congregational zeal, and all had trustees and administrators determined to give students proper training in the
ancient Way. They had success and failure. It was a small group of devout Williams students whose "Haystack meeting" inspired the founding of the American Board of Foreign Missions; Williams might justly
claim that the whole world had been evangelized from its hills. But as
Harvard had discovered even under theocracy, students, even future
ministers, were not invariably devout in their conduct. They fussed about
the meals served in their college commons, stole turkeys, absented themselves from chapel, and when forced to attend, absented themselves in
spirit by "writing obscene doggerel on the fly leaves of hymnals, by ex-
pectorating in the chapel aisle," that being an account of the conduct of
some students at the sanctified Williams.

The same students could be profoundly stirred by a conviction of sin
that would have pleased Jonathan Edwards, when a visiting revivalist
caught their attention. Later in the nineteenth century the restless found
a new outlet for adolescent energies when athletic sports became respectable even in colleges of the most pronounced religious emphasis.

Oberlin: Mother of Western Colleges

After the Revolution, when Congregationalists joined the westering
movement, they took their zeal for education with them, eventually to
the Pacific Coast. Their way was cleared by the Northwest Ordinance
of 1787, which a minister from the Ipswich area, Manasseh Cutler,
helped frame and astutely lobbied through Congress. Besides prohibiting
slavery in the Northwest Territory, the ordinance advocated that education be "encouraged." Congregationalists knew how to encourage it.

The new territory drew waves of settlers from both New England
and the South. Where the former predominated, academies were set
up in the old classical pattern. Thus Marietta, Ohio, founded by veterans, at once founded Muskingum Academy, which evolved into Mar-

ietta College. When Yankees were outnumbered by Southerners such efforts sometimes languished. Frontiersmen from Kentucky might be willing to expose their young to a term or two of book larnin', but when they saw it begin with something so incomprehensible as Latin accidence, their interest faltered, and so did the academy.

But if some enterprises failed, zeal did not. Ohio University, chartered in 1804, and Western Reserve, in 1826, though hardly classed as "Congregational" institutions, owed much to followers of the Way. General Rufus Putnam of Marietta helped found the first, and a group of Connecticut men, who had vainly petitioned for a charter as early as 1802, were responsible for the second, the so-called "Yale of the West." In 1803 Yale graduates got authority to found the Erie Literary Society, which had collegiate aspirations; in 1816 it received aid from the American Education Society, newly formed in Boston, and a decade later Western Reserve opened its doors under the presidency of George E. Pierce, who like most of his staff was a Yale graduate.

These were secular institutions; militantly evangelist was Oberlin, which began late in 1833 thanks to the efforts of two Congregational ministers from Vermont, Philo Penfield Stewart and John Jay Shipherd. Inspired by the vision of a college dedicated to carrying out God's will, they had explored the most godless reaches of the Western Reserve, asking divine guidance. Nor were they dismayed when God identified the proper site in unpromising swamp country in Lorain County, Ohio. They set to work at once to achieve not only a "collegiate institution" but a town, both named for Jean Frederic Oberlin, an inspired pastor of Europe's Alsace.

The novel ideas of the founders of Oberlin were to be widely imitated and make it the mother of colleges in the West and South as Harvard had been the father of the Ivy League. Much of the work of clearing and building was assigned to the students. They would pay their way thus; at Oberlin originated the idea of systematic self-help, the policy of earn while you learn. Negroes were admitted, and more remarkably, so were women, of which more later. The emphasis was on manual labor, on training future missionaries to cope with the rugged work demanded of them by frontier conditions, but the collegiate department offered the classical languages and philosophies.

While classrooms and dormitories were still under construction, and the families of the staff thrust together in very close quarters, the school opened, and was so immediate a success that by its second year it had more than a hundred students, and soon a waiting list of applicants. One might have supposed that in an area so close to Kentucky the admission of students "regardless of color" would have caused trouble. And it did—to Cincinnati's Lane Seminary, whose students, wroth at discriminatory practice, seceded almost in a body and walked through the woods to Oberlin, led by their Abolitionist professor, Theodore Dwight Weld.

Soon graduates and some of the staff set forth to found other Oberlins farther west. "Father" Shipherd went to Michigan to found Olivet. Graduates founded Hillsdale College in Michigan, Ripon in Wisconsin, Northfield (later Carleton) in Minnesota, and assisted in the founding of Grinnell and Tabor in Iowa. After the Civil War, Oberlin's policy of learn while you earn was adopted at Kentucky's Berea and at the Negro school of Hampton Institute, Virginia.

"The Yale Band"

By this time the need for evangelizing the West and giving its young a Christian education was attracting as much attention among followers of the Way as the more exotic activities of the American Board of Foreign Missions. Samuel Mills, whose haystack prayer meeting had inspired the creation of the Board, had been visiting the frontier and reporting a degree of heathenism that equaled that of India and Ceylon. Something must be done to preserve the settlers from illiteracy and infidelity. The Connecticut Domestic Missionary Society had already been active in Ohio; after the formation of the American Home Missionary Society in 1826, theological students at Yale and at Andover Seminary gave prayerful attention to plans for forming companies of ministerial shock troops to win the West for God. Thus was organized the Illinois Association, better known as the Yale Band, and in Andover, the Iowa Band, both of which built not only churches but schools and colleges in their respective territories.

The Yale Band originated among seven students of the Divinity School in 1829, and their example inspired six others, all of whom reached Illinois between 1829 and 1833. They had corresponded with John M.

Ellis, who after working in Missouri had come to Illinois where he was already raising funds for a "seminary of learning" in Jacksonville. It was, wrote Ellis, his conviction that "evangelical truth and education must go hand in hand to the work of the world's redemption. . . . Bibles and tracts make their way but slowly and to little purpose when the community do not read."

In response the members of the Band had drawn up a compact: "We the undersigned hereby express our readiness to go to the State of Illinois for the purpose of establishing a seminary of learning as shall be best adapted to the exigencies of that country—a part of us to engage as instructors in the seminary, the others to occupy, as preachers, important stations in the surrounding country." Before they left Connecticut, the signers had raised an endowment of $10,000 and enlisted the support of the American Home Missionary Society.

In January 1830, while many of the Band were still preparing for the journey, the advance guard inaugurated Illinois College at Jacksonville. As at Oberlin its start was simple, precarious, and picturesque. Julian Sturtevant, one of the Yale Band, and local trustees met the student body of nine young men in the building later known as Old Beecher. There was no desk for the teacher, few benches for the students, and no heat. Since it was a January morning, Sturtevant made it his first order of business to set up the stove, with the aid of trustees and students. That task completed, he led his students in prayer and then inquired "into the intellectual condition of my pupils."

From such homely beginnings Illinois College grew in excellence and today boasts that a greater proportion of its graduates are listed in *Who's Who in America* than 98 per cent of other colleges and universities. But it had its growing pains. Members of the Band, and President Edward Beecher were too radical in their thinking to please some members of the community. In 1833 Beecher and two of his staff were tried before the presbytery on charges of "unsound teaching." They were exonerated, but the episode was unpleasant, and Beecher's outspoken advocacy of abolition gave offense. For a time such controversies hampered the growth of the college.

In the meantime Congregationalists within or without the Yale Band were establishing other "seminaries of learning." Jacksonville also had a female seminary, which was to merge with Illinois College in 1903 when the latter went coeducational. In 1835 one of the Yale men founded in Alton the Monticello Female Seminary, now a junior college. Other colleges included those at Rockford, Wheaton, and Knox College in Galesburg. And though the Congregationalists do not lay claim to the University of Illinois, a member of its Illinois College staff, Jonathan B. Turner, was a founder.

Efforts to found the classic concept of the New England academy succeeded only sporadically and then the academies usually became colleges. A more enduring result of this attempt was the growth of a high school system. The first township high school in Illinois owes its inception to John Howard Bryant, brother of the poet William Cullen, one of the Massachusetts men who founded Princeton, Illinois.

By the early 1840's when young men in their junior year at Andover Seminary looked to the home mission field, Illinois was too well provided with schools and churches to satisfy their craving to give service where the need was greatest. They consulted God in long prayer before they received the answer that their field lay beyond the Mississippi in what was now Iowa Territory; the youths formed the Iowa Band.

They numbered twelve, as did the disciples, though they were too modest to call attention to this fact. Until they had searched God's will, they avoided calling attention to themselves at all. They held their prayers and their deliberations at night in the seminary library, which had no lighting, and there, like godly conspirators, they assembled regularly in the dark.

Beyond the Mississippi

Once they had taken their decision, there was no need for secrecy. They obtained the blessing of the Home Missionary Society and corresponded with its representative already in the field, Reverend Asa Turner, who having been often disappointed of reinforcements, patiently answered their questions but couldn't resist a despondent comment, "I never expect to see any of you west of the Mississippi River as long as I live."

He was mistaken. In September 1843 Andover's South Church gave the Iowa Band a send-off, with no less than Dr. Leonard Bacon to preach the sermon. In early October they were on their way. Four of the twelve were detained, one permanently, but the roster was nearly complete. "Mr. D. Lane and Mr. A. B. Robbins, with characteristic foresight, had taken to themselves wives in view of losses from our original as might possibly occur." By November, after an arduous journey by train, Great Lakes steamer, and prairie schooner, they assembled in Denmark, Iowa, to receive their ordination from Turner.

Their imaginations had populated Iowa with dragons. There was the Mormon settlement at nearby Nauvoo, Illinois, from which missionaries went forth to entice Iowans. Thanks to Edward Beecher's recent preaching on the subject, they expected a quantity of hostile Roman Catholics. The territory even harbored a practicing atheist, Abner Kneeland, who also advocated free love. But these perils did not trouble them. The Mormons soon moved on; far from being infested by Catholics the place was inhabited by people who often had not the sketchiest notion of what faith they belonged to. Kneeland was an affable dragon, who courteously consented to debate with one of their number and whose followers were confined to the little village of Salubria.

More real were the agues and fevers which carried off the two young wives, the rigors of living on the four hundred dollars a year provided by the Home Missionary Society (supplemented by an occasional missionary barrel), the difficulty of assembling congregations and building meetinghouses (one minister was grateful for permission to preach in the corner of a saloon), and by their lack of privacy as boarders in one-room cabins, where the minister's study was marked off by the hanging of a blanket and the minister composed his sermons seated on a saddle.

Newspapers, reading matter of all kinds, were nearly impossible to obtain; yet as early as 1844 the Iowa Band, now organized into the Iowa Association of Ministers, met at Denmark to plan for founding a college, and set about to raise an endowment and find a proper location. Davenport was their first choice; its citizens pledged $1362 and thirteen building lots. In 1848 a beginning was made under the direction of Reverend Erastus Ripley. The pupils were probably then enrolled in the "preparatory department," as happened with most infant colleges of the West. (In 1846 when an ambitious school principal founded what he grandly named the University of New Mexico, he had no student beyond the elementary grades; yet the university eventually took root.) By 1850 there was progress: Ripley had twenty-eight pupils in his Latin course, and eight who studied Greek.

But the endowment was coming in driblets: $442.65 in 1849, mostly from the tiny stipends of the ministers; $152 in 1852, but then a year later munificence: $711 from local benefactions and $5080 from Deacon P. W. Carter of Waterbury, Connecticut. By 1855 Iowa College boasted four professors, but the city of Davenport was making ungracious difficulties. It had already thrust a road through the original grounds and now coveted the new site. In 1850 the hounded regents moved their college to Grinnell.

The town had recently been founded by Josiah Grinnell, to whom Horace Greeley had addressed his famous words, "Go West, young man!" The directive was apropos of Grinnell's difficulties in the East as a minister dedicated to abolition. He had been called to the first Congregational Church Washington, D.C. ever had only to be dismissed when he began by preaching abolition. New York congregations treated him no better. It was then that Greeley, assigning him to cover the Illinois State Fair, gave him his memorable counsel.

After exploring Missouri and finding it delivered wholly to Satan and slavery, Grinnell founded the Iowa town in his name, and through his articles in Greeley's *Tribune* attracted sober Yankee settlers. Among them he gathered a congregation, founded Grinnell Academy, and was contemplating a college when he found one ready-made, the beleaguered group in Davenport. In the thriving new town, whose founder became an active member of the board of regents, the college also thrived; eventually it took the name of its benefactor and became Grinnell College.

Other institutions were founded by Iowa Congregationalists. Grinnell had its academy, and the log church in Denmark, where the Band had been ordained, on weekdays housed a school taught by a New Hampshire girl, Eliza Houston. In 1845 the town opened an academy under another graduate of Yale Divinity School, Albert A. Sturgis. By the close of the Civil War this school had three hundred pupils, a staff drawn from Oberlin and Amherst, and was sending its graduates to teach throughout Iowa. In the early 1850's the newly settled town of Tabor, whose congregation, beginning with eight members, soon became one of the largest in the state, founded Tabor

College. The latter, "temporarily" suspending its classes in 1928, and thanks to the depression never resuming them, represented a failure rare among Congregationalist educators.

Advances continued in what had been the Northwest Territory. In 1846, two years before Wisconsin achieved statehood, what had begun as Beloit Academy was chartered as Beloit College. The Congregationalist settlers of the town on the Turkey River had signified their intentions a decade earlier when they laid out College Street. The town had been known as The Turkey until someone aspiring for greater dignity suggested a French phrase, probably Bel Endroit, which in local pronunciation became Beloit. The college's first president was a Yale graduate and Congregational minister, Stephen Peet. Across the Mississippi in Northfield, Minnesota, a Beloit graduate took over the direction of the town school which in 1866 became Carleton College; he was another Congregational minister, James W. Strong.

Manifest Destiny and the Way had reached the Pacific Coast. A Dartmouth graduate, George W. Atkinson reached the Oregon country in 1847 and two years later founded Pacific University at Forest Grove. In 1859 he was instrumental in the creation of Whitman College in Walla Walla, Washington. In the meantime he had worked as vigorously establishing a public school system as for the gathering of congregations.

Along the way Congregationalists founded Doane College in Crete, Nebraska, Yankton in South Dakota, and Colorado College at Colorado Springs. A notable success in California was Pomona, founded in 1887 by graduates of Williams, Colby, Dartmouth, Yale, and Oberlin, who skillfully addressed themselves to the task of creating "a college of the New England type."

One picturesque effort was the founding of a New England academy not far from the site of Custer's Last Stand and at almost the same time. This happened in Dakota Territory, just across the line from Montana in newly settled Spearfish. While General George Armstrong Custer was advancing to face the Sioux, pioneers were dodging Indian attacks to settle the towns of Deadwood, Lead, Central City, and Spearfish. Being godly men, they founded Congregational meetinghouses at once, and at Spearfish they founded an academy.

In 1880 it opened its doors to thirty-five students; a year later it was incorporated as Dakota College; in 1882, it closed its doors. It had depended on the aid of the Reverend J. W. Pickett, superintendent of the Congregational Mission of the Rocky Mountain District, and his sudden death in a stagecoach accident had deprived them.

Dakota College was dead, but on its site, and making use of its furnishings, South Dakota established a normal school in 1883, selecting Spearfish because of its citizens' zeal for education. The Congregationalists do not claim credit for what is now the Black Hills Teachers' College, but they might well do so.

Schools for Negroes

Perhaps even more remarkable was the achievement of the American Missionary Society in founding Negro schools in the South after the Civil War. As in the West, work had to start at the elementary level, but in a short time grade schools evolved into academies, some of which were said to have standards equal to those of the best in New England, and colleges of excellence. Hampton Institute, founded on the principles of Oberlin by a son of Congregational missionaries to Hawaii, General Samuel Chapman Armstrong, attracted so much attention among northern philanthropists that at one time it was said to be the best-endowed college in Virginia. Fisk in Nashville, Tennessee, Howard in Washington, and Dillard in New Orleans became universities.

Some day someone must examine in detail the story of the Congregational contribution to education. It is far greater than shown by the modest figures in the year books, a total of forty-seven colleges "historically associated" with the Way, only two dozen of which acknowledge a current relationship. It is true that other denominations outdistanced the Congregationalists numerically, the Presbyterians (partly as a result of the Plan of Union), the Baptists, and ultimately the Methodists when these recognized the need of an educated ministry.

But the official list ignores the more subtle contributions of the self-effacing Congregationalists, their cooperation with other sects, their influence in establishing public schools, their initiative in founding state universities and the land grant colleges. Jonathan B. Turner was the real author of the Morrill Act which made the latter possible; he had been working on the project since 1850 and saw one bill pass Congress in 1857 only to be defeated by presidential veto, until finally a bill sponsored by Representative Justin Morrill of Vermont was signed by President Lincoln in 1862.

One characteristic of the colleges founded by followers of the Way was that they did not bear a denominational name. Such modesty may have contributed to their success; parents of divers faiths who might hesitate to send their children to an institution designated as Southern Methodist, Presbyterian College, or Friends University, felt no such misgivings about entrusting them to one with a neutral name like Pomona or Grinnell. All such colleges were founded to provide a Christian education, but this term was never conceived in a narrow doctrinal sense. "Congregational" colleges rarely failed; their great attribute is not numerical superiority but excellence.

Women and the Oberlin Revolution

There was one blind spot in the educational vision of the seventeenth and eighteenth centuries: women were considered less educable than Indians. The original purpose of Dartmouth had been to indoctrinate the red man into white man's culture; Harvard, which sometimes admitted an Indian student, would not for centuries consider admitting a woman; it was not considered necessary to raise the female cultural level.

It was not that women were despised, in spite of the fact that Eve by tempting Adam was held largely responsible for the Fall. It was meet and desirable that women learn enough to read their Bibles, to write letters to absent husbands, to cast up accounts. Accordingly Samuel Sewall took his little girls to the current Boston Dame School; but it was his son's education that he anxiously supervised, coaching him to construe his Latin Testament in the hope that he would one day be acceptable to Harvard. No need for little girls to study the classical tongues; grammar school and Harvard were not for them. Harvard was in a sense a vocational school, designed to give ministers and magistrates the proper background to practice their calling. Woman's calling was in her home. That the Congregational Church would eventually ordain women into the ministry would have scandalized everybody but followers of Anne Hutchinson.

Some provision was made for girls beyond the elementary school level. Northampton was not alone in providing polite finishing schools for daughters of the elect in front parlors. Fathers who gave instruction in their homes did not always deny it to their daughters. Jonathan Edwards' father was as strict in teaching his daughters the rules of Latin accidence as his only son. Another Connecticut father actually presented his twelve-year-old daughter Lucinda Foote for examination at Yale in 1783. The reverend professors gravely examined the child and pronounced her "fully qualified except in regard to sex to be received as a pupil of the Freshman Class of Yale University." Not that they so received her. Apparently they undertook the experiment from amused curiosity and viewed Lucinda's accomplishments in much the same spirit that Samuel Johnson viewed a demonstration that a dog could be trained to walk on its hind legs. It could be done, but what for?

The opening of colleges to women on a coeducational basis came with the westward movement. The new communities in Ohio, Illinois, and Iowa were often nostalgic duplications of the villages from which the settlers had come, but there was an important difference. Horace Bushnell had rejoiced in the liberation of the little Ohio town he visited from old, restrictive traditions. One tradition that did not carry over to the West was the prejudice against higher education for women on an equal basis with men.

Oberlin pioneered in this as in other matters. It not only gave Negro students a wholehearted welcome, but opened its doors to another underprivileged group by enrolling women. This was a radical and revolutionary step. If women were to be educated to this extent—the proposition was still dubious—let it be done in nunlike seclusion, and not in promiscuous association with young men whose undergraduate misdeeds were well known. "This Amalgamation of sexes won't do," one critic warned Oberlin. "If you live in a Powder House, you blow up once in a while." The students, however, were zealous for their reputation. One youth caught propositioning a coed was drawn aside by his classmates and given twenty-five lashes.

By the time of the founding of land-grant colleges and universities in the West, coeducation was the order of the day. Iowa, whose corn fields were dominated by New England steeples, led the way in its university in 1855; Wisconsin followed in 1863, and later Indiana, Missouri, Michigan, and California. In 1874 even ivied Harvard made a first guarded gesture in recognizing the educability of women. It didn't, heaven forbid, receive coeds, but it did permit its professors to examine women and award certificates for studies pursued elsewhere.

The door swung lightly ajar could not be closed. Presently Harvard shared its staff with the young women of the upstart Radcliffe, though as was proper, in separate classes. At long last that was obtained which would have raised the hackles of the founders, men and women attending lectures together, sharing laboratory apparatus, studying in the same libraries, even sometimes pouring each other tea in the same common rooms. Harvard undergraduates could revenge their college's fall from dignity by eschewing the society at Radcliffe in favor of the Wellesley girls, who followed intellectual pursuits in maidenly seclusion without infringing on the prerogatives of men.

For there were women's colleges too, some growing out of "female seminaries" of higher caliber than front parlor finishing schools. Lyman Beecher's daughter Catharine, who rebelled against Calvinism after the death of her unconverted sweetheart, managed an excellent one in Hartford, and Mary Lyons in South Hadley founded in 1837 the seminary that became Mount Holyoke College. Some of her graduates went into the field to manage another Congregational enterprise, the schools set up by the New West American College and Education Society.

The New West

The New West, founded in 1874 with the grand purpose of educating and evangelizing the Southwest, cooperated with the Home Missionary Society, which simultaneously undertook to send its ministers into the region, but it differed in that its primary emphasis was on education and community service. It did not wait on invitation. On the contrary, the Archbishop of Santa Fe, founded and churched long before Plymouth was thought of, threatened excommunication to parishioners who accepted the opportunity offered by the young ladies from the New West, and the Mormon elders bristled at the invasion by "Gentiles."

It also differed from the American Board in that the venture was largely entrusted to females. The Board had indeed used women in its mission schools, but only under the close supervision of the male missionaries. Many young teachers from the New West worked at their own discretion. There were proper male auspices in Boston in the Congregational Ministers Union and its secretary, Charles R. Bliss, but even there and in branch offices like Chicago, many district officers were women. On the home front women labored to raise the wherewithal for their support; the Ladies Aid Society of the Phillips Church of South Boston furnished the funds for building the Phillips School in Salt Lake City.

Garbed in the voluminous costumes of the day, the girls made their way into the exotic New West; there were railroads for the longest part of the journey, but to reach the points chosen in Boston from study of the maps, most had eventually to transfer to stage coaches, buckboards, or even mules. They went into New Mexican communities where they didn't know a word of the language. Mormons spoke English, but at first were highly uncordial. Until a school proved its success, and sundry Ladies Aiders could raise funds for building, the schoolhouse had to be improvised. Often it started in an adobe hut; one in West Jordan, Utah, began in an abandoned saloon.

Puritan Schools for Mormons

The work in Utah was considered especially urgent. Here were native Americans who had erred strangely from the faith of their fathers. Their founder, Joseph Smith, born presumably under decent Congregational auspices in Sharon, Vermont, had supplemented his study of the Bible with a vision of golden tablets, whose secret hiding place had been revealed to him by an angel. Had these tablets been made available, ministers trained in the ancient tongues would have given them studious attention. Instead, after Smith had miraculously translated them (he had no classic training), they had been mystically withdrawn, and the orthodox classified Smith's *Book of Mormon* as romantic fiction.

There was a more damaging circumstance. In spite of the respect the

Puritans paid the Old Testament, they knew when to depart from it. No theocrat had considered following the practice of the patriarchs in the matter of plural marriages. Joseph Smith, and Brigham Young, another Vermonter, had done so not as mere permissiveness but as a high moral duty. It was as if having studied the headstones in Vermont burial lots, they had drawn strange conclusions from the fact that a New England patriarch sometimes lay there with four wives. On earth he had enjoyed their society consecutively, but at the Resurrection all would rise together. What was godly in Heaven was godly on earth.

Congregationalists did not accept this logic; neither did Presbyterians or Baptists, or for that matter the Roman Catholics. Plural marriage was adultery in their eyes, and existence here on a par with the scandalous practice of certain groups of Anabaptists in post-Lutheran Germany. Their missions abroad and among the Indians had worked hard to eradicate similar abominations. No less must be done for the Mormons.

The latter had founded the State of Deseret outside United States territory in order to be free of such interference. It was bad news when Manifest Destiny brought the American flag to fly over their sanctuary, and worse when federal laws were passed against polygamy. Eventually, in order to achieve statehood, they would renounce it, but not until 1893. When an attempt was made to gather a Congregational church in Salt Lake in 1865, and when nine years later the young women of the New West came to rescue their women from "degradation," they showed fight. A Sunday School superintendent of the church was murdered. The young ladies were not so roughly handled—the assumption that they would not be was one reason for entrusting the field work to them—but their welcome was not warm.

The elders issued a warning: "By promoting dissensions, inciting rebellion, bringing about disputes between the priests and the people, opposing polygamy and exercising an influence over Mormon girls, they expect to plant the first gun on Mormon soil." Nevertheless, under American territorial government, they could not forbid the schools, and these presently evoked the same admiration among Mormons that the thriving, well-ordered Mormon communities evoked from the Congregationalists. Utah was after all a success story, as notable as that of early

Massachusetts, and with a past as poignant as Plymouth; Puritans and their descendants would always respect success.

As of this date Utah had done little about education, and when the young women demonstrated their ability to conduct orderly classes, few Mormon parents hesitated to entrust their children to them. Academies opened in Salt Lake, Ogden, and Provo, and rural schools in twenty-three remoter districts, or "stakes" as the Mormons called them.

Soon the Latter-Day Saints were inspired by example to found their own schools. At Farmington the mission school found itself in unexpected competition with a well-managed academy set up by the stake. Near Ogden, community initiative raised a local schoolhouse and then asked the New West for guidance in setting up classes. It would be in Utah, as had already happened in some parts of the South, where the American Missionary Association found its services superfluous when local communities administered schools of their own. So far as the primary incentive was to educate, this was a consummation devoutly to be wished. In Utah there was the additional incentive of combating polygamy. But that could most wisely be left to federal law and the growing impulse among this order of saints to acquire a respectable national image.

In Arizona the New West made rapid progress, largely because the population included a substantial English-speaking element that welcomed education. Las Vegas was in this jurisdiction, and an academy there had such success in attracting Mexicans and Indians that an old Jesuit College indignantly removed to Denver. Founded in 1879, the academy flourished under direction from Chicago, and in 1890 moved its four hundred students into a three-story house. The students, drawn from all parts of the territory, scattered after graduation to communities which had consented to tax themselves for school support. There was a notable convert in this area: a Pueblo Indian who received ordination as a Congregational minister.

New Mexico, with its heavy preponderance of Mexicans and Indians, proved more difficult than Mormon Utah. Santa Fe, a lovely and ancient little city set at the foot of the mountains, looked promising, since it was the seat of territorial government. But it was also the seat of the archbishop, who had no ecumenical spirit at all, and forbade his parishioners to learn their letters from the Protestant heretics. One young woman had some success when she discovered that there was a sewing machine in town that no one knew how to use. She demonstrated the gadget, formed a sewing circle, and some of its members sent their children to her school. But Santa Fe never did well; after pouring more than two hundred thousand dollars of good Congregational money into it, the New West had to confess that the results were discouragingly incommensurate.

Albuquerque, a railroad town, did better, and there were villages where the young women, visiting the sick in their homes, helping lay out the dead, offering New England nostrums, recipes, and suggestions for home management, managed to build up modest little schools. And there were a few where the girls, perhaps less ingenious, perhaps scared by the unfamiliar language, customs, and the total absence of accustomed society, sat day after day in empty classrooms only to give up and go home. They were in a minority. The women of the New West had proved themselves not only as educable, but as resourceful educators.

XXI

UNITY IN DIVERSITY

"I *miss* hell!" an old lady once confided to her pastor. This would be after the Council of 1865 when Calvinism had been dropped as a denominational designation, and some Congregational pastors became in their preaching indistinguishable from their Unitarian brethren.

The lady had a point. There was a bedrock firmness in Calvinism. New England had been founded and had grown to greatness under the direction of people who entertained no doubts about the reality of the devil and his hell, about natural depravity and the dire necessity of regeneration. If this faith caused them to hang "witches," it had also impelled them to found Harvard, a public school system, declare independence of England, and write and ratify the United States Constitution.

Had the permissive liberalism of these later days softened and corrupted the vein of iron in the ancient faith?

In New York there was Lyman Abbott, who had given up the pastorate of the Plymouth Church to give full time to editing the *Outlook*. It drew some distinguished contributors, like his good friend President Theodore Roosevelt; and the liberalism of its editor embraced and attempted to reconcile science and religion. Darwin's *Origin of Species* had disturbed fundamentalist believers even more profoundly than the Deist philosophies of the eighteenth century. Abbott's grasp of science may have been superficial; if he was more advanced than Cotton Mather, it was not because of any superior depth of thought and research, but because the times had moved since Mather. In holding to Bushnell's concept that theology was essentially poetic, that the Book of Genesis presented symbolic truth rather than literal fact, he rescued many readers from the anguish of having to choose between their faith and their intellect. Darwinism would one day lead to a "monkey trial," but it would not originate under Congregational auspices.

Science itself was taking turns that might well revive hellfire Calvinism and a most painful apprehension of Doomsday. Abbott's contemporary, Dr. Sigmund Freud, was evolving a view of the human psyche that had much in common with concepts like infant depravity, predestination, and the need for redemption. "The truth shall make you free," Freud said in effect to sinners stretched out on his couch. Physicists were at work on the atom, and would presently apply their knowledge to an invention that would present all mankind with a choice between Doomsday and total regeneration. In Abbott's day it was still possible to regard human progress as inevitable and human nature as perfectible. Nor did young ministers in training who studied elements of psychiatry have Calvinist analogies in mind; they were only seeking the means of aiding distressed parishioners.

Science was not the only field that engaged the attention of the faithful as their world grew more complex. Others than Gladden and Abbott weighed the rights of capital and labor. A very old temperance movement took a new turn, waxed powerful, and in 1920 achieved an amendment to the Constitution prohibiting the manufacture, sale, or transportation of alcoholic beverage. American soldiers returning from the front to this situation were no more astonished than Edwards might have been, he, who while advocating temperance in drink as in all things, saw to it that his parsonage was kept well stocked with rum. This achievement was no permanent success.

World War I brought other problems. There was a tendency among some ministers, some congregations, to outdo the Friends in insisting that the only godly course was pacifism, originally advocated by President Wilson himself. This was not the whole story. In one of those Iowa communities that was a bit of New England transplanted, a minister born to German immigrant parents preached an Old Testament doctrine of hatred and destruction that antagonized his daughter. Little Ruth Suckow had been the embodiment of Bushnell's "Christian nurture"; the meetinghouse was as familiar and homelike to her as her mother's kitchen; she wrote her first childish stories in the study, while her father worked out next Sunday's sermon. Bred to the knowledge of God's loving kindness and the forgiveness of sins, she was estranged from both church and father when the latter preached vengeance. Only when the hysteria of war subsided as a spring flood returns to its riverbanks did she make peace with her father, and at long last with her faith. Such conflict and dismay were by no means limited to one Iowa parish.

A Corporation from the Council

The Council of 1865 had expressed a craving for unity among Congregationalists which did not vanish when the delegates went home. The Council established a committee which labored for years to elaborate a creed which all congregations, however far to the right or the left of Calvinism, could accept. It was followed by a permanent Council, whose permanence consisted of its meeting at regular intervals and functioning in the meantime under an executive committee and a number of standing committees.

This was their unity; but it operated against the old background of diversity. The congregations guarded their independence very much as the Bay Colony had guarded its own against king and bishop. So long as they accepted no other than Christ as its head, each was at full liberty to covenant according to its own lights, recite what creed was best adapted to its collective conscience, reject or accept Darwinism, accept or reject the resolutions of the National Council. Thus even when for pressing legal reasons the Council became a corporation, it functioned as one more autonomous body. The Council resembled the old ministers' associations on a national scale in that it provided fellowship between congregations and offered advice, but had no punitive powers.

The first meeting of the Council as a permanent body was in Oberlin, in November 1871. The 276 delegates represented 3000 churches with a membership of 312,000. It arranged for triennial meetings, standing committees, and adopted a constitution which was amended thereafter nearly as regularly as the Council met.

The Council of 1883, meeting in New Hampshire, essayed the adoption of a creed. Hitherto Congregationalists had been content to ratify creeds acceptable to the Anglican Church, such as the Westminster Confession. The Burial Hill Declaration had informally set forth principles; this was an attempt at a more formal statement. It had eloquence and beauty: "We believe in one God, the Father Almighty, maker of heaven and earth and of all things visible and invisible." It was designed to rectify the condition that Dr. Leonard Bacon had spoken of in 1865: "I have had some apprehension that some of our brethren . . . have an idea of Congregationalism that it consists in believing nothing in particular." But the new creed was long, better adapted for study in classes preparing for membership than for frequent recital in worship. In practice most congregations kept to the old Apostles' Creed; taken literally, it did not entirely correspond with belief, but it retained poetic validity.

It was shortly after 1883 that the Council, which had expressly limited its powers to avoid rousing local fears of anything like presbyterian control, was forced to incorporate itself as "The Trustees of the National Council of the Congregational Churches of the United States." A substantial bequest, and the growing responsibility of administering funds collected for ministerial relief, dictated the necessity of forming a legal body accountable to the law.

Ministerial relief was long overdue. A touching aspect of the problem had been presented to the American Board of Foreign Missions in 1857 when Lucy Butler had reported the death of her husband Elizur. He was the minister and physician to the Cherokees, whose loyalty to his charges and the Board had cost him a prison term in Georgia. He had never had the same standing with the Board as his colleague, Samuel Worcester, in those name the case was brought to the Supreme Court. In 1852 the Board had struck Butler a bitter blow by dismissing him from its service. From then until his death five years later, he and his Lucy had lived by taking in boarders, Butler helping with the household tasks. "How meekly and quietly that good man performed these daily duties!" wrote Lucy.

There was an implied reproach in these words, and it applied not only to the Board but to the congregations which made no provision for a pastor in his old age. Barring wealthy city parishes like Hartford and Brooklyn, where congregations couldn't do enough for pastors as well loved as Bushnell and Beecher, most ministers were ill-paid, often had to dun their parishioners to get what was promised them, and unless they had private means or published salable books, had small chance of providing for their old age. Some churches added "ministerial relief" to their benevolences, but the sums thus accrued were often so tiny that they could have contributed nothing more substantial than an occasional Thanksgiving basket.

The very phrase "ministerial relief" was condescending; it ill befitted the dignity to the heirs of the powerful oligarchy that had once guided New England. Yet relief was all that was available until the Council of 1917 set up an annuity fund. The plan had been originated in New Haven two years earlier in a vigorous campaign to raise an endowment. Initiative to provide pensions had arisen even earlier in Ohio, Wisconsin, and Southern California. Dr. Charles S. Miller became administrator of the fund, and laid the foundation for the later Pension Board.

Women into Ministers

In the 1890's the Council took a step that must have startled the ghosts of those who had condemned Anne Hutchinson; for the first time it authorized the ordination of a woman minister. She was the forty-year-old Amelia Frost, wife of George Frost, pastor in Littleton, Massachusetts. Her ordination took place there in February 1894, and from then until her death in 1915 she and her husband operated in tandem.

If such authorization was revolutionary, it was also way behind the times. As was characteristic of Congregationalism, innovation took place first not at the national but the local level. The *Congregational Year Book* of 1893 listed nine ordained women preachers in towns in the states of New York, Ohio, Illinois, Iowa, South Dakota, and Washington, seven of them in full charge of pastorates; it listed an additional thirteen "ministerial licentiates," largely in states west of the Mississippi. Nantucket had a woman preacher as early as 1880.

The first ordination had taken place before the Civil War, in September 1853, when the Reverend Luther Lee came down from Syracuse to South Butler in Wayne County, New York, to preach the ordination sermon for Miss Antoinette L. Brown. And behind this radical event, as one might have expected, lay Oberlin College, most radical of institutions.

Actually Oberlin was not as radical as all that. Its administrators preferred to steer young woman applicants away from collegiate studies into the "Female Department," into courses that began with English grammar, modern and sacred geography, and ended with the study of

Milton's poems and Wayland's "Moral Science with Lectures." Head-strong young women who insisted on the collegiate course received at commencement a certificate instead of a diploma and lived in the mean-time under restraints of strictest propriety.

The young women who came were headstrong indeed; they had to be even to get to Oberlin. Many had faced parental opposition, and those who did not had to make a long and difficult journey to the one institution where they could learn Greek. One female whom Antoinette Brown found when she reached Oberlin, and who became her confed-erate, was Lucy Stone.

Lucy was twenty-five when she entered the college in 1843; consider-ing that an early enrollee in the collegiate course had been thirteen, this was an advanced age. It was the measure of the difficulties Lucy had already faced; it had taken her nine years of hard work to earn the wherewithal just to get to Ohio, and even then, on the steamer between Buffalo and Cleveland, she had slept on deck rather than take a state-room. Born in West Brookfield, Massachusetts, she had begun teaching at sixteen at a dollar a week, later earned sixteen dollars a month, and improved her mind by studying every text she could lay hands on until at last she was prepared to apply to Oberlin.

Unlike Antoinette, Lucy did not aspire to the ministry; she would preach, but in a specialized field. Her motivation was nonetheless theological. Her father had scorned her studies; her mother, worn out with the bearing of nine children, had called her attention to the curse of Eve as proof that woman's whole duty was to submit herself to the will of man.

Young Lucy did not concur. She was not so irreverent as to contest Biblical authority, but it did strike her that man might have misin-terpreted it. God had not dictated the Book of Genesis in English. Like the legendary Boston woman who in old age took up the study of Hebrew so that in heaven she could compliment her Maker by address-ing Him in His native tongue, Lucy proposed to learn the ancient tongues for the express purpose of checking the validity of that transla-tion. She planned independent research in higher criticism.

Oberlin was a self-help school, else Lucy's nine-year savings could not have long maintained her there. She was allowed to earn her way by teaching a class of illiterates. They were fugitive slaves, members of one oppressed minority group, and they promptly objected to being taught by a representative of another. What could a woman teach them? Plenty. In Massachusetts Lucy had proved her ability to control any class, even during the difficult winter terms that drew in hulking bullies from the farms. She won over this class too, and earned such respect among the colored community in town that it got her into trouble with the college authorities by having her address them on the "Negro Fourth of July," the anniversary of the abolition of slavery in the British West Indies. Lucy was called before the Ladies Board of Managers for discipline and a reading from St. Paul's ban on a woman's speaking before men.

Lucy had some Greek by then, not enough for her purpose, but she held her own. The Ladies Board did not expel her, but when soon after a much younger woman entered Oberlin, she was warned against associating with Lucy. Naturally Antoinette Brown sought her company at once, and the two became fast friends and allies.

Antoinette was drawn to Oberlin by her ambition to enter the ministry. When on her completion of the Ladies Course (Lucy took her bachelor's certificate in the collegiate department the same year), the young woman and a classmate applied to the theological department, the authorities were in a quandary. Under Oberlin's charter they could not forbid these applicants, but to what end were these girls entering a blind alley? They tried dissuasion by quoting St. Paul. Antoinette countered by citing a higher authority, Jesus Christ, who in the parable of the talents had spoken of "that one talent which is death to hide." In her home in upper New York State she had been a natural leader in prayer meeting. She had further proved her talent for speaking, though illicitly, at Oberlin, where she and Lucy and other classmates had conducted a debating society off campus in the cabin of a colored friend.

Admitted to theological studies, the other girl very properly fell in love and married a minister. But Antoinette, reserving marriage for a later date (like Lucy she married a Blackwell), completed her studies, and what was almost miraculous, actually received a call, from the Congregational Church in South Butler. Luther Lee came to preach her ordination sermon.

His text was Galatians 3:28: "There is neither male nor female, for ye are all one in Christ Jesus." His title was "Women's Right to Preach the Gospel"; his intent to cite Paul against Paul to prove that the injunction against women's speaking out in church didn't mean what it had been taken to mean. "I cannot see how the text can be explained so as to exclude females from any right, office, work privilege, or immunity which males enjoy, hold, or perform. . . . If males may belong to a Christian church, so may females; if males may vote, then females; if males may preach the gospel . . . if males may receive ordination by the imposing of hands . . . so may females, the reason of which is found in the text."

He cited women prophets from the Old Testament: Miriam, Deborah, Huldah. He cited practice in the primitive Christian Church on the authority of Joel: "I will pour out my spirit upon all flesh, and your sons and daughters shall prophesy." He elucidated Paul's apparent injunction; the Apostle was not forbidding women to speak in public, but instructing them how to do so, always with the head covered. Paul's remarks were directed against disorder and confusion in worship, and so far as he bade women be silent it was only on such occasions as when they disputed the will of their husbands.

Another speaker at the ceremony was the abolitionist Gerrit Smith, whose friend John Brown had not yet been heard from. However, the event did not set a precedent; it was almost forgotten when much later women preachers became common, and even then "common" is too strong a word. Even after the formidable Lucy Stone's struggle for women's rights achieved a U. S. Constitutional amendment giving them the suffrage, Congregational women preachers remained in a minority. Most congregations preferred to call men; women who pursued theological studies usually went in for educational, missionary, or social work, or like Antoinette's classmate devoted their knowledge to helping a reverend husband. But women who craved a wider hearing could seek it. By 1889 the Hartford Seminary was accepting women on the same terms as men, and other theological schools followed suit.

Boston Priorities

The National Council and its standing committees continued the struggle to evoke a pattern of unity from what had grown up haphazardly. The problems were not unlike those that had faced the founders of the nation when they labored to join thirteen disparate colonies under the Articles of Confederation and then under the United States Constitution. States' rights, as it were, had to be respected, exemplified here not only by the autonomous churches but by the two major missionary societies; democratic procedure, that very laborious form of government for which the Congregationalists were partly responsible, had to be meticulously followed. Discontents that might lead to a secession like that of the Unitarians had to be avoided.

This national concept no more implied interference with local congregations than the federal government dictated to town meeting. The major problem was with the multiple benevolent societies, tract societies, publications, that over the years had sprung up independently, often with overlapping functions. Order was needed if only to insure that each receive proper support. One Council after another coped with the task by appointing committees: the Committee of Nineteen, the Committee of Twelve, the Apportionment Committee, the Strategy Committee. Wisdom was not always with them; some committees became victims of divided responsibility. But in the end budgets were achieved to make an equitable distribution of funds. The American Board and the American Missionary Society were persuaded to make concessions to each other. The latter ceded to the Board its foreign missions; the Board surrendered such Indian missions as lay within United States territory.

The meeting places of the Council symbolized its national scope: in 1898, Portland, Oregon; in the next session, 1901, Portland, Maine; at other times they met in Chicago, Des Moines, Kansas City, Los Angeles, Detroit. Boston was no longer the national center.

Yet Boston did preserve certain priorities. Here was the Congregational House. Established in 1857 in the handsome residence of Judge Charles Jackson on Chauncy Street, within a decade the quarters were too small. The building was sold to Jordan Marsh, and Congregational House took another site, eventually moving to its present one on 14 Beacon Street. Here there was ample space—for a time— to house the "rooms" of the American Board, which had also been peregrinating about Beacon Hill, the Congregational Library, and the Pilgrim Press.

What Happened to Puritan Austerity?

The churches had in the meantime outgrown their austere beginnings
and the Puritan aversion to ornament and grace. Much of the early
austerity had been dictated by need. The Pilgrims worshiped in a
fort not because they deemed a military background essential to worship, but because they needed a fort and a meetinghouse and lacked
the means to build both. The same circumstances produced the
"Lord's barns" of the Puritans. Worship could not wait upon the
completion of such dignified churches as they had known in England;
in a new community a preacher often gave his first sermon under an
oak or from a "pulpit rock." But the New England climate precluded meeting indefinitely in open air. A roof had to be raised, and
was, as soon as possible.

When the settlement prospered, the first crude structure was dis-
carded for a more commodious building with galleries and pews. Sentiment did not preserve so much as one of the originals; the Old
Ship Meetinghouse in Hingham, Massachusetts, represented not the
pioneer but the settled phase. At this time the churches were painted
whatever color pleased the congregation. The preference for white came
after the Revolution in the building of the classic churches that still
dominate many a village green. Old-timers returning from the West for
a visit to the homeplace were often shocked to see how many of the
loveliest, most "Congregational" meetinghouses now were Unitarian.

Other styles followed. The Greek revival, inspired by Thomas Jefferson, and reaching New England toward the 1830's, led to Doric
façades and a curiously wrought steeple. The Greeks happened not to
have gone in for steeples, and imitation here had incongruous results.
It was, however, preferable to some of the Neo-Gothic churches designed later in the century by architects with a weakness for abundant
gingerbread work. Congregations who went back to the early 1800's for
their model, to the period known variously as Federal, Late Georgian,
Post-Colonial, showed better taste. Nor has the evolution of style yet
ended; some congregations are passionately concerned with their building committee's decision to let the architect go "modernistic" after the
manner of Frank Lloyd Wright. "A monstrosity," some say, and look to

the classic white structure still preserved in the rear as a community house with nostalgia.

Interiors and the church service itself underwent similar transformation: choirs and a choir loft. A place was found for an organ, sometimes in the old gallery in the rear, sometimes forward, behind the pulpit and communion table, and the latter came more and more to resemble an altar.

Something like the litanies of the Book of Common Prayer was introduced in the form of responsive readings. Holy Days, once deemed pagan or Papist, Easter and Christmas, were no longer forbidden. Early in the settlement of Illinois a minister sought his association's sanction for letting his Sunday School have a Christmas tree. It was all that was needed to provide an opening wedge to admit Christmas trees, Christmas holly, and a bearded, red-clad saint not mentioned in the Book of Acts to distribute gifts to the children. When a new revulsion against Christmas came it would not be on the grounds of papistry but commercialism.

The little diamond-shaped panes of the early windows yielded to stained glass. Wherever a congregation could afford them, angels, Apostles, Good Samaritans looked down on the worship, and sometimes local saints. What would Thomas Hooker's parishioners make of the window commemorating and representing the pastor who led them to Connecticut, now placed in the classically elegant First Church of Hartford? Perhaps only that it is not much of a likeness; that is their own fault for never having induced their beloved pastor to sit for his portrait to a limner.

XXII

THE MERGING WAYS

In 1872 the aging Kaiser Wilhelm I received a letter that his secretariat hesitated to show him. It came from a German missionary to darkest America, one J. Lueder, and it asked His Imperial Majesty for bell metal for a church he was building in Duluth, Minnesota. At the moment when the Prussians had just vanquished France and faced the problem of administering the newly conquered Alsace and Lorraine, a missionary thought His Imperial Majesty had nothing better to do than supply a church in an obscure parish with a bell.

His Imperial Majesty was pleased to oblige. When he read the letter and Lueder's account of his work among "rationalist" expatriate Germans, many of whom mocked the faith of their fathers, he was touched; Lueden and his little congregation in Duluth got the metal, and when the building was ready, they cast it into a bell to call unbelievers back to faith.

It was not the first time that German-Americans had been concerned for a bell. Nearly a century earlier a congregation in Allentown, Pennsylvania had ripped up the floors of their church, the Zion Reformed, to hide from the British one that had become sacred to all Americans, Philadelphia's Liberty Bell.

After the Revolution and the restoration of the Liberty Bell to Independence Hall a great revival movement took place, comparable to the Great Awakening of Jonathan Edwards. It reached its climax toward the end of the century in Kentucky camp meetings. Clearings were made in the woodland, stands erected not for one preacher but many, tenting grounds prepared for the communicants, and the latter came, sometimes thirty thousand strong, to hear the preaching, and writhe and shout when the spirit descended upon them after the manner of Pentecost, and travail for their soul's salvation.

And what did all this have to do with Congregationalists? Nothing at the time. Heirs to the congregation that had left Leyden so that their children could hear the gospel in English instead of the "uncouth" tongue of the Dutch had no visible affinity with a church which until 1925 conducted its synods in German. Camp meetings were conducted in English, but they were accompanied, according to report, with sometimes scandalous excesses. Even at best their high emotionalism was repugnant to orderly congregations, many of whom now agreed with Bushnell that this type of evangelism defeated its own purpose. The prevailing Congregational belief in these days was that God spoke in a still, small voice, not in the storms of shouting and the earthquakes of stomping at camp meeting.

Yet all these circumstances were to reshape and revitalize the ancient Way. Not all the Pilgrims had landed in Plymouth; migrations had not ceased with the Great Migration to the Bay Colony in the 1630's. There were new pilgrimages, new pilgrims, and their voices were to be heard.

Not long after the Civil War, and with increasing momentum in the twentieth century, the centrifugal forces that had splintered the Holy Roman Church into a thousand warring fragments went into reverse and became centripetal. What was called the ecumenical movement was underweigh and gathering strength. It would bear upon the Congregationalists until in the early 1960's, in a momentous decision, the General Council would accept a once-hated designation: it became a synod, the General Synod of the United Church of Christ.

Earlier Plans for Union

The ecumenical movement was not essentially new. It can be traced to the body called a synod, there then being no prejudice against the term, which in 1648 framed the Cambridge Platform; though in England there had been sharp division between Separatists and Puritans, they drew together in this body to shape the polity of the Congregational Churches.

Conscious denominationalism was foreign to followers of the Way. Few churches called themselves Congregational until the orthodox needed a means of distinguishing themselves from the Unitarians. In early New England, Presbyterians and Congregationalists worked together, and in a sense considered themselves true members of the Church of England, purified of its corruptions. To be sure, when under Andros, Anglican worship was set up in Boston, quite unpurified of elements like cross, altar, candles, and vestments, the faithful took vehement exception.

On the Congregational side, the Plan of Union with the Presbyterians continued for nearly half a century, and Presbyterians and some others were welcomed to a place on the American Board and in its missions. Some members of the Council of 1865 deplored having to use the term denomination at all, and the Council of 1871 at Oberlin adopted a Declaration of Unity which contained an invitation to federation:

"As little as did our fathers in their day, do we in ours, make a pretension to be the only churches of Christ. We find ourselves consulting and acting together under the distinctive name of Congregationalists because, in the present condition of our common Christianity, we have felt ourselves called to ascertain and do our own appropriate part of the work of Christ's church among men. . . .

"We believe in 'the holy Catholic church.' It is our prayer and endeavor that the unity of the church may be more and more apparent, and that the prayer of our Lord for his disciples may be speedily and completely answered, and all be one; that by consequence of this Christian unity in love, the world may believe in Christ as sent of the Father to save the world."

The first response to this implicit invitation came from the Free Will Baptists. In New England many of this group had originated during the Whitefield revivals as one aspect of the New Lights. Their practice was still close to that of the older churches, and in the 1880's they seriously considered a merger. Eventually, however, they united with the Regular and General Baptist Churches.

Surprisingly the first real union came with congregations in the South, where the American Missionary Society had had little success in founding churches. These Southerners had originally responded to a different missionary effort, the one conducted by the Methodists and directed by the indefatigable circuit rider, Bishop Francis Asbury. Eventually they became dissatisfied with the service of circuit riders and the supervision of bishops. In 1852 Methodist worshipers in Forsyth, Georgia had withdrawn from the Methodist conference and reorganized as the Congregational Methodist Church. Their example was followed, especially after the Civil War, by churches in Georgia, Alabama, and Mississippi. The National Council of 1892 received an application from some of these churches and accepted them into membership. As in New England, local option prevailed and the movement was never unanimous; a few churches later withdrew from the fellowship.

In 1895 Chicago Episcopalians moved toward the "unity of Christendom" in its Protestant manifestations. Rejoining the Episcopalians might have fulfilled one hope of the Puritans, but though the matter was considered in a special, limited sense as late as the Council of 1923, union never took place. This was because of Episcopal insistence that Congregational ministers who served the communion to Episcopalians must first receive what they called a "valid" ordination from one of their bishops. The Congregationalists would have accepted second ordination as a matter of form, but non-sectarian though they were, they objected to the implication that their own practice was invalid.

At the same time a second plan of union with the Presbyterians fell through, as did negotiations with the Methodists and the Universalists. In the meantime events were moving toward union with groups of which many had not even heard.

"Blest Be the Tie that Binds"

The first was with the Christian Church, an amalgamation of three groups that had originated independently in the South, New England, and the Midwest. Their eventual union was ecumenical, since their respective beginnings were Methodist, Baptist, and Presbyterian.

The Methodist group gathered around James O'Kelly, probably Irish by birth, who during the Revolution had refused allegiance to George III, and after escaping from the British had served in the Continental Army. Converted soon after the war, he preached to Methodist congregations and became one of the most influential religious leaders in the South.

But the man who at the risk of his life had refused allegiance to

British majesty, was equally disinclined to obedience to the Methodist hierarchy, as exemplified by its conferences and its bishops. When in 1792 Bishop Asbury felt obliged to discipline the eloquent Irishman, and denied his right to appeal with the statement, "The government of this church is autocratical," O'Kelly seceded. He took with him twenty ministers and a thousand followers, who formed a group known as the Republican Methodists. No more than the old Puritans did they announce complete separation; when the mother church adopted a democratic polity they intended to return.

The second group formed in New England around Abner Jones, whose family had during the Revolution moved from Massachusetts to Vermont. He was a serious lad, who taught himself his letters, and in response to Baptist preaching suffered his first conviction of sin at the age of eight. His soul's birth pangs were long and agonizing; he was twenty before his doubts were resolved. In the meantime, study of the family Bible had convinced him that it did not authorize Baptist Calvinism. Since Baptists in this area were of the Free Will persuasion, no one accused him of heresy. His gift for exhortation made his services widely sought; when in 1801 he achieved his first pastorate in Lyndon, Vermont, Baptist ministers consented to ordain him on the express understanding that he was to preach not as a Baptist but as a Christian.

From Lyndon he went to Portsmouth, New Hampshire, where Elias Smith joined him in founding a Christian Church; in 1804 they tried to gather another in Boston. But the orthodox there, already troubled by the first signs of the Unitarian controversy, made it so difficult that Jones moved to Haverhill and then Salem. He was laying the foundations of the Christian Church, and its ideals were being set forth by the world's first religious periodical, *The Herald of Gospel Liberty*, founded by his colleague Smith in 1808.

Before that time the great camp meeting revivals had been taking place in the southern mountains, and finding a leader in Barton W. Stone, who in 1793 had been denied a license to preach by the Presbyterians because his thesis on the Trinity was deemed unorthodox by his examiners. Five years later the Methodists ordained him. He began preaching at camp meetings at Cane Ridge, Kentucky, and later evangelized Tennessee, Ohio, Indiana, Illinois, and Missouri. He joined a group of like-minded pastors in founding a new church on liberal doctrine: each communicant was given the liberty to follow the guidance of the Bible according to his own lights; Christian character, not creed, was the sole requirement of church membership; the churches would bear only one name, Christian.

It was Smith's publication that made these groups aware of each other and that led to an impulse to merge. Union was first arranged only through district and state conferences, whose delegates were so fearful of forming authoritarian bodies that they made it a practice to burn their minutes publicly at the close of each session. In 1817 they made a first move toward national organization, and three years later established an annual body, the United States Christian Convention, whose purpose was to "discuss, admonish, advise and urge but [not to] command or legislate."

The Christian Church was in the meantime expanding rapidly, especially in the Midwest. Its congregations, which held no heresy trials since they imposed no strict creed, were multiplying. On the frontiers their ministers functioned frequently as schoolmasters, and founded academies and even colleges. Antioch was established in Ohio in 1852 with the famous Horace Mann as its first president. In its liberalism it surpassed Congregational Oberlin; women were admitted without the fussy restrictions that chafed the spirit of Lucy Stone at the older college.

In the 1890's the "Christian connection" considered union with the Congregationalists, whose history and polity so much resembled theirs. The National Council of 1895 reported favorably on their qualifications: "They are a very earnest body of believers, passionately devoted to the Bible only, earnestly rejecting all doctrinal creeds . . . preaching gospel liberty against all imposition of dogma, and protesting against all sectarianism which divides Christians into followers of this or that human leader, they having no leader but Christ." A suspicion that the Christians were Unitarians was examined and rejected. It was true that they avoided the concept of the Trinity on the grounds that they did not find it in their Bibles, but they had declined Unitarian offers of assistance in the founding of Antioch.

But if the Congregationalists could accept the Christians, the reverse was not yet true. In 1898 a convention of the latter rejected the proposition; its New England delegates were accused of "selling out to the Congregationalists," a term too denominational to please the majority. The proposal was not revived until 1923, and it was not until 1929 that the two groups met in the Plymouth Church in Detroit to sing "Blest Be the Tie that Binds" in celebration of the birth of the United Church of Christ. The union had brought 1200 ministers of as many congregations and 120,000 members to the followers of the ancient Way.

Local churches of the older denomination could still call themselves Congregational at their pleasure. But Church of Christ was not a new name; it was what some of the earliest congregations in New England had called themselves. In cities large enough to have more than one parish, the practice had been to use the terms First Church, Second Church, and so on in sequence. Some, like the Brattle Street, took a geographical reference, others a nickname, for instance the Old Tunnel of Lynn, a title affectionately preserved when at long last the building was taken over by a congregation more ancient than that of its founders, the Congregation Anshi Sfard.

The Pennsylvania Dutch and the Reformed

Only Congregationalists who knew the so-called "Pennsylvania Dutch" or who lived in the Midwest had prior acquaintance with the massive group of churches which united in fellowship with the National Council of 1957 and transformed it into a synod.

Like the Christian Church, these newcomers represented a merger of older groups, the German Reformed, and the Kirchenverein of the German Evangelists; these had become the Evangelical and Reformed Church only in 1934, hardly twenty years before they sought fellowship with the Congregationalists. But their genesis was as old as Protestantism; their traditions went far back of the American Revolution, of the landing at Plymouth, or even the covert worship at Scrooby; one might trace their origin to the moment when Luther nailed his theses on the cathedral door in Wittenberg.

The first to reach America were members of the Reformed Church, whose relation to the Lutherans roughly resembled that of the Puritans to the Anglicans. They began coming in the early 1700's and most went to Pennsylvania, of which they had heard nothing but good. The Germanies were still recovering from the desolations of the Thirty Years' War; the rich farmlands available in Penn's Wood, the democracy and religious freedom established by its founder, promised opportunities that Germans could not hope for in Europe.

Unlike the Pilgrims and Puritans they did not come in congregations. They lacked the means. They came as individuals or as families, getting the passage money by binding themselves to a term of service as indentured servants. They were pious people, and when they completed their terms, got possession of land of their own, and founded communities, they craved an opportunity to worship.

They gathered their first congregation in 1720 in Whitpain Township under John Philip Boehm. He was only a schoolmaster from the Palatinate, but in the old country schoolmasters had been permitted to preach, and Boehm was happy so to serve. Presently his congregation came to him "with tears in their eyes," asking him also to baptize their children and celebrate Communion. This was beyond the authority of a schoolmaster, but Boehm could not deny human need. For five years he served Whitpain as unpaid pastor; then he ministered to a group of forty in Falkland Swamps, and eventually to thirteen congregations.

A Heidelberg tailor, Conrad Templeman, began similar work in Lancaster County. The first gatherings were in his home, where he read sermons and prayers and led hymns. Then he was asked to conduct services elsewhere and presently the devout tailor also found himself baptizing children. By that time he had met Boehm, who no longer officiated with misgivings, since his congregations had ordained him. Later when authorized ministers with strict ideas about protocol reached Pennsylvania, Boehm regularized his position by receiving ordination from the Dutch Reformed Church.

He and Templeman laid the foundations of the Reformed Church in America, allied at this time with the Classis of the Dutch Reformed. Its beginnings under the ministry of a schoolmaster and a tailor had much in common with early Plymouth, which so long had no ordained minister. The difference was that these homespun founders did not, like Brewster, refuse to administer the sacraments, and that their communicants did not endure the hardships of heroic little

Plymouth. Their hardships lay behind them, in the nameless miseries their forebears had undergone in the German religious wars and the long period of reconstruction. Pennsylvania was a success story from the start, its climate benign, its lands rich, its Indians friendly, its settlements intelligently administered and well supplied.

Yet the early years were not always easy. Sometimes an isolated community, craving to hear the Word, snatched at the first literate passerby and found itself nourishing a viper; sometimes new arrivals from Germany had ideas that clashed with theirs. Nevertheless the congregations multiplied and flourished. In 1747 they sent delegates to Philadelphia to conduct their first Coetus, that being the Reformed equivalent of a Congregational council. This group laid the groundwork for an organized denomination. The Coetus of 1793 represented 150 congregations and 15,000 communicants; some pastors were missionaries from Holland.

By then there were church schools, and since 1787 they had Franklin College, founded in cooperation with the Lutherans. They had had their own "great awakening," largely due to the efforts of the eloquent Philip William Otterbein. They had supported the war with England, sending their young men into the Continental Army and some of their pastors as chaplains. The church in Allentown had preserved the Liberty Bell, and one minister, finding German-speaking prisoners in a nearby camp, had preached to the Hessians on the error of their service with the British.

The Coetus of 1793 dissolved the connection with the Dutch Classis and converted itself into the Synod of the Reformed German Church in the United States of America. Henceforth its congregations were on their own, no longer relying on Holland and Germany to send missionaries or support. Successive synods consolidated their position in Pennsylvania, gathered congregations in the South, and above all, like the rest of the young nation, they looked to the West.

There were never ministers enough to serve the frontier as it accelerated its expansion through Ohio, Indiana, to the great plains, and drew communicants of the German Reformed to all these places. What ministers there were had to follow a practice something like that of the Methodist circuit riders, each serving many widely scattered groups, and gathering his flock under whatever shelter offered.

Like the first Puritans, they preached under trees, in real barns where some of the congregation sat in the hay mows. They preached in log cabins, town halls, once in a jail.

They founded churches, classis, synods; they founded schools and seminaries. And when the nineteenth century had run a third of its course, they ran into a new wave of German emigration which contained fewer pious tailors than men who mocked the very idea of worship. There had always been a rowdy element on the frontier; some of these newcomers were worse than rowdy; they made a creed of blasphemy. Fortunately the Reformed Church ministers also found allies; missionaries were coming direct from Germany to restore God to the godless.

Alliance with German Missionaries

The new wave of German emigration fell into two parts. The motivation of the first lay in the French Revolution, the upheavals of the Napoleonic wars and of the Industrial Revolution, then barely incipient in the Germanies, and the discontent with the unsuccess of the revolutionary movements of 1830. The second followed the equally disappointing revolutions of 1848. Some of the latter had been exposed to the *Communist Manifesto*. The nervous impression of Chicago Congregationalists that all German immigrants of this period were socialists, was exaggerated, but it was true of some. Such had even learned that religion was the opiate of the people.

That phrase had yet to be coined when the first wave arrived. But among good Lutherans there were also many who called themselves "rationalists," in emulation of the worship of reason set up during the French Revolution. For them as for Karl Marx, religion was associated with the oppression of the state, or rather the states, there being thirty-eight Germanies at this time, each with its own establishment, decreed by law and supported by taxation. The churches they knew upheld reaction and repression; they wanted no more of them when they got to America.

They craved fellowship, but most were content with the neighborliness of the German-speaking communities, their choral societies and social clubs. An occasional group set up a church dedicated to rationalistic principles. Some parents were said to ask that their children be baptized in the name of a trinity of their choosing: liberty, equality, fraternity.

Except for those who clung to the Lutheranism of the homeland, it was unlikely that pious tailors would arise among them. As much as the villages of Africa, India, and Asia, their little colonies became a challenge to the mission spirit, and missionaries came. American Lutherans came, especially from the Ohio synod. They were handicapped by the fact that in the eyes of the colonists they seemed to represent what they had left Europe to escape. The Congregational Home Missionary Society made an effort, to be defeated by linguistics. Such ministers as had studied German in their seminaries had only book learning of imperfect intelligibility to the people they tried to serve, and their unskilled ears could make little of what a potential parishioner tried to communicate. However, the Home Missionary Society found a way to success; it allied itself with missionaries from Germany.

In the summer of 1836 Horace Bushnell made the acquaintance of two German missionaries who were spending the summer in Hartford as guests of the Society. They were recent graduates of the seminary in Switzerland founded by the Basel Missionary Society under the inspiration of a pietist movement which sought to counteract the rationalist doctrine. These young men were neither the first nor the last representatives of what was to be called the Evangelical Church to reach America. They were on their way to redeem the souls of unbelieving Germans in St. Louis.

They had rough going. The German-American rationalists were not the usual order of frontier bullies whose indifference to religion derived from ignorance and could often be easily swayed with a rousing revival. Prevailingly literate, imbued with a rationale of their own, such Germans were unlikely to respond to the camp meeting approach. They were articulate, and published in St. Louis a paper in their own tongue, which included a prayer: "Lord, do not meddle with us. We will take care of ourselves."

They bedeviled the missionaries, placing a beer keg by the pulpit, holding riotous drinking parties outside the meetinghouse when a service was in progress, mocking Holy Communion: "We can drink our wine at the tavern and don't need the Lord's Supper." They committed acts of vandalism, sometimes burning a church under construction.

Even when in the face of such troubles a stable congregation was gathered, difficulties did not cease. In the old country the state churches had been supported by taxation; it was news to these people that here they were not only expected to listen to preaching but pay the preacher. Even the devout demurred, with the result that the earliest missionaries lived very meagerly indeed. They could not have lived at all without the support of the Home Missionary Society, and the support was conditional: each grant must be matched by funds raised by the congregation. It was no wonder that the pastor in Duluth, worn out by the superhuman task of inducing his flock to build a church, applied to the Kaiser for a bell. He was perhaps emboldened to do so by the fact that this monarch now ruled all the Germanies, the union having taken place at last.

Yet the missionaries were stouthearted men who did not quail before difficulty; their numbers were reinforced from abroad and eventually from their American seminaries. The first of these opened in Marthasville, Missouri, with the Congregational minister Horace Elijah Boardman as an instructor; thanks to the Civil War it was short-lived, but it revived to merge with the Melancthon Seminary, which became Elmhurst College in Illinois. Long before this time the missionary effort had won respect both in America and abroad. In 1852 the diet of the German Evangelical Church, meeting at Bremen, had collected two thousand books for the proposed seminary in Missouri, and the Prussian Emperor contributed fifty talers.

German parents wanted their children taught, and even rationalists were willing for them to learn the Heidelberg Catechism, so long as they received a good German education with it; moreover they were willing to pay for their attendance at the parochial schools. By 1840 there were enough pastors to impel a minister of a church near St. Louis to invite his fellows to a conference. Only five then responded, but this was the beginning of the Synod of the Northwest and of over-all planning for the organized Kirchenverein. A publication, the

Friedensbote, appearing first in 1850 with aid from Basel, became popular and accomplished further work toward cohesion.

In the 1930's, in response to the ecumenical movement among Protestant churches, representatives of the Reformed and the Evangelical synods began formal work on a plan of union. There were difficulties. The Evangelical Synod accepted the Augsburg Confession and the Lutheran and Heidelberg Catechisms, the Reformed the Heidelberg Catechism only. The polity of the Evangelical group, whose natural affinity was with the Lutherans, more closely approached the concept of a hierarchy, or at least a presbytery, than the more "congregational" practice of the Reformed. But in 1932–33 a plan of union was achieved stating that the two churches "under the conviction that they were in agreement on the essential doctrines of the Christian faith and on the ideals of the Christian life . . . do hereby declare their desire to be unified in one body." The union took place in Cleveland, June 26, 1934, and by 1938 was implemented by the adoption of a constitution "essentially presbyterian but functionally congregational."

Thus was formed the Evangelical and Reformed Church. As of this time the Evangelical membership was nearly 300,000, centering largely in the Middle- and Northwest, but extending also to California and Texas. It had come close to overtaking the older group, whose six synods represented a membership of nearly 350,000. Both churches had mission societies, foreign and domestic, they had schools and publications, and both, especially since World War I, were moving from the language of their origin, though it was not until 1925 that a president's report to the Evangelical synod was read in English. The Reformed Church had long since dropped "German" from its name.

Both groups had taken part in the ecumenical work of the Federal Council of Churches of Christ and the Interchurch World Movement. Both followed a polity not unlike that of the old Congregational Way. This was conscious decision on the part of the Evangelists, whose early missionaries, owing much to the Congregationalists, had looked into American history and recognized a spiritual kinship with the founders of Plymouth and the Bay.

In 1941 a tentative step was taken toward union with the Congregational Christian Church; sixteen years later the union took place.

A Fresh Statement of Faith

The delay had been caused by the opposition of some Congregationalists. Even the earlier union had caused friction. A legendary old-timer is said to have objected, "I've been a Congregationalist all my life, and no one's going to make a Christian of me now." Not all local churches had ratified the union. The merger proposed now was of proportions so massive as to threaten to overwhelm followers of the Way. The membership of the new applicant was "foreign," deriving from a nation with which in one generation America had twice been at war. Nor did Congregationalists like the term "synod," for all that they had once used it themselves. When a General Synod was arranged for 1950, representing both the Reformed and Evangelical Churches and the Congregational National Council, a Brooklyn church sued for an injunction and challenged in court the authority of General Council to act. Though the suit was settled in the Council's favor in 1953, it was not until June 1957 that the Uniting General Synod was held in Cleveland, Ohio.

Insofar as the protest had been aimed at enjoining the Council from legislating for the churches at large, it was justified; it was also superfluous. The Congregational Christian Church had no legal existence; the National Council was a corporate body and so were the separate churches, but the one had no more power over the autonomy of the other than it had ever had.

Even with the best of good will the delegates to the Uniting Synod had their difficulties in consummating a union. As one of them put it, "The New England boiled dinner and the Pennsylvania sauerkraut had to come to terms with each other." Yankee prejudice was aroused by the addiction of some Evangelical and Reformed leaders to their cigars; some of the latter shrank from what they considered affectation in Yankee turns of speech and accent. Theological terms required endless explication, as did the ominous "synod." It might have been easier for the Congregationalists if the Evangelical-Reformed had offered older terms like coetus or classis; but the one was hard to spell and pronounce and the other had the same connotations for the Reformed that synod had to Congregationalists. After all, the word meant nothing but assembly. Congregational prejudice gave way, and National Council became Synod.

The Synod of 1957 began work on a constitution for the United Church of Christ. It was completed in 1961 and submitted to the church conferences for ratification. This was not accomplished unanimously; one of the thirty-three Evangelical synods rejected it, and though a majority in each of the thirty-five Christian conferences approved it, each conference included dissenters. Thirty-nine of Massachusetts' 454 churches rejected the constitution, and so correspondingly in other states.

No compulsion was exerted on the abstainers. All congregations, assenting or not, managed their affairs in the old way and maintained fellowship through their ministerial associations through the state level. Only one privilege was denied the dissenter, representation on the National Synod.

The multiple Congregational boards followed a similar pattern. The American Missionary Society retained its independence; the powerful American Board, after prolonged soul-searching, entered the United Board for World Ministries, and moved its headquarters from Boston's Congregational House to the more modern building of the Interchurch Center on New York's Riverside Drive.

The churches were allowed their own latitude on creed, but a fresh Statement of Faith, somewhat in the spirit of the Burial Hill Declaration, was composed so that those congregations who would might make it a part of their service.

We believe in God, the Eternal Spirit, Father of our Lord Jesus and our Father, and to His deeds we testify. . . .

He seeks in holy love to save all people from aimlessness and sin. . . .

He promises to all who trust Him forgiveness of sins and fullness of grace, courage in the struggle for justice and peace, His presence in trial and rejoicing, and eternal life in His kingdom which has no end.

Blessing and honor, glory and power be unto Him. Amen.

ACKNOWLEDGMENTS

My thanks to all those who helped me round up the material on the Congregational saga. Among them, the librarians at the Connecticut State Library and the Congregational Historical Society who helped me with Horace Bushnell and Thomas Hooker; the Reverend E. E. Voelkel, pastor of the heirs of Hooker's congregation in Hartford, who kept me supplied with the excellent Hooker lectures; Miss Alice Phinney, who on a memorable Thanksgiving gave me a lift to the reconstructed Plimouth Plantation; the Reverend Arthur W. West-wood, Spearfish, South Dakota. And above all the Congregational Library in Boston, where Miss Corrine M. Nordquiest, librarian, and her assistants, Mrs. Evelyn Vradenburgh and Miss Eleanor Kruse, were never too busy to help me trace down an obscure reference. Barbara Morse gave me a hand with the proofreading.

SOURCES AND SUGGESTED READINGS

General

Atkins, Gaius Glenn and Fagley, Frederick L. *History of American Congregationalism.* (Boston and Chicago: Pilgrim Press, 1942)

Bainton, Roland H. *Christian Unity and Religion in New England.* (Boston: Beacon Press, 1964)

Barton, William E. *The Law of Congregational Usage.* (Boston: Pilgrim Press, 1923)

Dexter, Henry Martyn. *The Congregationalism of the Last Three Hundred Years as Seen in its Literature.* (New York: Harper and Brothers, 1880)

Walker, Williston. *The Creeds and Platforms of Congregationalism.* (Boston: United Church Press, 1960)

————. *A History of the Congregational Churches in the United States.* (New York: Charles Scribner's Sons, 1894)

The Pilgrims and Their Background, Chapters I–IV

Adeney, W. F. and others. *Early Independents.* (London, 1893)

Bradford, William. *History of Plymouth Plantation, 1606–1646,* ed. by Worthington Chauncey Ford. (Boston: Houghton Mifflin Company, 1912)

Davis, Ozora S. *John Robinson, the Pilgrim Pastor.* (Boston: Pilgrim Press, 1903)

Fleming, Thomas J. *One Small Candle, The Pilgrim's First Year in America.* (New York: Norton, 1964)

Marshall, George N., ed. *The Church of the Pilgrim Fathers.* (Boston: Beacon Press, 1950)

Morison, Samuel Eliot. *The Story of the Old Bay Colony of New Plymouth.* (New York: Knopf, 1956)

Nuttall, Geoffrey F. *Visible Saints, The Congregational Way, 1640–1660.* (Oxford, England: Blackwell, 1957)

Willison, George F. *Saints and Strangers.* (New York: Reynal and Hitchcock, 1945)

II. For a carefully detailed account of Brewster's work with the Scrooby congregation, see George F. Willison's *Saints and Strangers.* Harvey Wish, in his skillfully abridged edition of Bradford's *Of Plymouth Plantation,* provides insights in his introduction to the youth of William Bradford.

The account of John Robinson's leadership in Holland is largely drawn from Ozora S. Davis's biography. The quotation beginning "the custom of the church" is on page 255; the reference to Calvin, 247; "such was ye zeal . . .", 142. His doubts of the compact with Weston are from Bradford I, page 109; the fears of the colonists, from Bradford I, 57, 60; the parting, I, 125.

III. An account of the *Mayflower* voyage written by a historian with a knowledge of seamanship is S. E. Morison's *Old Bay Colony;* a recent, very readable account taking the Pilgrims through their first year is Fleming's *One Small Candle;* all this supplemented by the indispensable Willison.

The account of the Mayflower Compact, the settlement, the general sickness, Bradford I, 189–214.

The origin of New England town meeting is a moot point. The theory of the historian Edward Channing that it originated in Congregational Church polity has been contested by Charles Francis Adams and others in *The Genesis of the Massachusetts Town and the Development of Town Meeting Government,* Cambridge, Massachusetts, 1892. They trace it to the general court authorized by the Massachusetts charter. Certainly the meeting in the *Mayflower* cabin had something in common with town meeting, though Bradford never used the phrase.

The full text of De Rasières account of Plymouth is in the New York Historical Society *Collections* 2, Series II, 350. See also Willison, 265–66. Weston's annoyed comment is quoted in Bradford I, 233.

IV. The description of Morton of Merrymount and Weston's visit to Plymouth are in Bradford II, 46–58, and Willison, 274–84.

The gathering of the church in Salem is described in such detail as scanty records permit in O. E. Winslow's *Meetinghouse Hill,* 20–23; Willison, 84–85 gives an account of Fuller. Perry Miller (see *Orthodoxy in Massachusetts,* 125–35) discounts Fuller's part in "converting" Salem to Congregational polity.

For a description of the relations of Archbishop Laud and Charles I, see C. V. Wedgwood, *The King's Peace,* Chapter II.

John Cotton's farewell sermon is described by Miss Winslow, 8–10; the fears of his listeners by Hutchinson, I, 18.

Spellings have been modernized, barring an occasional exception introduced for flavor. Punctuation and capitals also follow modern practice; Colonial writers seldom capitalized pronominal references to the deity.

Massachusetts Bay and Theocracy, Chapters V–IX

Battis, Emery. *Saints and Sectaries.* (Chapel Hill: University of North Carolina, 1962)

Burr, George Lincoln. *Narratives of the Witchcraft Cases, 1648–1706.* (New York: Charles Scribner's Sons, 1913)

Gaer, Joseph and Siegel, Ben. *The Puritan Heritage.* (New York: New American Library, 1964)

Hooker, Thomas. *Patterns of Perfection.* (London, 1640)

––––––. *The Soul's Humiliation.* (Amsterdam, 1638)

Hutchinson, Thomas. *History of the Colony and Province of Massachusetts-Bay.* Edited by Lawrence Shaw Mayo. (Cambridge: Harvard University Press, 1936)

Johnson, Edward. *Johnson's Wonder Working Providence 1628–1651,* ed. by J. Franklin Jameson. (New York: Charles Scribner's Sons, 1910)

MacClure, A. W. *The Lives of John Wilson, John Norton and John Davenport.* (Boston, 1846)

Mather, Cotton. *Diary, 1681–1708.* Massachusetts Historical Society *Collections,* 7th Series, VII, VIII.

––––––. *Magnalia Christi Americana.* (Hartford, 1855)

Miller, Perry. *Errand into the Wilderness.* (Cambridge: Harvard University Press, 1956)

––––––. *Orthodoxy in Massachusetts, 1630–1650.* (Cambridge: Harvard University Press, 1933)

––––––. *Roger Williams.* (New York: Bobbs-Merrill, 1953)

––––––. *The New England Mind.* (New York: Macmillan, 1939)

Morison, Samuel Eliot. *Three Centuries of Harvard, 1636–1936.* (Cambridge: Harvard University Press, 1936)

––––––. *Builders of the Bay Colony.* (Boston: Houghton Mifflin, 1930)

Norton, C. E., ed. *The Poems of Mrs. Anne Bradstreet.* (Boston, 1897)

Parrington, Vernon Louis. *The Colonial Mind, 1620–1800.* (New York: Harcourt, 1927)

Sewall, Samuel. *Diary.* Massachusetts Historical Society *Collections,* 5th Series, V–VII.

Starkey, Marion L. *The Devil in Massachusetts.* (New York: Knopf, 1949)

Vaughan, Alden T. *New England Frontier, Puritans and Indians, 1620–1675.* (Boston: Little, Brown and Company, 1965)

Walker, George Leon. *Thomas Hooker.* (New York: Dodd, 1891)

Wedgwood, C. V. *The King's Peace, 1637–1641.* (New York: Macmillan, 1955)

Winslow, Ola Elizabeth. *Master Roger Williams.* (New York: Macmillan, 1957)

———. *Meetinghouse Hill.* (New York: Macmillan, 1952)

Winthrop, John. *Journal.* (Boston: Massachusetts Historical Society, 1930)

Specific References

V. Much of this chapter is based on John Winthrop's *Diary,* with supplements from the history of Massachusetts Bay by Hutchinson, who had access to sources otherwise unknown. (These included Bradford's *Of Plymouth Plantation,* which vanished during the Revolution, and was discovered nearly a century later in London.)

VI. Hooker's early career is described in Walker's biography, 37–38, 42–43; Walker points out that Mrs. Hooker's service in Esher was not necessarily menial. The puns and the anecdote about Hooker and Stone are from Mather's *Magnalia Christi Americana,* I, 337 ff. The description of Newtowne (Cambridge), from Walker, 73; the letter to Wilson on Hooker, Walker, 88; Ward's comment, Walker, 159.

The quotation on the soul's "love letters" is from Hooker's *The Soul's Humiliation,* 101. The Connecticut Historical Society has an interesting collection of Hooker's sermons; *Patterns of Perfection,* London, 1640, contains an irreverent "commercial" pasted in the flyleaf, advertising "Dr. Buckworth's famous lozenges."

The Thomas Hooker lectures, published by the First Church of Hartford, give many insights into Hooker's life and work.

VII. Roger Williams' early life is drawn from O. E. Winslow's *Master Roger Williams.* Hooker's comment on the cross and on praying with the "unregenerate" is from Walker's biography, 80–81.

Williams' remark on civil peace is found in Miller's *Roger Williams,* 129; his protest to Endicott, *ibid.,* 163.

A modern and elaborate account of Anne Hutchinson is found in Battis's *Saints and Sectaries;* her trial, 189–208; her "menopausal abortion," 247–48, 346–48.

VIII. Morison estimates the numbers of the ministers in the Bay Colony in his *Builders of the Bay Colony,* 184. The early days at Harvard are from his *Three Centuries of Harvard;* Shepard's early life and contribution to Harvard, 10–11, 15, 18. The School Act from the same source, 189; Child's activities, 245, 251, 255 ff. The New England "plague" that postponed the Cambridge synod is described by Hutchinson, I, 128.

Atkins and Fagley, in their *History of American Congregationalism,* describe the Cambridge Platform, 82–84 and 288 ff.

IX. Cotton Mather's experiences with the condemned are drawn from his *Magnalia Christi Americana,* II, 409–13; his sermon on punishment for sin, II, 392–93; on God's use of thunder, II, 363–72.

The account of the Salem witchcraft is drawn from my *Devil in Massachusetts,* which in turn is primarily based on the manuscript records preserved in the Essex County Courthouse in Salem, Massachusetts. Concerning the death of Giles Cory there is dispute; some historians claim he "stood mute" to save his property for his heirs; others say that whatever his intentions, it wouldn't have had that result. I like my own explanation.

John Wise, Jonathan Edwards, the American Revolution, Chapters X–XII

Baldwin, Alice M. *The New England Clergy and the American Revolution.* (Durham, North Carolina: Duke University, 1928)
Cook, George Allen. *John Wise, Early American Democrat.* (New York: Kings Crown Press, 1952)
Edwards, Jonathan. *Works,* Volume IV. (New York: G. &. C. & H. Carvill, 1830)
Starkey, Marion L. *A Little Rebellion.* (New York: Knopf, 1955)
Stowe, Harriet Beecher. *Oldtown Folks.* (Boston: Houghton Mifflin, 1889)
Trumbull, James Russell. *History of Northampton, Mass., from its Settlement in 1654.* (Northampton: N. L. Miller, 1902)
Winslow, Ola Elizabeth. *Jonathan Edwards, 1703–1758.* (New York: Macmillan, 1940)
Wise, John. *A Vindication of the Government of New England Churches.* Introduction by Perry Miller. (Gainsville, Florida: Scholars Facs., 1958)

X. The biographical material on John Wise is from George Allen Cook's biography; the quotations from Wise are from his works as stated.

XI. The biographical material is from Winslow's *Jonathan Edwards,* supplemented in the "bad books" episode and the inception of the Stoddard system by Trumbull's *Northampton.* Quotations from Edwards are largely from his *Works,* Volume IV: the description of the Northampton youth, 19–20, of Abigail Hutchinson, 63, Phoebe Bartlet, 64–69. His description of hell is from Perry Miller's *Errand into the Wilderness,* Cambridge, Massachusetts, 1956, page 176. Edwards' remarks on withholding the truth from his *Works,* 163–65, on excessive zeal, 213, 219, 165.

XII. The reference to the spinners of Litchfield is from Baldwin, 154–55; the protests of the Connecticut tax payers, 74–75; the incident in Hatfield, 159. In Book IV of her *Meetinghouse Hill* Miss Winslow devotes three chapters to the part of the clergy in the Revolution.

George Washington's disillusionment: John Corbin, *The Unknown George Washington,* New York, 1930, pages 110–13. The account of Shays' Rebellion is derived from my *A Little Rebellion.* Francis Brown has written an illuminating biography of Joseph Hawley.

Unitarian Separation, the Missions, Chapters XIII–XVI

Anonymous. *A Statement on the Proceedings of the First Church and Parish in Dedham Respecting the Settlement of a Minister.* (1818)

Beard, Augustus Field. *A Crusade of Brotherhood. A History of the American Missionary Association.* (Boston: Pilgrim Press, 1909)

Johnston, Johanna. *Runaway to Heaven.* The Story of Harriet Beecher Stowe and Her Era. (New York: Doubleday, 1963)

Lader, Lawrence. *The Bold Brahmins.* (New York: Dutton, 1961)

Smith, Frank. *A History of Dedham, Massachusetts.* (Dedham: Transcript Press, 1936)

Stacy, James. *History of the Midway Congregational Church, Liberty County, Georgia.* (Newman, Georgia, 1899)

Starkey, Marion L. *The Cherokee Nation.* (New York: Knopf, 1946)

Strong, William E. *The Story of the American Board.* (Boston: Pilgrim Press, 1910)

Walker, Robert Sparks. *Torchlights to the Cherokees.* (New York: Macmillan, 1931)

Wilbur, Earl Morse. *A History of Unitarianism.* (Cambridge: Harvard University Press, 1952)

XIII. The outraged protest to heating the churches is from Winslow's *Meetinghouse Hill,* 312; the account of the evolution of Congregational architecture is derived from Edmund W. Sinnott, *Meetinghouse and Church in Early New England.*

The dispute leading to the Massachusetts Supreme Court decision of 1820 is detailed in the anonymous *Proceedings of the First Church and Parish in Dedham,* and from Frank Smith's *History of Dedham.*

The history of the Unitarian movement and of the activities of Jedidiah Morse is from Wilbur's *History of Unitarianism;* the Plan of Union with the Presbyterians is described by Atkins and Fagley in their *History of American Congregationalism,* 142 ff.

XIV, XV. The account of the Haystack Mission and the plea of Judson to the ministerial association follow Strong's *Story of the American Board*. Details of Congregational interest in and contributions to the missions derive from exploration of the files of that fascinating publication, *The Missionary Herald*.

The story of the Cherokees is drawn from my own *Cherokee Nation* and Walker's *Torchlights to the Cherokees*. Both of us based our narrative on study of the mission letters and diaries in the Houghton Library at Harvard; I also went through the files of the *Cherokee Phoenix* in the British Museum.

XVI. The *Amistad* case and the evolution of the American Missionary Society is drawn from Beard's *Crusade of Brotherhood*. Bushnell's remarks on the Negro's future are from a discourse delivered at Clifton Springs, New York, November 29, 1860; it is in the Connecticut Historical Society.

Lader's *Bold Brahmins*, Chapters IV, V, VII has much about early resistance to the anti-slavery movement and the troubles of the Grimké sisters. Later chapters describe the change of heart. My source on Harriet Beecher Stowe is Johanna Johnston's biography.

Council of 1865, Horace Bushnell

Bushnell, Horace. *The Age of Homespun.* (1851)
———. *Christian Nurture.* (New York: Charles Scribner's Sons, 1862)
———. *Reverses Needed.* (Hartford, 1861)
Cheney, Mary Bushnell and others. *Life and Letters of Horace Bushnell.* (New York, 1880)
Chesebrough, Amos. *Reminiscences of the Bushnell Controversy.* (Typescript in the Connecticut Historical Society)
Congregational Council. *Debates and Proceedings of the National Council of Congregational Churches, held at Boston, June 1865.* From the phonographic report by J. M. W. Yerrington and Henry M. Parkhurst. (Boston, 1866)
Munger, Theodore T. *Horace Bushnell, Preacher and Theologian.* (Boston and New York: Houghton Mifflin, 1899)

XVII. This chapter is wholly derived from the *Debates . . . of the National Council*. Difficulties of the Credentials Committee, 150; Quint on England, 326; the gold rush, 304–6; conditions in Memphis, 309, in Missouri, 279, in Iowa, 310 ff. Ministerial gifts, 159; training, 470, Bacon on independent churches, 453; resolution on polity, 463. Bacon on the Burial Hill Declaration, 363; Unitarians, 246–48.

XVIII. The study of Horace Bushnell is based partly on the Munger biography but more on the pleasant grab bag of material collected by his wife Mary. The latter includes anecdotes by his friends and by his daughter. Much miscellaneous material, including the holograph of *Reverses Needed,* is available in the Connecticut Historical Society.

Expansion, Union, Chapters XIX–XXII

Dunn, David and others. *A History of the Evangelical and Reformed Church.* (Philadelphia: United Church Press, 1961)

Gladden, Washington. *Recollections.* (Boston: Houghton Mifflin, 1909)

Holbrook, Stewart H. *The Yankee Exodus.* (New York: Macmillan, 1950)

Hood, E. Lyman. *The New West Education Commission 1880–1893.* (Atlanta, Georgia: E. L. Hood, 1905)

Horton, Douglas. *The United Church of Christ.* (New York: Nelson, 1962)

Hosford, Frances Juliette. *Father Shipherd's Magna Carta.* (Boston: Marshall Jones Co., 1937)

Lee, Luther. *Woman's Right to Preach the Gospel.* (Syracuse, New York, 1853)

Rudolph, Frederick. *The American College and University.* (New York: Knopf, 1962)

Sinnott, Edmund W. *Meetinghouse and Church in Early New England.* (New York: McGraw-Hill, 1963)

Spinka, Matthew and others. *A History of Illinois Congregational and Christian Churches.* (Chicago: Congregational and Christian Conference of Illinois, 1944)

XIX. The story of the Congregationalists in Illinois is from the *History* by Spinka and others: woman's place in the congregations, 191; Sabbath-breaking, 129.

The account of Gladden is largely drawn from his *Recollections.*

XX. Much of the material on the Congregational founding of universities and colleges is drawn from Rudolph's book: the quote on Amherst, 55; the Williams doggerel, 76; Lucinda Foote at Yale, 307; the protest against coeds at Oberlin, 326.

The section on the New West movement is based on Hood's book.

XXI. Atkins and Fagley, 259, refer to the Congregational Churches in World War I; an intimate account of the moral problems involved is given by Ruth Suckow in her *Some Others and Myself* (New York, 1951).

Atkins and Fagley, Chapter XIX, describe the evolution of the National Council and the reorganization of the multiple boards.

The career of Amelia Frost is derived from the *Congregational Year Book,* 1916.

The experience of Lucy Stone and Antoinette Brown is from Hosford's book; a copy of Luther Lee's ordination sermon is in the Congregational Library.

XXII. J. Lueder's appeal to the Kaiser is in Dunn's book, 236–37; the rescue of the Liberty Bell, 50. Atkins and Fagley, Chapter XX, describe the ecumenical movement. Frederick L. Fagley, in *The Congregational Christian Churches,* Boston, 1946, Chapters XI and XII, describes the origin of the Christian Church; the union with the Congregationalists, Atkins and Fagley, 357–59.

The authority for the Reformed and Evangelical Churches is the history by David Dunn and others. The early history of the Reformed, Part I. Chapters 6 and 7 by Theophil W. Menzel in the same source describes the European background and the frontier beginnings of the Evangelical group. In Chapter XI, Carl E. Schneider describes the union of the two churches.

The union with the Congregational Churches to form the United Church of Christ is the substance of Douglas Horton's book: some of the difficulties in the union, 20–22; the creed, 66.

INDEX

H

Like a chain of fortresses, colleges inspired by Congregationalists grew across the land

WASHINGTON

Whitman College, Walla Walla

Pacific University, Forest Grove

OREGON

SOUTH DAK

Yankton Co
Ya

NEBRA

CALIFORNIA

COLORADO

Colorado College, Colorado Springs

Pomona College, Claremont

T

MEXICO

PACIFIC OCEAN

Miles

0   300

palacios